Sentenced to Die

Sentenced To Die

THE PEOPLE, THE CRIMES, AND THE CONTROVERSY

by Stephen H. Gettinger

Macmillan Publishing Co., Inc.

NEW YORK

Macmillan Publishing Co., Inc.
866 Third Avenue, New York, N.Y. 10022
Collier Macmillan Canada, Ltd.

Library of Congress Cataloging in Publication Data

Gettinger, Stephen H
    Sentenced to die.

    Index: p.
    Bibliography: p.
    1. Crime and criminals—United States—Biography.
2. Capital punishment—United States. 3. Criminal
justice, Administration of—United States. I. Title.
HV6785.G4   364.6'6'0922 [B]   79-4552   ✓ 1-83
ISBN 0-02-543070-X

First Printing 1979

Second Printing 1979

Printed in the United States of America

To my parents,
who gave and taught
only love and life.

Contents

Foreword

Steve Gettinger began this book believing he was opposed to capital punishment. After interviewing numerous Death Row inmates, judges, prosecutors, defense attorneys, families of victims, and many others, and after pondering the subject from every aspect, he's no longer so sure of things.

Not, as readers will quickly see, that his research swung him around to advocacy of execution; rather, it shook some of his assumptions, repudiated some of what he had thought of as facts, and taught him to claim no moral certainty for his view. As a lifelong opponent of capital punishment, I believe the book he has written will have the same effect on those who heed its harrowing pages.

Sentenced to Die is not a tract; persons who believe in or oppose capital punishment will not necessarily find their fundamental views changed, although I doubt anyone's attitude will remain wholly unaffected by it. It is a careful study of eight men on Death Row, the crimes they were accused of, the prosecutions and defenses they received, the kinds of people they are and were, the lives they led, and the attitudes they developed while waiting for the last dawn.

Each case leads Gettinger to a comprehensive factual study: from Jessie Pulliam, an epileptic black convicted of killing a white cab driver, to a review of the overwhelming evidence that death is a penalty most often visited upon blacks for killing whites; from Rich Hager, an Oklahoman who killed his wife's lover and then urged the state to execute him for his crime, to a chilling review of the various methods of execution, the rituals that surround the act, and ways in which the people on Death Row cope with their ordeal.

This method reinforces Gettinger's impartial presentation and underlines his reluctance to preach a sermon. For the more one studies the death penalty, those who receive it, how it is imposed and carried out, the supposed results—and the more unemotional and open-minded such a study is—the more compelling the case against execution by the state becomes. The sermon is not in Steve Gettinger's attitude, but in his careful detailing of the subject matter.

Few people have made a careful and unemotional study of capital punishment. On the contrary, it is the subject of the most intense emotionalism, both pro and con, and, in these days, of the most appalling political demagoguery from candidates who, if elected to office, would have little or nothing to do with the criminal justice system or the sentencing of offenders.

Few candidates advocate the death penalty on grounds of moral retribution or social revenge against murderers. The cry, instead, is usually that execution of "these animals" will deter others from committing heinous crimes, thus protecting society. Interestingly enough, in the era of television campaigning, this posture is often struck as a sort of high moral position—probably to avoid the possibility that the relentless tube may magnify the advocacy of death into something too bloodthirsty for a mayoral or congressional candidate.

Anyone who reads Steve Gettinger's book seriously will be hard put to believe that kind of pitch in the future. If the execution of people by the state "protects society" at all, it is only in the undeniable prevention of further crimes by the person executed. But death in modern times is reserved almost exclusively as a penalty for murderers, whose deeds most often were done in the heat of the moment. Most are unlikely to become "habitual" practitioners of that particular crime.

Gettinger's careful analysis strongly suggests that the idea of deterrence as a socially useful consequence of the death penalty is insupportable; but he concedes—as will any honest analyst—that "the evidence is not conclusive." Hans Zeisel of the University of Chicago has put the question in proper perspective: "The evidence we have is quite sufficient [that there is little or no deterrent effect] and the request for more proof is but an expression of an unwillingness to abandon an ancient prejudice" that the death penalty deters.

While on the Oklahoma Death Row, Rich Hager told Gettinger rather colorfully that "as far as being a deterrent, it's about as much deterrent as that door over there. They been killing for hundreds of years. I don't care if you took four hundred of 'em out there tomorrow and strung 'em up, electrocuted 'em, gave 'em lethal injections—they're still gonna kill people."

But the cruelest hoax in the current political fashion of promising death is the premise that somehow this will make the streets safer, the old folks more secure in their homes, daughters less liable to rape. Capital punishment will not remotely have such an effect, even if practiced on a scale far greater than when executions were common in this country.

For one thing, in no jurisdiction, federal or state, is it seriously proposed that the death penalty should be the proper punishment for anything other than certain murders, perhaps an airplane hijacking, or treason. These are not the crimes that people fear; even the incidental killing that results from some lesser crime is not often punished by a death sentence. Robbery, burglary, mugging, assault, rape—these are the crimes that have turned city life into a nightmare and of which so many Americans (now including even those in smaller towns and the countryside) are justifiably afraid. But these are not the crimes to which the death penalty applies, or that even its supposed deterrent effect is likely to reach.

For another thing, even in those jurisdictions where the death penalty has been constitutionally upheld—at this writing, only Georgia, Florida, and Texas—and even in the case of crimes for which it may be imposed, only a tiny fraction of those convicted actually are sentenced to death. Of that fraction, fewer are executed. And when and if people begin to be executed again in this country, each one will have fended off the final moment for months, usually years, through an all-but-limitless variety of appeals, stays, hearings, and other legal devices. If deterrence, as all authorities agree, results only from sure and certain punishment, the death penalty is the least effective instrument conceivable.

Such arguments will not, unfortunately, deter the demagogues. Neither will Steve Gettinger's book; but reading it might make voters, whatever their instincts upon first opening it, at least somewhat more aware of the complexities and ambiguities of this issue and hence less vulnerable to political con men. From Richard Nixon's promise in 1968 to end crime in the streets by the use of wiretapping, through all those campaigns against "liberal judges" and "soft on crime" processes like the Miranda rule requiring arrested persons to be informed of their rights, down to the current fad for the death penalty, the search has been for a "quick fix"—something painless and outside ourselves that would put a stop to crime, or at least cut it back to the level of the fabled "good old days."

But there is no quick fix. Whatever the answer to crime in America, it certainly does not lie outside ourselves or our society, in the telephone tap or the electric chair. So let those who will, make what Steve Gettinger calls "at bottom a moral choice" in favor of capital punishment. That is their right. But if less were heard about "protecting society" and "deterrence" and if less heed were paid to those who pander these phrases, perhaps we could get down to the real and deeply troubling questions involved.

"It is my view," Gettinger writes after his long travail among murderers, victims, and moral conundrums, "that pragmatic considerations, however important, will ultimately yield to moral ones in making a choice on whether or not to support capital punishment"—to the understanding of which, it seems to me, his book makes an illuminating contribution.

TOM WICKER

Introduction

"I had it in my hands to snuff out his life or let him live. And it's a horrible feeling to have."

The life in question belonged to a fifteen-year-old boy—an A-student and altar boy—who had been convicted of the rape-murder of a little girl. The speaker was a woman, recalling the experience of sitting as a juror to decide whether he should be put to death in the electric chair.

The decision in that case was particularly excruciating, but the feeling is no less horrible whenever society takes in its hands the power to extinguish a life. There are no easy answers to the dilemmas presented by capital punishment.

What should we do in the case of a loving father whose secret torment drives him to butcher his pregnant wife and three of his children? Should his deeply felt desire to be punished by death for his crime affect our decision?

Or what about a man accused of what his own lawyer called "the most dastardly crime known to man—poisoning his own son for money"? How much indirect circumstantial evidence do we need to overcome reasonable doubt about his guilt?

What if there is no reasonable doubt—as in the case of a panicked robber-rapist caught in the act after shooting a policeman?

Then there is the problem of racism and its role in the history of capital punishment. When a black youth shoots a white cab driver in a Southern town, what effect will the legacy of segregation have on the outcome?

This book focuses on eight such cases. They tell unpleasant stories containing much horror, little humor, no heroes. They yield no pat answers. I present them not to pander to sensationalism, nor to build an airtight case for or against capital punishment, but to challenge those who think their minds are made up. Too often the debate on capital punishment has been obscured by hysterical rhetoric or sterile statistics. This book attempts to add a human dimension, to show the flesh-and-blood realities of murder and its punishment.

Each case raises particular problems, some of which are explored in the general discussion that comprises the second half of each chapter. There, I have tried to sum up the history, evidence, and opinions relating to the broader question of whether or not the United States should return—after a decade-long suspension—to the practice of killing those criminals we hate and fear the most.

More is at stake in this debate than the lives of these individuals (seven of whom were alive at the time this was written), or the lives of the five hundred seventy-five men and women who, in early 1979, had been sent to Death Rows in various states. For hundreds of years, capital punishment has aroused heated debate among legislators, theologians, lawyers, judges, social scientists, and citizens at large. This is an issue that cuts through to some of mankind's greatest philosophical questions: What is the value of human life? How is it best honored? Why do human beings act the way they do? How much power should we have over the lives of our fellow men and women?

These questions have not been answered during the moratorium on executions, and they have not been resolved by the laws that aim to revive the death penalty. In some cosmetic ways it will be a "new" death penalty, with elaborate legal procedures to hone and sanitize our social surgery. Several states have even scrapped their electric chairs. Instead, they will sedate the condemned inmate and strap him into a hospital stretcher, where he will be given a lethal overdose of drugs.

But at bottom it will be the same punishment as practiced throughout the centuries, however packaged. It will still confront us with the same questions that bedeviled the "old" death penalty: whether executions prevent future crimes; whether the few people sentenced to death are truly the worst criminals, or only the unluckiest ones; whether our legal system is adequate for making life-or-death decisions; whether we have any alternative ways of punishing the most serious murders.

It is my view that these pragmatic considerations, however important, will ultimately yield to moral ones in making a choice on whether or not to support capital punishment. After all the studies, arguments, and anecdotes have been offered, challenged, and digested, the decision will depend on individual interpretations of justice. But, abstract as these principles might be, they must be translated into decisions deciding the fates of individual human beings. What I ask of the reader, in making his or her choice, is this: In order to support capital punishment, you must be able to look in the eyes of a condemned man, recognize his humanity, see how he got to that point—and still tell him he must die. In order to oppose capital punishment, you must confront the horror of murder, feel the loss, fear, and outrage—and still be able to look the victim's relatives in the eyes and say that the murderer must live.

I was not searching for moral dilemmas, legal problems, or case histories when I first visited Death Row, the end of the line in our society. I went there, in 1976, to do a magazine article on the mood as the inmates waited for the U.S. Supreme Court to decide the constitutionality of capital punishment. But I found myself unable to ignore questions that went beyond what were the inmates' daily schedules and how many cigarettes they smoked, and so I forced myself to sit in the electric chairs and the gas chambers, to speak with the weeping relatives of the condemned, to confront judges, jurors, prosecutors, and executioners. It has not been fun. One day I had the experience of informing a man on Death Row that the U.S. Supreme Court had turned down his appeal. He had heard on the radio that some cases had been decided the previous day, but his lawyer had not called him. He grilled me concerning the morning newspaper articles until I reluctantly admitted that yes, his name had been included, and yes, he had been turned down. He thanked me politely and stood impassively, but he could not hide what was in his eyes. And as I was leaving Death Row a few minutes later, a porter came running up to the guard: "Bob just got some very bad news and would like to see the counselor right now!"

I would be less than candid if I did not admit that I began this project thinking I was opposed to the death penalty. This was as much as anything a matter of personal taste and I was not particularly well informed. In doing the research for this book my opinions have been seriously challenged, and while I have not found enough evidence to change my mind I recognize that it is still an open question. I have tried to keep in mind the warning of lawyer Michael Meltsner, who noted that abolitionists such as himself often "perceive themselves as a small embattled band with a special gift of moral superiority. . . . Such attitudes are not always conducive to winning friends or influencing people." I have tried to be fair.

The scope of this book is limited to the crime of murder. I do not consider whether the death penalty should be retained for treason, genocide, or other special crimes. Even so, no collection of case histories, however large, can fairly represent the human tragedies we call murders. These stories cover a broad range, and they are more typical of capital cases than Charles

Manson or the Rosenbergs, whose names are frequently brought
up in public debate. But they leave large gaps. Only one of the
eight cases, for instance, involves a black man, whereas half of
those sentenced to death are black. All of these condemned
inmates are male, yet some women have been sentenced to
death and their special problems deserve attention.* Since all
of these cases *did* result in a death sentence, there is a missing
dimension to this book—since for every crime resulting in a
death sentence, several other similar ones get lesser punishments. But the reader should be able to see whether these cases
could logically have had different outcomes, and how they compare with the crimes detailed in our daily newspapers.

These profiles can only attempt to capture the highlights of
actual cases. They are based on many sources: court transcripts,
newspaper clippings, interviews with victims, relatives, prosecutors, judges, jurors, police officers. None should be considered
the last word on any case. I have had to ignore some important
details, and I could not ferret out all the inaccuracies, untruths,
and missing information that lie behind these deeds. I do
not consider it outside the realm of possibility that one of these
men might someday be proven innocent; stronger cases than
these have been fabricated in the past.

One problem with investigating murder cases is that many of
the people involved—surviving victims, relatives, and criminals
alike—would rather not have their private tortures paraded before the public. Some victims' families, for instance, did not
want to relive their experiences for publication. They have a
right to silence; for them, it is time to forget. But for us, it is
time to pay attention; these executions will be performed in our
names. To minimize embarrassment and to protect the innocent
from the idly curious, I have changed the names of victims, inmates' relatives, witnesses, and others whenever necessary. In

* Women comprise less than one percent of those executed since 1932.
Throughout this book, I have chosen to use masculine pronouns when
referring to unspecified defendants.

the end, no amount of attention can either deepen or heal the wounds they have already suffered.

In every case (except the opening one, where the central figure has already gone to a far higher court) I have given the condemned inmate a chance to speak for himself. I do not pretend to have an intimate knowledge of these men. In several cases, only a single interview was possible. Frequently, the interviews were short, conducted in trying circumstances, and based on incomplete information. For the most part, I found these men to be frank, cooperative, and serious. In one area they were anything but candid: discussing the details of their crimes. Usually, they had been instructed by their attorneys not to do so, and I did not challenge this decision. On the other hand, the men were always willing to confront questions that most of us try to avoid: the meaning of life, what happens to us after death, whether we are afraid to die. I found their answers fascinating, and frequently I have included their thoughts on these subjects even though they have no direct relevance to the major theme of the case. Whatever one thinks of condemned men, one must admit that they have a unique perspective on these matters. They are, after all, the only people in our society to be given notice of exactly when and how they will die.

There are two basic premises that must be kept in mind throughout this book. Without agreement here, future discussion would be chaotic.

First: *The issue is not whether murder is to be punished, but how.*

No one is proposing that the people in this book go unpunished. People guilty of the crimes described here should not be on the streets tomorrow, or next year, or even within the decade. Some people would have us believe that imprisonment is hardly punishment at all. One book jacket declares, "Charles Manson and Richard Speck are watching color TV, eating filet mignon at the taxpayer's expense, and looking forward to parole." This is silly, grimly so. I have visited some eighty prisons in the past three years. I have yet to find a country club; I have yet to hear a warden speak of a "good" prison; I have yet to see a prison where I would willingly spend the night. Some prisons are worse than others—some are medieval horrors—but in all cases the physical deprivations are secondary to the loss of freedom.

The other part of this premise is that, in a frequently used phrase, *death is different*. As Justice Potter Stewart wrote, "Death, in its finality, differs more from life imprisonment than a one-hundred-year prison term differs from one of only a year or two." Advocates of capital punishment agree that no matter how long the term, no matter how bad the living conditions, imprisonment can never equal death as a punishment.

Second: *We are considering the fate of human beings.*

Some demagogues would have us believe that we are not discussing human beings at all, but rather "beasts," "monsters," "mad dogs," "vermin," or "mutations." One tract begins: "Do creatures like this deserve to live?"

But the choice of noun dictates the answer. The same mental gymnastics that define people as nonhuman were used to justify slavery a century ago, and, more recently, to justify outrages committed against "gooks" or "pigs."

Power, Simone Weil observed, is the capacity to transform a living person into a corpse—that is, into a thing. Through our laws and our electric chairs, we are taking upon ourselves that power. But even if we do so, we cannot forget that as long as they are alive, these condemned men are human. It would be nice if we could get rid of evil by defining it out of the human species, declaring that anyone who does these horrible things is not human. But it will not work. The capacity of man to do evil, no less than good, is what defines us as human.

Sentenced to Die

CHAPTER ONE

● *"This is my time"*

Profile: Luis José Monge

"Let's do it!"

With his last words, Gary Mark Gilmore showed as little regard for his own life as he had for the lives of the two young fathers he had killed during his robberies. Gilmore, a truculent professional convict, had hijacked the nation's headlines for months with his demand to "get hisself capital-punished."

Now, seated facing the firing squad, he did not flinch as a black hood was drawn over his head and a paper target was pinned to his breast. A few moments later, four rifle bullets ripped through his heart. He was pronounced dead at 8:07 A.M., January 17, 1977.

The deathwatch of the decade was over. Even as Gilmore's eyes were being removed from his corpse for corneal transplants, his literary agent (an innovation in execution rituals) described the death scene to a battalion of eager reporters. This was big news. It had only been two and a half months since the nation elected a new president, but in that period Gilmore's name had appeared on the front pages of many newspapers more often than Jimmy Carter's.

Gary Gilmore's death meant that capital punishment had returned to the United States. It had been nine years, seven months, fourteen days, and twelve hours since the last American had died as punishment for a crime. During that moratorium, many Americans had thought that there would never be another execution. By the mid-1960s the supporters of capital punishment were in the minority in public opinion polls, and executions had become rare events. Defense lawyers found ingenious ways to stall the executioner, and their efforts bore fruit in 1972 when the U.S. Supreme Court declared all existing death penalty laws unfair and therefore unconstitutional.

The nation's mood changed, however. Capital punishment came back into public favor, and the Supreme Court decided that newly drawn laws had overcome its objections. By the time Gilmore's demand to have himself put to death hit the front pages, people wanted blood. A Harris Poll showed that seventy-one percent of those questioned favored Gilmore's execution.

But quite a few people, who bore no affection for Gilmore, were profoundly disturbed by the events in Utah. One of them was a young man in Colorado, a few hundred miles southeast of the prison where Gilmore was killed. He had a special interest in the case.

"I'd just as soon my father had stayed the last person executed," said Frank Monge, a twenty-eight-year-old man with a wispy beard and dark, sad eyes. "I say that even though Gilmore's death might take him out of the limelight."

The limelight has been a painful glare for Frank and his six brothers and sisters. Their father was known for years as "the last man executed in the United States." But they remember him for other things.

"My parents were extremely loving parents, and caring," Frank said in a low, halting voice. "My mother was going to have her eleventh child. My father was a disciplinarian, but he shared his time with us in so many activities. We had the good times—the days playing softball, the days kite-flying. So many activities. The love was there."

Frank's voice trailed off. He was eighteen when his father died. Now he had a wife and child of his own, a job, and ambitions to go to law school.

"Talk to anybody that knew him, or worked with him," Frank continued. "He was a good man. He did so much for the church. He was a giving person. How can you have ten children and not be?

"He had a problem. And we sure as hell didn't know about it. We were just loving children, just getting by."

Frank paused and took a deep breath.

"There's no. . . . He was a good man. I don't know how else to say it."

Those who knew him say that Luis José Monge (pronounced mon-gee) lived for his family. Perhaps that was because he'd missed so much family life as a child. Born in Puerto Rico in 1918, his parents died when he was eleven and he was sent to Brooklyn, New York. There he shuttled from home to home, living with various relatives. Luis quit school after the tenth grade. In November 1940, when he was twenty-two, he joined the Army Air Corps. He was assigned to Lowery Air Force Base near Denver, Colorado. There he met and fell in love with Dolores Mitla; they were married in 1944. The couple settled in Denver, and two years later they had a son. Now Monge had a family, and he wanted a home life for them that was better than his own youth.

He also wanted to make it a large family. By 1961 there were nine children: seven boys and two girls. Monge bought an aged but solid two-story brick house; there was not much room, but the family never lacked anything. Monge worked as a door-to-door insurance salesman, and he was good: personable, reliable, outgoing. Entering middle age, Monge, with his black hair and brown eyes, was handsome. At five-feet-seven-inches, he weighed a trim 150 pounds. His only physical problem was his asthma, which bothered him occasionally.

The asthma didn't prevent him from keeping up with his active youngsters. Sports were a passion with him, and a way to spend time with the children. With the girls he played volleyball and Ping-Pong; with the boys he played baseball in the summer, football in the fall. He didn't compete with his children or try to be their pal; he was always the coach, the instructor. As such, he was idolized by his family, and by the neighborhood children as well.

The same relationship governed the home. Monge liked to play with the children, but he was a stern disciplinarian when necessary. He enjoyed presiding at festive Sunday dinners, which took place after the family attended Mass. Often they heard him sing in the choir, for he had a fine voice and enjoyed church activities. He was active in the men's organization, the Holy Name Society. His only interest other than his family and his church was bowling, which he did once a week.

In April 1961, Luis Monge seemed the prototype of the middle-class family man.

Then he disappeared. One evening he failed to come home from work and the family was worried. The next day, Dolores called the police. A week passed, and Monge's friends feared that he might have been kidnapped or killed. But over the next few weeks, clues began drifting in from other states indicating that he was all right. His car was found ablaze in St. Louis. In Baton Rouge, Louisiana, he had been briefly detained by the police for vagrancy, then he moved on. His absence was a mystery to the family and the police. There seemed to be no reason for him to run away: no thievery, no gambling, no other women, no alcoholism, no family fights.

Then, after two months, Monge came home. He told his children that he had suffered an attack of amnesia and had forgotten who he was. When his memory did come back he was so ashamed, he explained, that he worked for a month in New Orleans to build up cash and courage. The children, overjoyed at his return, accepted Monge's explanation: "Everything went hazy."

In a short while, Monge was again a pillar of the community. He found a new job as a driver-salesman for a furniture company. He rejoined the church, resumed bowling. Another daughter was born. He was again the loving father.

Too loving. That was Luis Monge's problem. For several years, he had been sexually attracted to his daughter, Janet. By the time she started school, he had begun to play special games—teasing, touching, secret games—with her. Janet soon told her mother that something was going on, and Dolores confronted her husband. He confessed his problem, begged forgiveness, and promised to control himself. For several years he had been successful. But then the pressures began to mount again, and in 1961 they seemed unbearable. Rather than give in, Monge had run away from home.

For a time after his return, Monge was fine. But then the problem resurfaced. Dolores soon found out, and so did the oldest daughter, Anna. Dolores consulted the family priest about it, and warned her husband that he had one more chance. The next time it happened, she said, she would tell others and bring public disgrace upon him. Monge knew that she meant it.

Only the mother and the two daughters had any knowledge of the torment that plagued Luis. To the others, he was still their strong, loving father. In the spring of 1963, there were ten children, with an eleventh due in August. The oldest was eighteen, a high school athlete about to graduate. Anna was sixteen. Then came Richie, fifteen, and Frank, fourteen. Janet was thirteen; Teddy, eleven; Guy, eight. Freddie, at six, was a favorite of his father's, perhaps because he was dependent and slow to learn. Then there were Thomas, four, and Tina, the eleven-month-old baby.

The night of Friday, June 28, 1963, everyone went to bed early except Luis. Dolores slept in the double bed in the first-floor bedroom. In a crib in the same room was the baby. Upstairs, Anna and Janet shared a bedroom with Thomas. The other six boys shared three rooms, except for Teddy, who was away at summer camp.

Luis stayed downstairs by himself until about eleven-thirty. He climbed the stairs and entered the first bedroom, where his daughters lay asleep. He went over to Janet's bed and sat down. Gently, he reached under the covers for her sleeping body. Soon he was very excited. A voice rang out in the darkness:

"What are you doing?"

Janet was still asleep, but her sister was not. Anna was sitting up in bed, staring at him.

Luis explained that Janet's feet had fallen to the floor as they sometimes did; he said he was just tucking her in.

"No, you weren't," the girl said accusingly.

Monge stood up and stalked out of the room. His mind was racing. She knew. He knew that she knew. She would tell her mother, and Dolores would tell others. He would be disgraced, and the whole family along with him.

Monge went back down to the living room in a panic. Soon he calmed a bit and began to search for ways out of his predicament. What about running away? No, he thought, he didn't have the strength. Anyway, it was too late; the deed was done. For an hour and a half, Monge paced the living room.

At about 1:15 A.M. he had made up his mind. He saw only one way to save his family from humiliation. What he did is best described in Monge's own words, as recorded by the police a few hours later:

So then I started thinking and thinking more and more and then I thought the best thing was to kill them and myself, too.

So I went to the back porch and got this heavy poker that I used and I hit my wife four or five times over the head and then I put a towel on her mouth so that the kids would not be hearing the noises.

And after she was dead, I cleaned her up and then I went down in the basement and got my stiletto that I got in New Mexico in 1956 and I stabbed my little baby girl. She started crying and I covered her mouth also until she was dead. I took her into the bedroom and cleaned her up some and then I put her in bed with the mother.

Then I went upstairs to the girls' room and took Thomas out of his bed. He sleeps in that room. And I took him down in the basement and choked him and then I covered his mouth up until he was dead. Then I brought him upstairs and put him in bed with my wife.

And then I went up into Freddie's room and brought him down into the basement and let him stay there for a while. Then he woke up and I told him to go back to sleep. He was just about asleep and then I hit him twice with the poker. And he started crying, "Daddy, Daddy." Freddie was my favorite. He was a little retarded, perhaps, but he was my favorite. And then he cried "Daddy, Daddy" a couple of times and I held him down until he didn't move any more. And then I got the towel and cleaned him up and took him upstairs and put him with his mother.

I couldn't go on any more. I had intentions of killing the whole family. Then I was thinking of fixing the car and killing myself with carbon monoxide.

Monge started for the garage to kill himself with carbon monoxide fumes from the car, but he could not. The pathetic cries of his favorite child had brought him to his senses. He called his brother, and then the police. "I've just killed my wife and three of my kids," he told the dispatcher at 2:30 A.M. "You'd better come over before I kill somebody else."

Within five minutes, three police officers arrived at the house. There they found Monge in a chair in the living room, rocking back and forth and moaning. In the bed in the back room they found the four bodies, neatly laid side by side with arms folded across their chests, covered with a sheet. Monge, alternately calm and hysterical, showed the policemen the murder weapons and related what he had done. He was soon hustled off to the police station. Relatives arrived to take care of the other children.

At the station, Monge recounted the murders over and over, in excruciating detail. The detective began by asking Monge what his thoughts were when he hit his wife.

"I felt I had to kill everybody, including myself," he answered.

"Didn't you feel remorse?" the detective asked.

"I had no remorse at the time. It is just when Freddie cried."

"How do you feel about it now?"

"I should be dead instead of them. I should have killed myself in New Orleans."

"Did you feel it was wrong at the time?"

"Yes."

"Why did you feel this way?"

"Because it was not right what I did to kill my family."

"You stated that you were going to kill yourself. Why didn't you?"

"I can't answer that. I thought it was best I turn myself in. God didn't want me to kill myself."

"What do you mean, God didn't want you to kill yourself?"

"He let me kill my family, but didn't let me kill myself."

"But He didn't tell you to kill your family, did He?"

"No, but He could have stopped me."

"What was the reason behind this?"

"I'm just a sex maniac. I hadn't committed any crimes or assaults with anybody that wasn't willing, but now I know I'm just a sex maniac."

"As I understand it, the reason behind this was fear of discovery?"

"Fear of public discovery. I figured that my wife said that if it happened again, she would let everyone know."

Ten days after the crime, Monge made an appearance in court. He asked to be allowed to plead guilty to the charge of murder in the first degree. "I would appreciate it if it would not cost my children any more grief," he said. "I want to get this matter over with as soon as possible. I know I am guilty. Nothing whatever under God is going to change that. Let God's will be done."

But the judge would not accept Monge's plea. He insisted that Monge consult with a lawyer, and the next day he appointed two prominent Denver attorneys to the case. They conferred with Monge and, despite his misgivings, convinced him to let them direct the case. The following day, they entered a plea of not guilty by reason of insanity. Monge made it clear that he did not think he was insane, and that such a finding would only add to his shame. He wanted no excuses. He told the judge that if he were found sane he would insist on pleading guilty; he wanted to avoid a trial, "which would just be added misery and disgrace for my children."

The judge told Monge that he would consider a plea at the appropriate time. He warned Monge, however, that there was no way to avoid a trial. In Colorado, a jury had to decide the penalty for first-degree murder. It was either life imprisonment or death in the gas chamber. Even if Monge pleaded guilty, a jury trial would have to be held to decide the punishment. But first there would be a psychiatric examination on the question of insanity.

Monge was sent to the Colorado State Hospital for thirty days for the examination. Psychiatrists there found that Monge was legally sane at the time of the crime because he knew what he was doing and that it was wrong. A lesser degree of mental illness made no difference under the law. The judge, wanting to be careful with the case, ordered a second examination by a private psychiatrist. He, too, found Monge sane.

Monge acted as if he had won a victory. He again insisted on pleading guilty. On October 23, 1963, he appeared in court and signed a statement admitting the murder of his wife. No charges had been entered in the deaths of the three children. After some questioning of Monge, the judge accepted the plea.

Then the judge produced a surprise. Instead of sending Monge back to his jail cell, he ordered that the prisoner be brought back to his chambers. Waiting for him there were his seven children, along with their aunt and uncle. This was the first time Monge had seen any of them since the night of the crime. It was, as one of the children recalled later, "a sobbing, traumatic session," but there were no confrontations. The children had already forgiven their father. Once again he was the head of the household. One by one, they came to Monge;

he hugged and kissed each child. The reunion lasted about half an hour.

Monge's children had given him the forgiveness he needed, but there was still the matter of punishment. Monge did not shrink from the death penalty. What he did fear was the inevitable publicity of the trial. When he wrote to the judge to thank him for arranging the family visit, Monge asked one more favor: that the judge ask the news media to suppress the details of his crime. "My children have suffered too much already because of my mistakes. Ask them for me to please spare them any more shame and suffering."

The trial to decide Monge's punishment began on November 13, 1963. Monge had no illusions about his chances to avoid the death penalty; indeed, he did not seem to want to avoid it. Monge did allow his lawyers to argue on his behalf, but they were fighting a losing battle. Monge contested nothing and the prosecution introduced enough evidence to shock any juror: the murder instruments; the detailed confessions; photographs of the murder scene; testimony by the police officers who first arrived. Monge's lawyers fought to exclude the most graphic evidence and lost. They had decided not to introduce psychiatric testimony because it did not seem helpful to their client and because it would open up the subject of incest, which so far had been mentioned only in passing. While the prosecution took four hours to present its case, the defense took only fifteen minutes. No one was surprised when the jury returned with a death sentence. Monge took it calmly.

But soon Monge had a change of heart. In the month between the trial and the formal sentencing, he asked his attorneys to prepare an appeal. He wanted a new trial. He wanted to fight; he wanted to live.

On December 18, 1963, the date of sentencing, Monge declined to say anything before the judge imposed the sentence. He showed no emotion when the judge sentenced him to die in the gas chamber during the week of March 15 to March 21,

1964. (By Colorado tradition, executions are carried out on the Friday of the appointed week—March 20, in Monge's case.) Monge knew that the appeal would automatically earn him a reprieve.

March 20, 1964 found Luis Monge at the Colorado State Penitentiary, with his appeal under consideration by the state supreme court. Inside, Monge was confined in a small cell on the second floor of a small building known as Cell House Three, the maximum-security building of the prison. Monge joined four other men on Death Row. One floor above them was the green steel gas chamber; in August, one of the inmates was led upstairs and executed.

In his cell, Monge kept photographs of his children, along with a borrowed house plant and two parakeets. He spent much of his time praying and talking with the prison's priest. For diversion, he wove frames for photographs from cigarette wrappers. He constantly scoured his cell for lint, which bothered his asthma. In the evenings he would watch television with the other men. He wrote letters to his children, and on weekends they made the 120-mile trip from Denver to visit him.

The appeal filed by Monge's attorneys centered on the admissibility of photographs and other evidence at the trial. On November 1, 1965, it was denied by the Colorado Supreme Court. During the time his appeal was under consideration, Monge's thin desire to live ebbed away. He did not want to pursue further appeals, and his attorneys withdrew from the case. The Colorado Supreme Court rescheduled Monge's execution for February 1966.

But in January, Monge received an unsought reprieve. The Colorado legislature had called for a referendum on whether to abolish the death penalty, and Governor John Love issued a stay of execution to all condemned men until the voters could decide the issue in the fall.

Opponents of the death penalty in Colorado were optimistic about the chances for abolition, and they waged a vigorous campaign. But abolitionist sentiment waned when a series of spectacular crimes swept the nation and the state. In July 1966, Richard Speck killed eight student nurses in Chicago. On August 1, Charles Whitman shot forty-four people from a tower at the University of Texas, killing fourteen. Colorado had several gruesome murders, two of them only a fortnight before the election. On November 8, 1966, Colorado voters decided to retain the death penalty by a margin of two to one.

Monge's execution was then reset for June 2, 1967. He seemed resigned to death as spring approached. He hoped that the publicity would soon be over, and that his family would be spared further agony. "It's the will of God," he announced on several occasions.

Early in 1967, however, Monge—who had been without an attorney for a year and a half—was persuaded by his neighbors on Death Row and by Rollie Rogers, the state's chief public defender, to enter another appeal. Rogers found a crusading, experienced private attorney to handle the appeal. It was drawn up with an eye toward getting the case into the federal courts, so it centered on constitutional questions regarding the death penalty law. But the attorney, not fully aware of Monge's distaste for publicity, threw in an alternative motion, based on a bitter offhand remark by Monge: If he were to be executed, the appeal stated, then it ought to take place at noon in front of the Denver City Hall, and it ought to be televised. This motion, intended to depict capital punishment as a repugnant act, backfired. The newspapers bannered this aspect of the appeal, and once again the Monge case made the front pages. The publicity outraged Monge and his family. In early April, Monge firmly ordered the attorney to abandon the entire appeal, and to cease further efforts on his behalf. Monge had resolved that it would be better for his children to say that both their parents were dead than if they had to admit that their father was serving a life sentence in prison. Besides, Monge was still tormented by the acts he had committed, and death offered release.

Monge's execution was officially set for the week beginning May 28. By tradition, the execution would take place at 8:00

P.M. on Friday, June 2. But Monge asked the warden of the penitentiary, Wayne Patterson, if he could be quietly executed at the beginning of the week, to minimize the suspense and publicity of the event.

Patterson was tempted to comply with the request. It was within his legal authority. He respected Monge and knew that he was prepared to die. In addition, Patterson was opposed to the death penalty, based on his religious convictions. He had never seen an execution.

But Patterson decided that he would not break tradition. Only a few weeks before, another inmate had won a reprieve from the governor on the day before his scheduled execution. Who knew what the governor might be thinking about Monge's case? And perhaps Monge would change his mind. If the execution were to occur, it would have to be at 8:00 P.M. on Friday, June 2.

Saturday, May 27:

Warden Patterson assembled two dozen prison officials on the third floor of Cell House Three, directly above Monge's cell. They were there for a dress rehearsal. The process of execution is a complex ritual, one that is difficult for the executioners as well as the condemned. If the occasion were to retain any dignity, Patterson felt, then it should go smoothly. He had to learn what to do, since by state law he had to be the executioner, the one who would pull the lever to release the cyanide pellets into a vat of acid, thereby producing the deadly fumes.

Sunday, May 28:

Luis Monge went to the chapel for Mass. The warden previously had waived the rule requiring solitary confinement for Death Row prisoners so that Monge could attend church. He and the priest had become quite close. Monge went to confession with the other Catholic inmates that Sunday morning, then served at Mass as an altar boy

In the afternoon there was a special event. By Colorado custom, the ceremonial "last meal" for condemned men takes place on Sundays, several days before the execution date, and visitors are allowed. Quite a few men had eaten their "last meal" and then were spared by reprieves.

At noon, Monge was escorted to the prison hospital's visiting room. There he warmly greeted his seven children. Four other relatives were present, as well as the prison priest and a favorite guard. For the banquet, Monge had chosen the menu: tossed salad, fried chicken, corn on the cob, French fries, and ice cream with fresh strawberries.

Only once was the significance of the occasion mentioned, when some of the family asked Monge to try for a reprieve. They knew it would almost certainly be granted, since no one in state government was particularly anxious to execute Monge. But the father remained firm: "This is my time," he said. "I'm ready to die. And I don't want any of you to attend my funeral or claim my body."

The rest of the meal was gay and loving. Monge wanted to know about school and sports events. He presided over the feast as he had ruled over many Sunday dinners at home.

Finally at four o'clock it was time to go. The children came to him one by one. Monge hugged each child and bestowed a farewell kiss. He gave each one a photograph with a frame he had made in his cell from cigarette wrappers. Only then did some of the youngsters break down and cry.

Monday, May 29:

Monge returned his borrowed plant to his Death Row neighbor, who was being taken to Denver for a court hearing and would be gone all week.

Tuesday, May 30:

A psychiatrist interviewed Monge. Under Colorado law, a man could not be put to death if he were unable to understand what was happening to him, and why. The psychiatrist certified that Monge was sane. This last obstacle cleared, Monge made rounds to say good-bye to those at the prison who had been kind to him.

Wednesday, May 31:

Monge had a last visit with his eldest son. When he left, the son took his father's possessions, including his two parakeets.

Thursday, June 1:

Monge telephoned his brothers, who lived in a distant city. He gave away his wristwatch and wrote letters. He also prayed with the priest, as he had been doing twice a day all that week.

Friday, June 2:

Monge awoke at about 6:30 A.M. after a good sleep. During the day, he was allowed to wander the corridor of Death Row, chatting with the other prisoners. One of the men had his thirty-fifth birthday that day, so Monge purchased some cigars. The men smoked them and drank soda pop. In the afternoon, Monge visited and prayed with the priest. He did not eat supper, although he had taken breakfast and lunch with the other prisoners. As the evening drew on, a fierce thunderstorm raged outside.

At 6:00 P.M. the chatter began to die down.

At 7:00 P.M. the priest returned. The two men talked and prayed.

At 7:45 P.M. Warden Patterson entered the cell area of Death Row. Monge hurried out to greet him, but the warden solemnly stopped him. "Mr. Monge, first I must read you this statement," he said. The warden then read the death warrant:

". . . and that upon a day and hour in said week, to be

designated and fixed by said warden, the said Luis J. Monge be taken from said place of confinement to the place of execution within the confines of said penitentiary, and then and there the punishment of death shall be inflicted by the administration of lethal gas until he shall be dead. . . ."

"Good-bye, and God bless you," Patterson concluded. The men talked a moment, and then they began the procession out of Death Row. In Cell House Three, the proverbial "Last Mile" was actually only a few dozen yards—out of the cell area, up one ramp, back up another. Warden Patterson led, followed by Monge, then the priest, finally some prison guards. As he left Death Row, Monge bade farewell to the men who stayed behind. Going up the ramp, the warden kept to a slow, deliberate pace; Monge, trying to walk faster, almost stepped on his heels.

At 7:58 P.M. the group reached a small cell on the third floor. This was known as the preparation cell. Inside, Monge knelt for a few moments, then rose and stripped off his gray prison pants and shirt. He was given a clean pair of white shorts and canvas sandals, which he put on. His hair had already been cut short, so it would not harbor any traces of gas. Monge formally thanked the warden for his help, and apologized for occasioning his first execution.

In Denver, Governor Love remained near the telephone in the Executive Mansion.

The prison switchboard stayed open in case the governor should issue a last-minute reprieve. But Love had said he would act only at Monge's request. A telephone extension waited next to the gas chamber.

The witnesses—seventeen reporters and seven officials—were ushered into the area around the gas chamber. The reporters went to a window that looked on the back of the chair; the officials would watch from the front. The witnesses had already seen hospital orderlies bring small plastic buckets to the third floor; these were to hold organs removed in the autopsy.

In the preparation cell, two doctors attached electrodes to Monge's arms and legs that would monitor his heart once he was inside the sealed chamber. As the doctors finished, Monge turned to one of them with a quizzical look.

"Doctor," Monge asked innocently, "will that gas in there bother my asthma?"

Everyone was taken aback for a moment, but then the tension exploded. The men burst out laughing. Monge had provided his own comic relief. The doctor thought of an appropriate reply: "Not for long," he said.

The laughter subsided quickly.

Then it was 8:00 P.M. Monge rose, took a deep breath, and strode out of the cell. He walked by himself, making a beeline for the oval opening in the green metal tank a few yards away. Monge climbed in and sat down in a white sheet-metal chair. Behind him, peering in through a window, were the reporters.

Two guards entered the chamber. They placed a black mask over Monge's eyes. A smile played on his lips. They strapped him to the chair with leather belts. The priest entered. He bound a rosary securely around Monge's wrist. The warden and the deputy warden entered by turns to whisper something in Monge's ear, then left. Finally, the priest leaned over.

"Are you ready, Luis?"

"Yes."

"Are you sorry for all your sins?"

"Yes, Father."

The priest clambered out, then began a prayer for the dying. The door clanged shut. Everyone looked over to the warden, who stood with his hand on a large lever.

Watching the rest of the proceedings, one of the doctors occasionally looked down from the window to make scribbled notations on an official form. This would later be taped into the prison's leather-bound, gold-stamped "Execution Log." Here is what he wrote:

Chamber locked	8:036
Sodium cyanide enters acid	8:047
Gas vapors appear	8:05
Prisoner apparently inhaling gas	8:05

Prisoner apparently unconscious	8:09
Prisoner certainly unconscious	8:09 8
Movements of prisoner's body: Coughing, very little movement of body—head jerking, pink foam at lips	
Heart stopped	8:20
Exhaust valve opened	8:34
Drain valve opened	8:35
Air valve opened	8:36
Chamber door opened	8:56
Prisoner removed from chamber	8:58

The day his father's crimes were discovered, Frank Monge, then fourteen, had insisted on delivering his newspapers as usual. On the front page of his newspapers were headlines reading: "Father of Ten Kills His Wife, 3 of Children." One of Frank's customers stopped him to ask if there was anything she could do to help. The boy answered, "Just pray for my mother and my father."

Four years later, at 8:00 P.M. on June 2, 1967, Frank was on his knees in a chapel with the rest of his family. "We prayed for about an hour," Frank recalled later in an interview, "just sending his spirit on." The children respected Monge's wishes and stayed away from the funeral. The body was buried on Woodpecker Hill, the prison's cemetery.

After their father's death, state child-care agencies tried to separate the orphaned children and place them in different foster homes. The children succeeded in winning permission to stay together with an aunt until the eldest son was of age to assume legal responsibility.

There never was any question, Frank said, of whether the family could forgive Luis for his crime. "We loved our mother tremendously, and our brothers and our sisters, but we loved him, too. That never stopped. He was obviously a sick man. We forgave him right away. But nobody stopped to ask how the family felt about it all."

The last time he saw his father, at the formal "last meal," he recalled it as "fantastic, just a good family gathering. It wasn't really that somber an occasion; we were feasting. The final good-byes, of course, were very, very hard."

Frank went on: "I know, in fact, that we could have gotten a stay of execution. But my father didn't want it. Because he didn't want his family to suffer any more. Those were his words."

Frank thought that even if there had not been publicity surrounding the case, his father still might have chosen to die. "He'd done a hell of a deed. I certainly wouldn't want to live with that on my conscience."

Although all the children opposed the execution at the time and tried to argue their father out of it, now Frank said, "I'm happy and content with his decision. I know he did that out of love. He wanted to die for his family."

Frank opposes capital punishment; he thinks it is morally wrong. "It might have been the best way for him, though. To have to live with his acts on his conscience?" His voice drifted away, then returned. "I think he became adjusted to dying. He worked out a rapport with his Creator. It takes a hell of a lot of courage to say, 'Yes, I'm ready for death.' I'm positive he's into a better situation now."

Frank sighed.

"I don't know. I don't know if it was a punishment or a favor. Like I say, I'm content with his decision."

Punishment or favor, it is ironic that Luis Monge and Gary Gilmore, so different in personality and in their attitudes toward publicity, should stand as markers at both beginning and end of the moratorium on capital punishment—and especially ironic because each so relentlessly sought a punishment that is supposed to be so fearful.

A final irony: Monge, like Gilmore, donated his eyes as a last payment to society. His corneas were implanted in the eyes of two nearly blind inmates, one of them a boy from the state reformatory. Colorado officials say the transplants were successful. A decade later, a day after Gilmore's execution, a doctor unwrapped the bandages from the eyes of a young patient in Utah. The youth blinked and then exclaimed: "My God, this is wonderful. I can see!"

The operations took place only a few hundred miles apart. The recipients do not know where the corneas came from. Perhaps some day they will pass on the street. The eyes of Luis Monge will glance into the eyes of Gary Gilmore, blink, and pass on.

The Return of the Executioner

Punishment began as revenge. Soon after man began to kill his fellow-man for self-defense or advantage, he learned to kill for retaliation. It was a good way to warn off predators. Eventually, the practice of killing in order to avenge a wrong was elevated into a religious duty and a family obligation. Blood feuds were sometimes carried on from generation to generation. But as men organized into societies, revenge had to be regulated. The precepts of the Book of Exodus—"If any harm follows, then you shall give life for life, eye for eye, tooth for tooth, hand for hand, foot for foot, burn for burn, wound for wound, stripe for stripe"—introduced the principle of proportionality corresponding in degree to the offense. In other words, a life could not be taken for the loss of an eye. This early formula— *lex talionis*—was an important advance. It was a key element of the Code of Hammurabi (1750 B.C.), one of the earliest civil codes. As government developed, the state took over from the victims the right to mete out punishment.

Death was a frequent punishment in ancient societies. Anthropologists point out, however, that death was often reserved for offenses that threatened the existence of the state—treason and blasphemy. (Blasphemy could bring down the wrath of the gods upon an entire people.) Wrongs suffered by individuals— including murder—were sometimes punished by banishment or fines paid to the family of the victim. Revenge had begun to be tempered by other principles—restitution and the welfare of the entire group. Some societies forbade the use of execution as punishment except in the most exceptional circumstances. During the time of the Roman Republic, from the fourth to the first century before Christ, Roman citizens could not be executed without a special grant of power from the Senate. Regimes in China, Sumeria, and among the Slavs abolished capital punishment entirely.

Some of our most celebrated historical figures met death by execution. Socrates drank his hemlock for the crime of impiety. Jesus Christ was crucified for claiming to be the king of the Jews. Joan of Arc was burned for witchcraft. Sir Thomas More was beheaded for treason. (These, at least, were the formal charges.)

The use of capital punishment increased dramatically in Europe in the Middle Ages, under the influence of religious fervor and the determination of monarchs to demonstrate absolute power over their subjects. In England, Henry VIII is said to have executed some seventy-two thousand people. The apex of fear came in the seventeenth and eighteenth centuries with England's "Bloody Code." Under it hundreds of offenses could be punished with death, including picking pockets, consorting with Gypsies, or impersonating a Chelsea pensioner. Children were hanged for stealing bread or disobeying their parents. A sense of proportion was preserved, in a way, since the more serious offenders (such as traitors) were subjected to tortures such as drawing and quartering, while common criminals were merely hanged.

The morality of officially sanctioned killing has been debated for hundreds of years. Cicero, Caesar, St. Augustine, and Sir Thomas More all criticized capital punishment. But the modern abolitionist movement began in 1764 with the publication of the essay *On Crimes and Punishments,* by the Italian rationalist philosopher Cesare Beccaria. In his essay he set out several themes that have formed the core of opposition to the death penalty ever since: that it is immoral for the state to resort to killing; that executions are not necessary to protect society; that long years of servitude provide a stronger deterrent example; and that a hanging only creates sympathy for the criminal. His basic argument was that the death penalty sets the wrong example: "To me it is an absurdity that the law which expresses the common will and detests and punishes homicide should itself commit one and, in order to keep citizens from committing murder, order a public one committed." Beccaria's radical proposal stirred intense debate in Europe, and several governments were inspired to limit or to eliminate the death penalty.

In America, Beccaria's ideas were eagerly welcomed by the Quakers in Pennsylvania. Most of the American colonies had emulated England's sanguinary example. The religious roots of some colonies had inspired the return to biblical standards; offenses such as denying the true God or cursing one's parents merited execution. Pennsylvania had tried to severely restrict the use of the death penalty, but the Crown had stepped in to require a more rigorous code. Shortly after independence, Dr. Benjamin Rush, a signer of the Declaration of Independence, brought Beccaria's ideas to an influential audience when he read a paper calling for abolition of the death penalty to a gathering of intellectuals at Benjamin Franklin's home. This paper, "Considerations on the Injustice and Impolity of Punishing Murder by Death," is considered the genesis of the abolitionist movement in the United States.

In the nineteenth century, antislavery crusaders such as Horace Greeley and William Lloyd Garrison made the abolition of capital punishment a companion cause.

The abolitionists won some victories. In 1836, Maine put so many restrictions on the death penalty as to render it obsolete. In 1846, Michigan became the first state—and the first jurisdiction in the English-speaking world—to abolish the death penalty for murder, but it kept it on the books for treason. Several other states followed within the next few decades. But in the face of labor unrest, hatred of immigrants, and fear of socialism at the turn of the century, the abolitionist movement faltered. Some states that had repealed the death penalty rein-stated it, usually after some particularly heinous crime.

Several controversial executions in the twentieth century helped to revive the cause of abolition and make it a tenet of liberal progressivism. In 1921, Nicola Sacco and Bartolomeo Vanzetti—poor, immigrant Italian peddlers who believed in a rudimentary anarchy—were convicted of a robbery-murder in Massachusetts. At their trial, anti-Italian prejudice and hysteria about anarchism played a greater role than the scant evidence linking them to the crime. Millions of Americans were con-vinced Sacco and Vanzetti were innocent. By the time they were executed in 1927, their plight had become what Felix Frankfurter called "one of those rare *causes célèbres* which are of international concern." The night they died in the electric chair, there were riots in several American cities, not to mention Paris, Buenos Aires, Vienna, Prague, and Geneva. Millions of people became committed foes of capital punishment.

A generation later, the case of Julius and Ethel Rosenberg aroused the same kind of controversy, and attracted more con-verts to the cause of abolition. In an atmosphere of public hysteria and political opportunism, they were convicted of giving the Russians the secret of the atomic bomb. Whether they were guilty of anything at all is still a subject for heated argument, but it is clear that even if some spying had taken place, the Russians did not profit from it; the documents they were accused of transmitting were worthless. But once again rallies around the world failed to stop the executions; the Rosenbergs were executed in New York's Sing Sing Prison on June 19, 1953.

Some seven years later, more people joined the abolition-ist cause after the execution of Caryl Chessman in California. There were no political overtones in his case—he had been convicted of kidnapping with injury to the victim—but many people were riveted by his twelve-year battle to avoid execution. Chessman had always proclaimed his innocence of the crimes he was accused of (there were marked irregularities in his trial) and on Death Row he turned into a best-selling author. By 1960 the death penalty was no longer possible for kidnapping, but Chessman nevertheless lost his dramatic battle on May 2, 1960—even as the telephone rang, too late, with a reprieve from a federal judge.

Over the previous century, even if the abolitionists fell short of their goal, they succeeded in changing the use of capital punishment. Gradually the number of crimes for which death could be given were reduced. Juries were given the power to choose between imprisonment and death. Violent and torturous methods of inflicting death were abandoned.

Perhaps the most interesting development, however, was the end of public executions. In the past, since executions were intended to deter potential criminals, great efforts had been made to insure that as many people saw them as possible. As the Roman historian Seneca put it, "The more public the punishments are, the greater effect they will produce on the reformation of others." In Europe, the heads of executed criminals were frequently displayed on stakes for the edification of the populace. In England, the bodies were "gibbeted"—suspended from trees in iron cages, where they remained for months or years. Crowds of thousands assembled to witness executions.

But public executions did not produce the intended awe in the spectators. Instead, they were carnivals of bloodlust and destruction. It was reported that pickpockets plied their trade on the crowds gathered to watch the hanging of a pickpocket; drunken melees often followed an execution, lasting long into the night. All in all, it seemed that the example of publicly administered violence only inspired violent behavior in those who witnessed it, and that it cheapened life. Executions were finally hidden behind prison walls not so much because they offended public taste, but because the public liked them too much. Pennsylvania, in 1834, became the first state to hide its executions. The last public execution took place in Owensboro, Kentucky, in 1936, attended by some twenty thousand citizens.

The result of all this has been an unmistakable trend away

from capital punishment. The federal government began keeping reliable statistics on executions in 1930. That year, 155 Americans were killed by the states. Executions rose to a peak in 1935, when 199 people were killed. During that decade, an average of 167 Americans were executed each year. This dropped to an average of 129 during the 1940s, 71 during the 1950s, and 36 during the first half of the 1960s. Then the toll declined even more sharply: from 15 executions in 1964 to 7 in 1965, 1 in 1966, and 2 in 1967. After that, there were no more.

This trend paralleled what was happening in the rest of the world, except that the United States lagged behind many other nations. In 1965, Great Britain suspended capital punishment for a trial period of five years, and in 1969 abolition became permanent. Canada, Italy, the Scandinavian nations, West Germany, and most of Latin America have abolished capital punishment. In France, executions were reserved for the most extraordinary of crimes. A survey of 101 nations showed that between 1958 and 1962 only South Africa, Korea, and Nigeria had executed more criminals than the United States. Most Asian and Arab countries, however, retain capital punishment, as do the communist powers.

How did the decade-long moratorium on executions in this country come about?

The main factor was a shift in strategy by the abolitionists. Until the 1960s, the core of opposition had come from religious groups. They mounted public education campaigns, lobbied, and helped support individual defendants whenever they could. They had an important impact on the formation of public attitudes, but they were not able to come close to their goal.

But with the civil rights movement came a new source of abolitionist energy. From colonial times, racial prejudice had all too often been closely tied to capital punishment. Some state laws provided that certain crimes were punishable by death for blacks but not for whites. After the Civil War, whenever local animosity was not satisfied by the courts there was always the possibility of lynching. Some thirty-five hundred lynchings were recorded between 1880 and 1940; an equal number probably occurred but were not documented.

It did not take long for the civil rights movement to expand its concern from discrimination in schooling and public accommodations to the problems in the criminal justice system. Soon the organizations began supporting black defendants in capital cases.

The civil rights struggle was also important in opening up the courts as an avenue for redressing social injustice. Ever since the Supreme Court outlawed school segregation in *Brown* v. *Board of Education* in 1954, the Court applied the litmus test of Chief Justice Earl Warren—"Is it fair?"—to more and more areas. In the field of criminal law, the Court found to be unfair many practices of police, prosecutors, and judges. But the Warren Court did not confront the divisive issue of the death penalty. It reviewed only a few appeals of capital cases, and decided them on technical grounds.

In 1963, however, three justices, in a dissent written by Justice Arthur Goldberg, indicated that they might be interested in looking at the constitutionality of the death penalty for the crime of rape. Executions for rape had long been reserved almost exclusively for blacks who had assaulted white women. While Goldberg did not raise this point, his interest struck a responsive chord among civil rights lawyers.

These two currents—civil rights activism and reliance on litigation—were potently joined in one organization, the Legal Defense Fund of the National Association for the Advancement of Colored People (NAACP). For many years, the LDF, as it is known, had been the legal warhead of the civil rights movement. In 1966, after several years of uncoordinated efforts in individual capital cases, the LDF attorneys decided to mount an all-out effort to fight the death penalty.

The goal was to convince the Supreme Court that the death penalty had become "cruel and unusual" and was therefore unconstitutional. They began looking for test cases to appeal to the Supreme Court. At the same time, they encouraged social scientists to gather evidence regarding discrimination in sentencing and the deterrent effectiveness of capital punishment. In the meantime, they used every legal tactic at their disposal to stall all executions in the country. This last effort was crucial if the judges (and the public) were to be persuaded to take a fresh look at a time-honored practice that received little attention. It proved to be the easiest to implement, as attorneys found a host of issues that could lead to endless rounds of hearings in state and federal courts.

At first the Supreme Court accepted some test cases, but refused to decide them on the basic issues of racial discrimination and cruelty. Instead, it overturned many sentences on narrower grounds. One of the most important of these decisions was the *Witherspoon* case, decided in 1968. Here, the Court looked at the traditional practice of excluding from the jury those who expressed reservations about imposing a death sentence. At the original trial of William Witherspoon, forty-six potential jurors had been dismissed because they evidenced even the mildest distaste for the death penalty. The judge had begun the process by announcing: "Let's get these conscientious objectors out of the way without wasting any time on them." The Supreme Court declared that any jury assembled under these standards would inevitably be a "hanging jury." Since this "death qualification" was standard procedure in most states, hundreds of condemned men were spared by the ruling. Various other legal challenges managed to keep the executioner at bay.

In 1971 the Court finally announced that it would review the central question of the constitutionality of the death penalty. It accepted for review four appeals, of which the case of William Henry Furman, convicted in Georgia of accidental murder during a burglary, became the lead case.

At stake were the laws of forty-one states and the federal government—and the lives of more than six hundred condemned inmates. The inmates' arguments were largely developed by Anthony Amsterdam, a Stanford University law professor who had worked with the LDF to mastermind much of the legal assault on capital punishment.

The major point argued by Amsterdam was that the nation's "evolving standards of decency," to use a phrase from an earlier Court decision on cruel and unusual punishment, had rendered the death penalty obsolete. Its use had withered away in many states. Death sentences were returned in only one of every twelve cases where they were possible. Moreover, it was applied selectively and only to the poor and to racial minorities—to "a few outcast pariahs"—in violation of constitutional standards of equal treatment. Finally, Amsterdam argued, the death penalty was disproportionate for offenses where no life had been lost. (Two of the four cases involved convictions for rape.)

The legal attack focused on the procedures by which defendants were sentenced to death. Juries had the discretion to decide, virtually by whim, which defendants would die and which would suffer imprisonment. Jurors made this choice in secret, without standards to guide them, at the same time deciding the issue of guilt or innocence. This system, Amsterdam argued, was an open invitation to discrimination and arbitrariness in sentencing.

In rebuttal, the attorneys for the states responded that capital punishment was explicitly authorized by constitutional language concerning the deprivation "of life or limb"; that racial discrimination had not been proven in any of the cases before the Court, and that abolition was a matter for state legislatures, not the courts.

In June 1972, the Court spoke, but not with a unanimous voice. The vote was five to four; each justice wrote his own opinion and together they totaled fifty thousand words. The most important result was this: no one could be executed under any of the laws then in force. The death penalty laws of all the states were declared unconstitutional.

Only two justices, William J. Brennan, Jr., and Thurgood Marshall, went so far as to say that capital punishment was inherently unconstitutional. The other three in the majority—

Potter Stewart, Byron White, and William O. Douglas—concentrated on the procedures involved. Justice Stewart concluded that the sentence of death had become "cruel and unusual in the same way that being struck by lightning is cruel and unusual. For, of all people convicted of [capital crimes], many just as reprehensible as these, the petitioners [were] among a capriciously selected random handful. . . ." Justice Douglas wrote that death was an impermissible punishment if it was given on the basis of "race, religion, wealth, social position, or class, or if it is imposed under a procedure that gives room for the play of such prejudice." The statutes before the Court all failed that test, he concluded.

The dissenting justices—all Nixon appointees, as were none of the prevailing justices—protested vigorously. The Court was usurping legislative powers, they said. How could it be said that society abhorred a penalty that its elected representatives so regularly enacted? Chief Justice Warren Burger warned that by condemning jury discretion the Court was condemning mercy; the result, he said, would be a rash of inflexible mandatory sentences. But only Justice Lewis Powell had anything good to say for the death penalty. Burger and Justice Harry Blackmun said they would not hesitate to vote against it if they were legislators, but they did not feel they had the power to overturn the judgments of the states.

The *Furman* decision aroused elation among abolitionists, consternation among prosecutors, and confusion among everyone. Lester Maddox of Georgia called it a "license for anarchy, rape, and murder." Many observers on both sides saw it as the end of capital punishment forever. But as lawyers studied the opinions, they realized that the Court had not ruled on capital punishment *per se*—only on the procedures used to impose it.

Supporters of capital punishment set about immediately to revive the institution. Within a few months, a million Californians had signed petitions to put the question of capital punishment on the fall ballot; the measure passed by a two-to-one margin. In December 1972, Florida called a special session of the legislature to deal with the problem; it passed over-whelmingly a new capital punishment bill. In the spring, President Nixon took aim at "soft-headed judges" who put the blame for crime on society rather than on criminals; he called for a new law providing the death penalty for certain federal offenses. Voters in Colorado and Washington approved reinstatement of capital punishment by large margins.

It was apparent that the Supreme Court would have to tackle the issue again. Did the new statutes overcome the standardless, discriminatory discretion that led to the *Furman* decision in 1972?

State legislatures generally chose one of two approaches to deal with the problem. Either they made death mandatory upon conviction for a specific crime, or they tried to provide standards to guide the jury in making its decision.

North Carolina exemplified the broadest application of the first tactic. A death sentence was automatic upon conviction for first-degree murder, rape, armed robbery, or nighttime burglary. Other states, such as New York, took this approach in a more limited fashion, making death follow only upon conviction of an extreme crime such as murder of a police officer.

The second system, providing guidelines for the jury, was pioneered by Florida and Georgia. They established a two-stage trial procedure. The first part of the trial determined guilt or innocence of the charge. The second stage followed only if a conviction was returned. It was a separate hearing to determine whether certain specified aggravating circumstances (e.g., the murder took place in the commission of a rape, or was especially torturous to the victim) or mitigating circumstances (e.g., diminished mental capacity, or youth) were present. The presence or absence of these factors would determine whether the defendant was sentenced to life imprisonment or death.

At first it appeared that the mandatory system would be more likely to pass the test of *Furman*. Indeed, in his dissent Justice Blackmun had warned that the result would be mandatory "legislation that is regressive and of an antique mold, for it eliminates the element of mercy from the imposition of punishment." This approach seemed to lead to more death sentences, as North Carolina demonstrated by leading the nation in imposing them. However, no one could doubt that ample discretion remained elsewhere in the criminal justice system—principally with prosecutors—to allow for the free play of whim and prejudice. Mandatory sentencing also raised a specter that had disturbed lawmakers and jurists for centuries: When a jury sympathized with a particular defendant or thought the punishment disproportionate to the circumstances of the crime, it would acquit a guilty defendant of all charges rather than send him to the gallows.

In the years following *Furman*, social scientists strove to gather data that the Court might find useful: data on race, deterrence, public opinion, and discretion. In April 1975, the Court listened to this evidence and to the new arguments of Amsterdam and the state attorneys general on a case that was to test the new procedures. But the decision was put off because of the illness (and later the resignation) of Justice Douglas, the Court's leading liberal.

Douglas was replaced by John Paul Stevens. The Court decided to hear five test cases together. The appeals from Georgia, Florida, and Texas involved "guideline" statutes; appeals from North Carolina and Louisiana concerned mandatory sentencing.

The oral arguments were heard in March 1976, by which time more than 450 people were confined on Death Rows across the nation.

Anthony Amsterdam again led the fight for the NAACP Legal Defense Fund. He argued that the new procedures merely proved the impossibility of deciding life-or-death questions impartially. Both systems, he argued, provided a smokescreen of fairness behind which blacks and impoverished defendants would be hurried into the execution chambers. He called capital punishment an "atavistic butchery which has run its course." In response to questions from the justices, Amsterdam said that no law could meet the standards set down in the *Furman* decision, and that capital punishment should be banned forever as cruel and unusual.

The attorneys for the states contended that the new procedures were fair, and that they were overwhelmingly supported by public opinion. The federal government's solicitor general, Robert Bork, argued on the side of the states: "I do not see how capital punishment can be unconstitutional just because it is used carefully."

The Court's decision was announced two days before the Bicentennial in 1976. By a vote of seven to two, the guided discretion, two-stage trial procedures of Georgia, Florida, and Texas were upheld. By a vote of five to four, the mandatory sentencing systems of North Carolina and Louisiana were struck down.

In the next chapter, we will look at the specifics of the laws that were upheld. But here we should examine the Court's position on the major question: whether capital punishment can ever be constitutional.

Justice Stewart, who had helped to overturn the old capital punishment laws in *Furman*, wrote the majority decision in what became known as the *Gregg* decision. (Tony Leon Gregg was the inmate appealing the Georgia law. The Florida case involved Charles Proffitt; the Texas case, Jerry Lane Jurek.) First Stewart took note of a long chain of Supreme Court decisions upholding death sentences. While the definition of what is "cruel and unusual" can change over time, he found strong evidence that the death penalty had not reached this point. "It is now evident that a large percentage of American society continues to regard [death] as an appropriate and necessary criminal sanction." The fact that thirty-five state legislatures enacted capital punishment laws after the *Furman* decision, he said, proved that the public still supported the death penalty. Stewart dismissed the evidence regarding the deterrent power of the penalty as unclear. He sidestepped the issue of racial discrimination, and concluded that he could not interfere with "the community's belief that certain crimes are themselves so grievous an affront to humanity that the only adequate response may be the penalty of death."

In an emotional dissent, Justice Marshall lamented the decision. "First, the death penalty is excessive," he said. "And second, the American people, fully informed as to the purposes of the death penalty and its liabilities, would, in my view, reject it as morally unacceptable." Justice Brennan, also dissenting, said that the punishment of death should be relegated to the history books next to barbarities such as the rack, the screw, and the wheel.

Lawyers for Gregg, Proffitt, and Jurek were able to stall execution of their clients through new appeals. But then Gary Gilmore came on the scene with his demand to be executed. Playing to a mesmerized national audience, he insisted on foregoing his appeals and being executed immediately. The Supreme Court declined to interfere. Gilmore, with characteristic charm, spurned attempts by his mother and the LDF to save his life: "I wish my mother, the niggers, and the sons of bitches would butt out of my life. They are all a bunch of cowards." The shots that ended Gilmore's life were sharp punctuation marks to the Supreme Court's decision restoring capital punishment. In January 1977, the moratorium on executions was over; capital punishment had returned, in practice as well as in theory.

Why did the death penalty come back?

The most obvious answer is crime. In the early 1960s, when public support for capital punishment was declining, the United States was enjoying a relatively peaceful period in comparison with other decades in our violent past. Even so, our propensity for violent crime shocked the rest of the world. But then crime rates rose alarmingly. During the moratorium, homicides went from twelve thousand annually to eighteen thousand. A citizen of the United States is ten times more likely to be murdered than a citizen of Japan or Denmark. (Japan retains capital punishment; Denmark does not.) Researchers at the Massachusetts Institute of Technology calculated that if the murder rate keeps on increasing at its recent pace, a child born in Detroit in 1974 stands one chance in fourteen of dying by murder. As law professors Norval Morris and Gordon Hawkins wrote, "The United States may or may not be the land of the free, but it is certainly the home of the brave."

Between 1968 and 1973, homicides rose forty-two percent; other threatening crimes increased even more. In 1968, and again in 1972, Richard Nixon demonstrated that fear of crime was a potent political issue. At first, liberal politicians pooh-poohed the crime rise or characterized it as a racist issue—only to find themselves out of office. By 1976, liberals such as New York's Ed Koch discovered that the easiest way to project a "tough guy" image was to advocate capital punishment, even if it had nothing to do with the office for which they were running (in Koch's case, mayor of New York City).

As Charles E. Silberman demonstrated in his insightful book *Criminal Violence, Criminal Justice*, not only was the increase in crime real, but so was its racial component. Blacks had always had a higher crime rate than whites, but it had been mostly confined to their own community, where it had been ignored by white authorities. In the 1960s, however, emboldened by their leaders' defiance of white authority, embittered by empty promises of progress, and isolated from bulwarks such as the church or strong family life, black youths turned their anger toward white victims. "After 350 years of fearing whites, black Americans have discovered that the fear runs the other way, that whites are intimidated by their very presence; it would be hard to overestimate what an extraordinarily liberating force this discovery is," Silberman noted.

Fear—especially fear tinged with racial suspicion—inspires drastic action. *Do something!* people demanded. For more and more frightened Americans, that "something" became the final solution: execution.

Other forces contributed as well. The country's economic recession turned people's attention back to looking out for their own welfare. The pendulum of justice had swung too far, many people felt. A pronounced backlash against the social concerns of the 1960s developed. Resentment of protesting blacks, demonstrating students, and social change in general became orthodox. The major argument of the 1960s—that the death penalty was given principally to the young, the poor, and the black—suddenly fell on deaf ears. The proposition was no longer shocking—it merely seemed to describe the criminal class. The 1970s seem to have been a decade preoccupied with self, and the plight of a few repulsive people did not inspire much sympathy. The death penalty became a symbolic issue, one that expressed American society's growing intolerance.

CHAPTER TWO

The Empty Chair

The petitioner argues that the imposition of the death penalty under any circumstances is cruel and unusual punishment in violation of the Eighth and Fourteenth Amendments. . . . The petitioner next argues that the new Florida sentencing procedures in reality do not eliminate the arbitrary infliction of death that was condemned in *Furman*. . . .

We reject this argument. . . . The judgment before us is affirmed. *It is so ordered.*

—*Proffitt* v. *Florida*
96 S. Ct. 2060 (1976)

Profile: Charles W. Proffitt

This is the language of the U.S. Supreme Court. Measured, impersonal, dispassionate, it is intended to cut through the particulars of a specific case to broad constitutional issues. Human tragedy and human frailty are not the stuff of which the Supreme Court's weekly conferences are made.

But the language should not obscure the fact that what the justices "so ordered" was the death of one man: Charles W. Proffitt. The justices had never seen him, and for all the thousands of pages that had been submitted in his case, little was known about him. In all of the courts that had considered his fate, Proffitt himself had never spoken. Not one witness had testified on his behalf. The man, the crime, even the victims— all were shunted aside as the lawyers debated. But it was constitutional to kill him.

Pam Margolis was restless in the early morning hours of July 10, 1973, and kept waking up to check the clock. She knew she had to get up at six o'clock so she could be on duty an hour later at Tampa General Hospital, where she worked as a nurse. It was only three o'clock when she leaned over her sleeping husband, Ronnie, to check the clock radio on the table next to him. She went back to sleep. Ronnie was a high school wrestling coach, and he didn't have to get up as early as she did.

For a couple that had separated two months before, the Margolises were on pretty good terms. This was the fifth time she had spent the night at her husband's apartment, the same apartment they had shared before the separation. That evening they had gotten together for dinner with friends. At ten o'clock that evening, Ronnie and Pam had gone to bed. Even with the lights out, things weren't completely dark in their one-bedroom apartment due to the street lights outside.

Pam tossed and turned and woke up again at four o'clock. This time, she asked her husband to give her his watch so she wouldn't have to keep leaning over him to check the time. She put the watch on a table beside her. A little while later, Pam woke again and glanced at the watch; it was a quarter to five. *Another hour to sleep*, she thought, and lay back down.

She dozed for only a few minutes. This time, something had disturbed her sleep: a noise. Moaning. Her husband often talked in his sleep, but this was different. He was groaning loudly. Pam sat up and turned to her husband. He was leaning on his elbow, with something in his free hand that looked like a ruler. And he was moaning.

"What's the matter, baby?" Pam asked.

Suddenly a human figure popped up from below Ronnie's side of the bed. It was a man. He ran around to Pam's side of the bed and hit her in the face. She tried to cover her head with her arms, but the man struck her three times, hard. Her nose started to bleed. The man dashed out of the bedroom, through a sliding glass door in the living room and disappeared into a parking lot.

Pam sat on the bed and felt around; it was wet. She ran around to the other side and switched on a lamp. Then she saw that her husband was covered with blood. It was not a ruler he held in his hand; it was a large knife, and he had pulled it out of his chest. Pam rushed to the telephone and called the police. Then her nursing training took over, and she pulled her husband off the bed and onto the floor so she could give him artificial respiration. She pounded on his chest for cardiac massage, trying to keep his heart going. Ronnie just stared. Pam decided she needed help, so she ran through the living room, fumbled with the bolt on the door and dashed to an apartment across the hall. She beat on the door until the neighbor came. They rushed back to Ronnie and took turns giving artificial respiration. Ronnie never moved. A few minutes after five, a policeman arrived. Ronnie was rushed to the hospital. He had been stabbed in the chest three times— two shallow wounds and one that punctured his heart. It was a little after 6:00 A.M. when they gave up. Peter Margolis, Ronnie's brother, was asked to make the identification. He went into the hospital room and a policeman lifted the sheet. Peter stared at the gaping wound and at the white face of his brother's body.

There seemed to be no motive for the murder. It could have been burglary, but nothing had been taken, and Ronnie had not awakened and surprised the intruder. The police found expensive stereo equipment untouched in the living room, $142 in Ronnie's pants pocket, and $50 in an ashtray. The man had apparently entered the apartment only to kill. Yet Margolis had no known enemies.

Police recovered four fingerprints from the sliding glass door, but three were smudged and worthless. Only one was good. Mrs. Margolis gave a description of the attacker: a white male, medium height, average build. He was wearing a striped shirt, long-sleeved with the sleeves rolled up to the elbow, and gray or khaki pants. He had light brown hair. But she hadn't gotten more than a fleeting glimpse of him and doubted that she would be able to identify him in a lineup.

At about a quarter after five that same morning, Susan Proffitt woke up in the bedroom of a mobile home six and a half miles away from the Margolis apartment. Her husband, Charles, had just come into the trailer. He was wearing his uniform—a white short-sleeved shirt and gray pants—for his job as a shipping clerk at a trucking firm. He was not wearing any shoes. When he rushed into the bedroom, he pulled a suitcase out of a closet and started throwing clothes into it. He stripped off his uniform and got into some other clothes. He was in quite a hurry. While he was packing, he spoke excitedly to his wife.

The conversation woke up Jane Gregory. Only a thin plastic wall separated her bedroom from the Proffitts'. A friend of Sue's, she shared the two-hundred-dollar monthly rent with them while her husband was away in the army. Jane sat in bed and listened to the agitated voices in the next room. After a short conversation, she heard the door slam, and then the sound of someone getting into a car. Jane got out of bed and rushed into the kitchen. In tears, Sue Proffitt entered, exclaiming, "Oh, my God!"

"Yes, I know," said Jane. "I heard."

"I'll have to call the police."

"Well," said Jane, "do what you think you have to do."

Then Sue went outside and spoke to her husband. He drove off, and Mrs. Proffitt called the police.

The Florida Highway Patrol found Proffitt's beige sedan at about 6:30 A.M., abandoned near the interstate a few miles north of Tampa. It was nine days before anyone heard from Proffitt. On July 19, Sgt. Robert Drayman of the Stamford, Connecticut, Police Department got a telephone call. It was from his half-brother, Charles Proffitt. "Meet me at the railroad station," Proffitt said. "I want to turn myself in." Drayman met him at the station and they exchanged unemotional greetings. ("We were never very close," Drayman said.) Proffitt looked tired. "Let's go," Drayman said.

Proffitt didn't fight extradition back to Florida on the charge of murdering Ronnie Margolis.

Proffitt was indicted for first-degree murder, and held in the Tampa jail for trial. He did not think he would be convicted, and even told his wife to buy two plane tickets to take them out of state when the trial was over. This assessment led to two decisions he would later regret.

One decision came when his wife visited him. She brought a message from the prosecutor. He was willing to plea bargain; if Proffitt would plead guilty to second-degree murder, he would be sentenced to a "life" term with parole possible after seven years. If convicted of first-degree murder, the lightest sentence possible was twenty-five years in prison. The alternative was the death penalty.

Proffitt turned down the offer. He said he was innocent; moreover, he had some idea of the strength of the evidence against him and he did not think it was enough to convict him.

The other mistake was to ask for help. In the winter of 1974, Proffitt asked to see a psychiatrist. The jail officials sent for Dr. James Crumbley, an internist in private practice who handled medical services for the jail. Dr. Crumbley had training in psychiatry, and he screened prisoners' complaints to see if they should be referred to outside psychiatrists for help.

Dr. Crumbley came to see Proffitt, and they talked for fifteen or twenty minutes. Two weeks later, they talked again. Proffitt later came to regret that he had ever asked Dr. Crumbley for help.

The trial of the state of Florida versus Charles William Proffitt opened on March 11, 1974. The prosecutor was William Plowman, the chief assistant to the state's attorney (equivalent to the district attorney) for Tampa. Proffitt's case had passed through the hands of several defense lawyers. The one who ended up taking the case to trial was Rick Levinson, a young assistant public defender. A couple of years out of law school, he had never seen a capital trial before. But the two-stage trial procedures of the Florida capital punishment statute were new to everyone, even the judge, Walter Burnside, Jr.

Jury selection went quickly. The trial began with the testimony of a pathologist who described the wounds that killed Ronnie Margolis. Next came a series of police technicians; they told of taking fingerprints from the sliding glass door in the Margolis apartment. But the fingerprints did not match Proffitt's.

The first major witness was Pam Margolis. She described the night of the murder—waking up to find her husband stabbed, being hit, getting help. She was asked if she could identify the man who struck her, and she said she could not.

In his cross-examination, Levinson probed her description of the attacker. The major difference was that she remembered a long-sleeved pinstriped shirt with rolled-up sleeves, whereas Proffitt's shirt, entered into evidence, was white with short sleeves. His shirt bore an insignia on the pocket; she did not recall one.

An FBI lab technician testified that there were two small bloodstains on the shirt Proffitt left at his trailer, but there was not enough blood to establish a type.

The most important witness was Jane Gregory. Levinson had tried to keep her testimony out of court. He had argued that the conversation between Proffitt and his wife was privileged because of the marital relationship; the testimony should also be barred, he said, because it was hearsay. But the judge had ruled that Mrs. Gregory could testify.

"What was the first thing you remember hearing?" Plowman asked her.

"He said he killed a man."

"Did he say how he had killed the man?"

"With a butcher knife."

"Did he say why he had killed the man?"

"He said he was burglarizing the place."

Mrs. Gregory went on to say that Proffitt had mentioned hitting a lady and knocking her out.

The prosecution called one more witness, Dr. Crumbley, but the judge would not allow the jury to hear his testimony. The prosecution rested its case.

Now it was time for Levinson to present the defense. He began by making a motion to have the case dismissed for lack of evidence. The judge turned him down. Immediately Levinson announced, "The defense would rest."

"The defense rests?" the judge asked somewhat incredulously.

"Yes, sir," Levinson replied.

So Proffitt and his lawyer had decided to rely on final arguments to poke holes in the prosecution's case. They pointed out that there was no evidence to place him in the Margolis apartment. In essence, the case boiled down to the word of one witness, Jane Gregory, who said she had heard Proffitt confess, against—nothing.

The jury quickly found Proffitt guilty.

Under Florida's new capital punishment law, a separate hearing was required to decide whether Proffitt should be sentenced to death in the electric chair or to life imprisonment, with parole impossible until he had served a full twenty-five years. The law included a list of "aggravating circumstances" that could justify a death sentence. The ones that could be applied to Proffitt's case were: if the murder occurred during a burglary; if Proffitt had created "a great risk of death to many persons"; if the crime was "especially heinous, atrocious, or cruel." There were also "mitigating circumstances" that could justify the lesser sentence. These related to a defendant's age, prior record, and mental health. The jury was to balance these factors and decide which were greater.

Judge Burnside began the hearing immediately after the jury brought in its guilty verdict. The prosecution had the first round, and it recalled Dr. Crumbley. At this stage, Levinson and Proffitt waived objection to his testimony. Apparently they hoped the doctor would say something favorable to Proffitt. Perhaps he could explain how this senseless crime came about.

Dr. Crumbley testified that Proffitt had called for him because he had an "uncontrollable desire" to kill someone, and he wanted help. In two fifteen-minute interviews, Dr. Crumbley said, Proffitt described the killing. "[Proffitt] told me that the tension and the feeling was one which could not be resisted and that once the deed had been done he felt a great deal of relaxation." Proffitt said, according to Dr. Crumbley, that the victim was a total stranger to him.

The prosecutor hardly had to ask any questions to cement the fear growing in the jury's mind. But to make sure they got the point, he asked, "Is it your opinion that, based on his statements to you, this man is a dangerous man and could be a danger in the future to society?"

"Absolutely," the doctor replied.

Levinson rose for cross-examination. He did not choose to attack the doctor's testimony, or his qualifications for making such judgments. In fact, the attorney tried to strengthen Dr. Crumbley's status as an expert. Apparently he was hoping the doctor would convince the jury that Proffitt had acted "under extreme emotional duress"—one of the mitigating circumstances spelled out in the law. In response to Levinson's questions, Dr. Crumbley said that he felt Proffitt had been acting under duress and that he couldn't help himself. "I'm certain at the moment and at the time that this occurred, this individual was overwhelmed with a force over which he had no control," Dr. Crumbley said. Levinson elicited the doctor's opinion that Proffitt could be treated for his problem and cured of it.

It did not require a master courtroom strategist to find a hole in this plea for mercy. Plowman's cross-examination was short. He asked whether proper psychiatric facilities were available for disturbed inmates in the Florida prison system. Dr. Crumbley admitted that he had no knowledge of such facilities.

Proffitt (for reasons never explained) had told Levinson that he did not want any witnesses to testify in his behalf at this stage of the trial. So after hearing a plea for mercy by Levinson, the jurors retired to consider Proffitt's fate. The jury deliberated for an hour and a half behind closed doors. It returned at 7:25 P.M. to say that Charles William Proffitt should be sentenced to death.

Judge Burnside, however, bore ultimate responsibility for the sentence. Apparently dissatisfied with the lack of information on Proffitt, he ordered two local psychiatrists to examine him. Each doctor talked to Proffitt for less than an hour. One psychiatrist limited his report to the judge to a brief opinion that Proffitt was legally competent at the time of the trial, and that at the time of the crime he probably could distinguish right from wrong. The other report was more detailed—and damning. The psychiatrist described having a conversation with Proffitt similar to Dr. Crumbley's: "He admits to a long-standing compulsion to kill someone, but this compulsion did not involve a break in reality testing and did not involve psychosis in that he always knew that murder was a crime and that he would be answerable for it. He has a long-standing sociopathic personality characterized by resort to violence as a solution to his life problems. . . . He had three rather chaotic marriages and has generally lived his life outside the usual standards of society. Mr. Proffitt states that he believes he is capable of killing again, that his main reason for killing on this occasion was that he 'just wanted to see what it would feel like.' "

Three days after receiving these reports, Judge Burnside sentenced Proffitt to death.

In his written findings, the judge said specifically that none of the mitigating circumstances, not even "emotional duress," was present. He found four aggravating circumstances:

1. "The murder was premeditated and occurred in the course of a felony (burglary).

2. "Proffitt has the propensity to commit murder.

3. "The murder was especially heinous, atrocious, and cruel.

4. "Proffitt knowingly, through his intentional act, created a great risk of serious bodily harm and death to many persons."

The end of the trial was only the beginning of the legal route for Proffitt. But it was the last time he would be present at any of the deliberations concerning his fate. From now on his life was in the hands of the lawyers.

The Florida law called for an automatic review by the Florida Supreme Court. Judge Burnside's findings were sent there, along with a transcript of the trial.

The appeal, of course, is an allegation that serious errors were made in the conduct of the trial, errors that deprived the defendant of a fair trial. But the law implied that the Florida Supreme Court was to look not only at the technical aspects of the trial, but also at the fundamental fairness and equity of giving the particular defendant the death penalty.

Proffitt's attorney raised eleven points of appeal in his brief. Most of these involved minor disputes over the judge's rulings. The attorney charged, for instance, that the judge had erred in permitting Mrs. Gregory to testify. These points related to the validity of the conviction; if the court agreed, the case would have to be sent back for a new trial—and without this evidence a conviction would probably be impossible to obtain.

But another challenge was made to the death sentence. If the justices agreed, then Proffitt would be resentenced to life imprisonment. The gist of this argument was that the trial court had ignored evidence of the mitigating circumstance of extreme emotional duress, and that the judge had also exaggerated the aggravating circumstances. After all, one of the cited aggravating circumstances (Proffitt's "dangerousness") was not included in the law. Also, the stabbing of a sleeping man conceivably was not "especially atrocious, heinous and cruel" in that the victim may well have felt little or nothing. (Under later Florida Supreme Court rulings, it would appear that this circumstance was reserved for more extreme situations.) It was also arguable that the murder was not really part of a burglary, since Proffitt apparently entered the premises only for the purpose of committing murder. Finally, the attorneys argued that the striking of Mrs. Margolis did not really constitute a great risk of death, and that she certainly did not constitute "many persons."

All of the briefs—these charges and the reply from the state— were filed with the Florida Supreme Court by October. On November 12, 1974, the court heard oral arguments. Six months later, it handed down its opinion. Proffitt lost his appeal by a vote of six to zero. The opinion was relatively brief. The testimony of Mrs. Gregory was upheld; all of the technical violations were dismissed. The argument on the judge's sentencing decision was held to be without merit.

The next step for Proffitt was to appeal to the U.S. Supreme Court. Several other Florida inmates had already done so. In August, the case was assigned to an experienced public defender, Jack Johnson. In September, he got the U.S. Supreme Court to stay Proffitt's execution until an appeal could be filed. This was a routine matter.

At the same time the Florida cases were being filed, a trickle of death penalty cases from other states had been reaching the Court. Sooner or later, the Court would have to decide the constitutionality of these new laws.

In November 1975, word came down that the Supreme Court had agreed to review cases from Texas, Georgia, Louisiana, North Carolina—and Florida. It would decide the constitutionality of those states' death penalty laws, and of capital punishment itself.

The Florida case that was chosen was Proffitt's. A twenty-six-year-old attorney working on the case told a reporter: "Usually, most lawyers work for years before they are heard by the Supreme Court. We're fortunate to have this happen so early in our careers."

When it accepts a case, the Supreme Court has the luxury of deciding beforehand the grounds on which it will hear arguments, and of excluding others. In Proffitt's case, it announced that there would be one question. "Does the imposition and carrying out of the sentence of death for the crime of first-degree murder under the law of Florida violate the Eighth [cruel and unusual punishment] or Fourteenth [due process applied to the states] Amendments to the Constitution of the United States?"

Some of the finest legal talent in the country was lined up to argue that it did. The NAACP Legal Defense Fund, with Anthony Amsterdam leading the way, fronted the assault. While the LDF did not directly represent Proffitt, it coordinated strategies in all five cases and filed a friend-of-the-court brief on Proffitt's behalf. Proffitt was represented by Jack Johnson and Clinton Curtis, two veteran public defenders.

Opposing Proffitt's attorneys was the attorney general of Florida, Robert Shevin, and his legal staff. Shevin was one of the most fervent advocates of capital punishment to hold public office in America. Shevin was known to be interested in running for governor, and it was suspected that he saw the death penalty as a good issue on which to garner votes. But it appeared that his stance was really one of personal moral conviction; his own father, the keeper of a small store, had been shot to death by a robber. Whatever his motivation, Shevin was not afraid to confront the issue directly, or to be emotional in his arguments. He had even visited Death Row at the Florida State Prison to tell Proffitt and the other condemned inmates that he would do what he could to see that they were executed.

Proffitt was in his cell on March 31, 1976, when oral arguments in his case were heard by the Supreme Court in Washington, D.C. Law students packed the gallery of the imposing Supreme Court building to hear the most controversial case of the year argued. Oral arguments might seem superfluous in a case where the legal briefs added up to hundreds of pages, but they are crucial to the Court's decision-making process. They present an opportunity for the opposing attorneys to fix attention on the central issues, and they also give the justices a chance to question the two sides. Sometimes a whole case will turn on one question.

Proffitt's case was the last of the five to be argued. Amsterdam had already presented the main attack on capital punishment, and he had been questioned at length by the justices. Clinton Curtis spoke for Proffitt, and he limited himself to the unique aspects of the Florida law. Robert Shevin personally presented the state's case.

After the oral arguments were over, the only certain thing was that a decision would not be made quickly. Attorneys for the inmates had little hope that the death penalty would be declared unconstitutional once and for all, but they did hope that some—perhaps even all—of the laws before the court would be found defective on narrower procedural grounds.

Proffitt is anything but imposing in person. With his receding hairline and deferential manner, he seems slight, insignificant. His sardonic pessimism was the kind that goes over well in neighborhood taverns; he was the kind of guy with whom to trade beers. Funny, frank—and nervous.

"Yeah, I'm getting a little anxious, yeah," he said in an interview two months after his case was argued. "It's getting a little nervous back there. You can feel it. People are scared. What do you expect?"

How do you feel about being out in front on this?

"I feel rotten about it. I just don't understand how in the world they picked me."

Proffitt was asked how he would feel if he did get a life sentence. After all, that would mean at least twenty-five years in prison, and many people say they would rather die.

"That is bullshit—*that is bullshit*," Proffitt snapped. "There ain't a man back there that wants to die."

Ever since he arrived on Death Row, Proffitt has maintained, in answer to questions, that he was innocent of the murder of

Ronnie Margolis. On the advice of his attorneys, he did not discuss details.

Sometimes when he got into the exercise yard, he would wander over to the fence and stare at a little building across the way. That was the Death House, and the guards left the blinds up in the window so the inmates could see the electric chair. "Old Sparky," they call it with grim jocularity. "You can get a pretty good look at it," Proffitt said. "Power control on the side. It's unnerving sometimes. Sometimes I go over there just to look at it. It's something you got to face; it's not going away. I have no desire to see it firsthand, however, right up close."

As June boiled toward July, Florida's Death Row turned into a pressure cooker, and it wasn't just the heat. While the rest of the nation prepared to celebrate the two-hundredth anniversary of the republic, the condemned inmates waited anxiously to learn their fate. The Supreme Court usually announces all of its decisions by the end of June. The rulings are handed down each morning at nine-thirty. At that hour, every radio in the sixty cells of Death Row was turned up, and the chatter died down. There was no news on Monday, June 28; no news on Tuesday; nothing on Wednesday. June was gone. There were still several cases on the Court's calendar, and the justices kept meeting. But it was possible that they would carry the cases over to the fall term.

On Friday, the Court convened an hour later than usual. A clerk distributed a sheaf of announcements, and included were the decisions in the five capital punishment cases. At 11:20 A.M. the radios in the cellblock announced the news: the Supreme Court had approved Florida's capital punishment law. The execution of Charles Proffitt was constitutional.

Newsmen converged on the prison, clamoring to talk to Proffitt and ask other inmates what it felt like to know they were going to die in the electric chair. Proffitt was allowed to go to the lieutenant's office to make a collect telephone call to his

attorney, and a newsman followed him in, trying to listen to
the conversation. Proffitt asked him to leave. After the call,
Proffitt held a press conference. "I expected it," he said grimly.
"It's all over but the crying, I guess. I sure hope I see Christmas."

The next day, in another interview, Proffitt seemed startled by
the media circus of the day before. "The reporters, I tell you,
they didn't know me or anything about me. And the stupid
questions they were asking me—'What was your crime?' 'How
did you do it?' It's really funny how impersonal they were."

The decision, he said, made "one hell of a two-hundredth
birthday gift—happy birthday America." Of all the days in his
thirty-one years on earth, he said, this "certainly wasn't the
best." Did he think the justices of the Supreme Court had paid
any attention to him as an individual?

"Naw, they look at me as just another case, another name on
a piece of paper. That's what society is coming to, it's all paper.
You just get a number and that's it."

*Do you feel differently now than you did a couple of days
ago?*

"Yes, I feel a little bit different—very uncertain about my future. Things don't look too good; they really don't look good at
all . . ."

His voice trailed off. He was taking frequent drags on a
cigarette.

Are you saying you don't have a lot of hope?

"No, I don't carry too much hope . . ." He shivered at the
unaccustomed air conditioning of the interview room. "You
just have to take one day at a time. I guess as the time gets
closer—I imagine you would get a little bit more nervous."

Didn't you say once that they'd have to drag you to the chair?

"I didn't exactly say they'd have to drag me down. I said I
just can't picture myself standing there and saying, 'Okay, let's
go.' Their idea of being a man is to walk right on down there to
it. My idea of being a man is fighting for my life."

Would you struggle?

"I imagine I might, but I really don't know how I'm going to act when the time comes. That's one of the things that bothers me most: I really don't know how I'm going to act."

How about your wife—is it bad for her?

"It's worse for my wife. She's an emotional girl. I've tried to prepare her, but . . . I tried a little humor on the phone to her last night, but it didn't work."

If you're executed, will you try to donate your body to science?

"No, because your whole body would be shot. When you're electrocuted your blood boils, your whole body goes into convulsions, and it just destroys all your organs." Proffitt paused to light another cigarette. "Personally, I'd rather be shot. No suffering, no pain, no nothing."

How about if somebody offered you a pill?

"I'd take it, I'd take it; go right to sleep."

Does that mean you'd commit suicide if you had the drugs?

"No. I have no death wish. I don't want to die. I'm like everybody else; I want to live."

What do you think happens after you die?

"You're dead. That's it. Rot in the ground."

Do you think you might turn to religion when the time comes?

A slight exasperation broke through. "I'm not a religious man; I just can't see how anybody can do that. Look, if there was a God, how the hell could he put a man in a situation like this? Or allow a man to do what he does?"

Are you afraid to die?

Proffitt took a drag on his cigarette and returned his questioner's gaze. "I'm afraid to die this way—helplessly, without a chance, without a fighting chance. It's frustrating. It's more than frustrating; there is nothing you can do. This is a dying you just can't do anything about. It's a different kind of dying, I guess."

Proffitt was not dead yet. There was one more chance: the governor and cabinet of Florida could grant clemency, commute his sentence to life. Here, Proffitt would at last get a chance to speak for himself.

Only at this final stage did any information about Proffitt himself emerge. The Florida Probation and Parole Commission was given the job of investigating the case. Officials interviewed everyone connected with it. They assembled background information: how Proffitt had been one of a set of twins born in New York; how his father had begun drinking heavily; how his parents' marriage had foundered. Proffitt had been shuffled among several homes and foster homes; he dropped out of school and got into trouble. When he was eighteen he was convicted of breaking and entering, an offense he said stemmed from a drunken craving for a hot dog that led him to break into a friend's residence to get one. He had two quick marriages, then one (with Sue) that seemed to work. Her father was living in Florida, and he invited the young couple to move there for a new start. They did, and Proffitt got a job with a trucking firm.

The Parole Commission interviewed some people who spoke on Proffitt's behalf. His wife, weeping during the interview, tried to do what she could. "Chuck was a good person to me," she said. "He worked every day, took care of me, and he made sure we had a roof over our heads and our bills were paid. I remember when we lost our baby [an infant girl born to the couple had died two days after birth], I was really sick for a long time. He worked two jobs to pay our medical bills." Obviously at a loss for words on such a grim occasion, she groped. "I could say a lot of things. I could say the law is unfair. To me there were just so many things that were done wrong. But like you said, they don't want to hear that any more. That's all over with now. All I know is that I love my husband, and I just don't want to see him killed."

There were letters, too. From the half-brother to whom Proffitt had surrendered: "I ask you as a man to reach out and feel the pulse of my mother and sisters who look but have difficulty seeing, who listen but fail to comprehend, who look to God and now to you for the life of our own."

Even Proffitt's father scrawled a few rough lines pleading for his son's life.

But the most desperate plea came from Proffitt's mother. Some said she had always had a special closeness to her son. In her letter she described the worries of an alcoholic husband, her own illness, and other family troubles. "When I came home after six weeks in the hospital, I was bedridden for at least four weeks. He was my nurse, my angel of mercy. . . . He suffered a lot, my son did. It just seemed that tragedy and heartbreak kept him from happiness. . . . Now his life is in your hands. He means everything to me and his family. His suffering is mine. I beg you to spare his life."

In his interview with the investigators (conducted with his attorney present), Proffitt tried to describe his temperament and problems. "Sometimes I feel like, you know, just striking out at someone—just hurting someone," he confessed. "I remember one time I got this pet. It was a little cat—a kitten. This was in California. His mother got killed and I was taking care of it. I got to drinking and the cat did something I didn't like so I picked it up and threw it against the wall. Then I immediately went to it, picked it up, loved it as best I could, and it turned out all right."

This, Proffitt went on, was only one of several instances when he did "things that just don't make sense." Often, he said, people would tell him about these "crazy things, stupid things" he did and he wouldn't remember. They usually happened when he was drunk. And, he said, that was fairly often. Things had gotten to the point where he would drink a couple of six-packs before going to work, then drink during work and finish off the day with a binge after work.

But sometimes he blacked out even when he wasn't drunk.

"I'd be sitting at home and my wife would be talking to me and I'd just go into a trance. She would shake me and I'd snap out."

In prison, Proffitt continued, he experienced severe headaches. They got so bad that, when ten aspirin failed to help, he just gave up and endured them. "Weird dreams, too. I have some pretty, pretty weird dreams."

His attorney introduced Proffitt's will into evidence. It included a few lines that constitute Proffitt's only direct statement about the crime for which he was condemned:

I have not believed myself completely normal in my mind. Alcohol, severe headaches and blackouts have bothered me. I did, for example, have episodes of blackout during the period of July 9–10, 1973, during the approximate time Ron Margolis met his death. . . . Even though I have told my attorney, in the presence of a witness, that I have no recollection of stabbing Mr. Margolis to death, I recognize that my chances of escaping electrocution are poor. Before that final event comes, I want to say these two things: I am truly regretful Mr. Margolis died; and also, I desire to make a contribution to medical science to help determine from a study of my being how mental abnormalities, if they exist, can be detected and successfully treated before tragedy strikes.

The attorney brought up the fact that shortly before Ronnie Margolis's murder, a couple who lived about a half mile from the Margolis apartment reported an attempted break-in to their house. Two men were involved in this incident, and one of them matched Proffitt's description. Perhaps Proffitt had not been alone, the attorney said; the presence of another man would account for the unmatched fingerprint found at the apartment.

The Parole Commission also solicited statements from the relatives of the victim. They expressed eloquently their frustration with the whole process.

Ronnie Margolis's father, weeping at times during the interview:

Let's tell how the victim feels. A father would rather be buried
than to bury his son.

Have we forgotten who committed the crime? Who's the criminal
and who's the victim?

The people in this community are up in arms. We have no quarrels
with the judicial system. We have no quarrels with our police force.
We do have a quarrel if we do not execute Proffitt and people of
his nature. Then society has lost. And there is no way back. We
might as well go back to the ancient days of vigilante justice. The
only mercy that could be given at this point is that which God
himself can give. I have none to give.

The brother, who had to identify Margolis's body at the
hospital:

I've lived for several years now with that image: the gaping wound,
and the senselessness that an innocent bystander happened to be in
the wrong place at the wrong time.

Have the victims in this crime become so obscure that we forget
what the criminal has done? But nobody takes into consideration
that every time this issue is brought up in public, we have to live
this thing over and over and over again—that I have to flash back
an image that rides through the night, and look at the body of my
brother, lifeless.

There's nothing that can be done for the person who is dead, but
you must realize that the families of these people who have been
murdered have to live with this year after year. We have to look
across the table at each other on special occasions and see an empty
chair.

Gentlemen, my family and the millions of other people like them
around this country and around the world cannot really come to
peace with themselves until this matter is concluded—when Charles
Proffitt dies. Perhaps that will relieve some of the burden that my
family carries for the loss of their child.

But another view was expressed by Pam Margolis. In an interview with a television newsman, submitted to the clemency
board, she said that at first she had wanted to see Proffitt executed. But then, she said, her training as a nurse had caused
her to change her mind:

Well, you see now how much society does to keep people alive. And you know what extent they will go to. You know, you just learn to live with the fact that you are to preserve life. I don't feel that it will add anything to kill Charles Proffitt. I was just going to say that I feel that justice has been done by putting him in prison for the rest of his life.

On February 21, 1977, the Parole Commission made its recommendation to the governor and the cabinet. It advised that mercy should not be extended to Charles Proffitt. But even though Proffitt's execution had been approved by the U.S. Supreme Court, his death warrant was not the first signed by Governor Reubin Askew. That doleful distinction went to John Spenkelink. And as abolitionist attorneys found new grounds on which to appeal Spenkelink's execution, Proffitt's case was suspended pending the outcome. He saw three Christmases after the Bicentennial, and hoped to see more.

The "New" Death Penalty

In 1976 the Supreme Court decided that it was possible to sentence someone to death and still abide by the U.S. Constitution. But it is not easy. Comparing the operation of the new death penalty laws with the Court's own standards, one can ask whether they will long withstand renewed challenges from abolitionist attorneys.

In the old days, things were simple: After hearing the evidence the jury would consider whether the defendant did it. If so, then the jurors used their best judgment to decide whether he deserved to live or die.

Too simple. In the 1972 *Furman* decision, the Supreme Court found the results to be arbitrary, with too much room for prejudice. Such a system was unfair and unconstitutional.

Some states responded by taking away the jury's power to punish murder with anything less than death. But in 1976, the Court rejected these mandatory sentencing schemes. Current moral standards required room for mercy, the Court declared:

"Fundamental respect for humanity . . . requires consideration of the character and record of the individual offender and the circumstances of the particular offense."

What the Court required, then, was the exercise of guided judgment, so that similar crimes would get similar punishments. The states whose laws the Court approved—Georgia, Florida, and Texas—had adopted some rather complex procedures to reach this goal.

In trying to resurrect the death penalty in 1972, the first step state legislators took was to define the types of murder for which the death penalty could be used. In doing so, they focused on particularly serious crimes and tried to rule out acts of passion.

Here are the types of murders for which many states decided the death penalty was appropriate, followed by examples of recent cases in which they were invoked—including some that show how broadly these categories can be interpreted in practice:

• Mass murders, or situations where the lives of many people were threatened, even though only one death had resulted.

The Alday Murders—Three robbers systematically slaughtered, over the course of several hours, six members of a Georgia family.

Charles Proffitt—A blow with the fist to the wife of the murder victim was interpreted as "great risk of death to many persons."

• Murder committed to escape from imprisonment or lawful custody.

Ignacio Cuevas—A group of prisoners took over part of a building at the Texas State Prison at Huntsville, and held two guards hostage for several days. The guards were killed, and when police finally stormed the building, all of the inmates except one were killed. The survivor, Cuevas, was sentenced to death, even though there was no evidence that he had personally participated in the murder of the guards.

• Assassinations, or killings "to hinder governmental functions."

Elwood Clark Barclay and Jacob John Dougan—Professing to be the vanguard of a "black liberation army," they chose—apparently at random—a white victim and killed him. A note pinned to the body, and messages to radio and television stations, proclaimed that "the revolution has begun" and called for an all-out race war. The trial judge found that this constituted an attempt to hinder the operations of government.

• Killing for money, or hiring others to kill.

Philip Lindquist—Convicted of murdering a pregnant woman for $3,500, he was hired by the woman's husband, who wanted to collect on an insurance policy.

James Whitmore—The jury decided that he had hired a security guard to kill his girlfriend. But in a separate trial, another jury ruled that the guard had acted in self-defense.

• Murder by a prisoner serving a life term.

Johnny Harris—Serving five consecutive life terms in an Alabama prison, he was part of a melee in which a prison guard was stabbed twenty-seven times. There was no direct evidence showing that Harris had actually done the stabbing, but participation in the riot was enough under the law.

• Especially cruel killings. The Florida law refers to murders that the jury considers "especially heinous, atrocious or cruel." The Georgia law specifies murders that are "outrageously or wantonly vile, horrible or inhuman in that [they] involved torture, depravity of mind, or an aggravated battery to the victim."

Johnny Paul Witt—With a codefendant, he was convicted of kidnapping an eleven-year-old boy and hauling him to a remote area. There the boy was sodomized, castrated, and mutilated with a knife. He suffocated on a gag.

John Spenkelink—An ex-convict drifter, he was convicted of shooting his traveling companion, a crime partner who had been terrorizing him for several days.

• Felony-murders—killings that take place during the commission of another felony (robbery, rape, burglary, arson, and kidnapping are frequently listed). These crimes account for the bulk of death sentences, although circumstances sometimes overlap.

John Evans and Wayne Ritter—These professional robbers shot an Alabama pawn shop owner to death in front of his two children when he reached for a pistol to defend himself against a hold-up.

Sandra Lockett—She drove the getaway car in a robbery in which a storekeeper was killed when he drew a gun. The triggerman, in exchange for a life sentence, testified against her, and she was sentenced to death.

The type of crime is not the only thing the jury is to consider. The defendant must be given an opportunity to present other information that might convince the jury to spare his life. The Florida law, which is the most specific on this point, directs the attention of the jury to several "mitigating circumstances." These factors can outweigh the existence of aggravating circumstances such as those outlined above. They include:

• The victim had voluntarily cooperated with the defendant (such as two men who step out of a bar to fight it out with knives).
• The defendant was only a minor accomplice in the murder.
• The defendant was under "extreme mental or emotional disturbance."
• The defendant was particularly young.
• The defendant had no previous criminal record.
• The defendant was mentally or emotionally ill—not enough to be legally insane, but enough for the illness to have contributed substantially to the crime.

Some states, such as Georgia, do not spell out the mitigating circumstances, but they allow the jury to consider anything it wants to. The procedure in Texas is a bit different; there, instead of specific circumstances, the issue for the jury to decide is whether the defendant is dangerous—"whether there is a probability that the defendant would commit criminal acts of violence that would constitute a continuing threat to society." Texas courts have interpreted this to allow virtually any mitigating information to be presented in rebuttal.

Procedures such as these, the Supreme Court said, effectively guided jurors in deciding which defendants should live and which should die by providing standards. "While these questions and decisions may be hard," Justice Stewart wrote, "they require no more line-drawing than is commonly required of a factfinder in a lawsuit."

Another innovation of the new laws was the two-stage trial. Jurors would no longer decide the question of punishment at the same time they decided whether the defendant was guilty. Instead, a separate hearing would be held to determine punishment only after the defendant had been found guilty of murder. At the second hearing, the jury could hear evidence that might not be admissible in the earlier portion of the trial. For instance, defendants frequently decline to testify on their own behalf at their trials. This is a constitutional right, and it is often exercised by those with prior criminal records because if they do take the stand, the prosecutor can bring up old convictions to alarm the jury. But under the old system, a defendant who chose not to testify against himself risked having the jury condemn him with little knowledge of who he was. Now, he can refuse to testify during the first stage of the trial and then, if he is found guilty, take the stand to plead for his life.

The Supreme Court praised this two-stage ("bifurcated") procedure, calling it "an informed, focused, guided, and objective inquiry into the question whether he should be sentenced to death."

In some states, the jury's decision is final. In others, it is only advisory; the judge can overturn it. In Florida, in the first two years of the new law there were eighteen cases in which judges ignored jury recommendations for mercy and sentenced the defendant to death. Finally, the Florida Supreme Court had to warn the judges that they could do so only when the case for doing so was "so clear and convincing that virtually no reasonable person could differ."

The process does not end with the judge's verdict. The new laws generally provide for an automatic appeal of the sentence. The appeals courts are supposed to make sure that the same standards are applied to different cases. Georgia went so far as to require the Georgia Supreme Court to compare death sentences with sentences handed down in similar cases. "The provision for appellate review in the Georgia capital-sentencing system serves as a check against the random or arbitrary imposition of the death penalty," Justice Stewart wrote. "If a time comes when juries generally do not impose the death sentence in a certain kind of murder case, the appellate review procedures assure that no defendant convicted under such circumstances will suffer a sentence of death."

On the surface, these laws seem unambiguous and neutral. The standards have the veneer of hard choice about them: either the murder occurred during a robbery or it didn't; either the defendant was a prisoner or he wasn't. But in practice, the laws have frequently been difficult to interpret.

What, for example, distinguishes a murder that is "especially heinous, atrocious and cruel" from one that is not? Is any murder not heinous? In one case the Florida Supreme Court said that a single shot to the head did not meet this criterion, but in other cases it has upheld sentences where this is exactly what happened.

The Florida case that dealt with this circumstance in greatest depth was a bizarre one. Thomas Halliwell was convicted of bludgeoning to death the husband of his lover, then cutting up the body and trying to dispose of the pieces. The court ruled that the mutilation of a dead body did not meet the criterion of "especially heinous, atrocious and cruel." "The attainment of a new depth in what one man can do to another, even in death," the court wrote, was not enough to justify a death sentence. When the victim died, the opinion continued, "the crime of murder was completed and the mutilation of the body many hours later" (with a saw, machete, and fishing knife) did not matter. An "especially heinous, atrocious and cruel" murder had to involve torture to a living victim, the court said.

Equally difficult to interpret have been the provisions regarding mental illness as a mitigating factor. The Florida Supreme Court, for instance, once ruled that the very fact that a crime was "especially heinous, atrocious and cruel" constituted evidence of a severe mental illness. (This was in the case of a man who had been raping his three daughters for fourteen years.) But another inmate who had his death sentence upheld by both the Florida and U.S. Supreme Courts had spent thirteen years in a mental institution before his crimes.

The Supreme Court doubtless hoped that it had settled the capital punishment issue once and for all in 1976. But in the next two years it had to redefine its position in several new cases.

One Florida case involved Daniel Gardner, who had been found guilty of bludgeoning his wife to death in a drunken rage. The jury recommended a sentence of life imprisonment, but the judge overturned it, relying partly on a confidential presentence report. Gardner's attorneys were not allowed to see the report or challenge its allegations. The U.S. Supreme Court decided that this violated the constitutional right to confront witnesses and overturned the sentence. The most interesting thing about the case, however, was that it visibly angered the justices, making them wonder if the Florida system was as fair in practice as it seemed in theory. At one point during the oral arguments, Justice Stewart, who had written the opinion upholding the Florida law, barked at the state's attorney, "This court upheld that statute on the representation of the state of Florida that this was an open and aboveboard proceeding. This case gets here, and it's apparent that it isn't." As if to prove the justice's point, the Florida Supreme Court responded to the ruling by eliminating presentence reports altogether from capital cases. Thus the state is willing to deprive people of life on the basis of less information than it uses to choose between probation and jail for drunk drivers.

Another Supreme Court ruling set a more important precedent. In a Georgia case, the Court concluded that death was an excessive, and therefore "cruel and unusual," punishment for the crime of rape. While the Court made no mention of the shameful history of racism in the use of capital punishment for rape (see Chapter Seven), it did note that only a handful of states attempted to punish rape with death, and that even in Georgia ninety percent of those convicted of the most serious charges of rape were punished with imprisonment. "Rape is without doubt deserving of serious punishment; but in terms of moral depravity and of the injury to the person and to the public, it does not compare with murder, which does involve the unjustified taking of human life," the Court's opinion said.

In 1978 the Court handed down a ruling that cast doubt on whether it was at all possible to do what the earlier decisions had required: establish a truly fair procedure for deciding whether to impose a death sentence. The case in question involved an Ohio woman, Sandra Lockett, who (according to testimony presented at her trial) helped plan the robbery of a pawnshop. She remained inside an automobile while her two companions went into the store. According to testimony, the shopowner grabbed for the gun held by one of the men and it went off (accidentally, they claimed). The man was killed; all the perpetrators were caught. Ms. Lockett, a woman of limited intelligence, refused a plea bargain, but the man who had fired the gun accepted the offer and was sentenced to a life term. He testified against Ms. Lockett at the trial. She was convicted and sentenced to death. The question was whether it is fair to execute someone who, in the words of Professor Charles L. Black, Jr., of the Yale University School of Law, "did not kill anybody, did not try to kill anybody, did not suggest that anybody be killed, and did not know that anybody would be killed."

Under the felony murder rule, it was fair. According to this ancient doctrine of law, a person is fully responsible for any death that occurs during a felony in which he or she participates. A robber can be convicted of first-degree murder if a storekeeper kills his partner; in one case, a man was convicted when his partner committed suicide upon being caught. Many legal scholars have criticized the felony murder doctrine, especially as it applies to capital cases; they would require that the prosecution be required to prove an intent to kill in order to sustain a first-degree conviction. This is what Ms. Lockett's attorneys asked the Supreme Court to do.

The Court was in a touchy position. It would be difficult to countenance the execution of Ms. Lockett, yet if the Court overturned the felony murder doctrine it would wreak havoc within the criminal justice system.

What the Court did was to overturn the Ohio capital punishment law. That law allowed only three mitigating circumstances to avoid a death sentence: that the victim helped to inspire the offense; that the defendant was under duress; or that the defendant was mentally ill or simple-minded. This did not leave enough room for mercy, Chief Justice Burger said, writing for the majority. The Court concluded that "any aspect of a defendant's character or record and any of the circumstances of the offense that the defendant proffers" should be allowed to justify mercy, at the discretion of the judge or jury. This decision forced many states to revise their laws.

Justice Rehnquist—the only justice who would have allowed the execution of Ms. Lockett—pointed out that with the *Lockett* decision "the Court has gone from pillar to post." In the 1972 *Furman* decision, the Court condemned a totally discretionary system because it led to arbitrary decisions. In 1976, the Court condemned inflexible mandatory procedures but upheld the principle of "guided discretion." But when Ohio tried to guide juries too much, the law was overturned. "By encouraging defendants in capital cases, and presumably sentencing judges and juries, to take into consideration anything under the sun as a 'mitigating circumstance,'" Justice Rehnquist wrote, "it will not guide sentencing discretion but will totally unleash it." The implication was clear: death sentences will be handed out unpredictably, just as under the old system. And if that occurs in practice, then the Court someday will have to declare the new laws unconstitutional.

That, of course, is precisely what the opponents of capital punishment have been predicting all along: that it is impossible to devise precise standards that can be uniformly applied. In the words of Professor Black, "No society is going to kill everybody who meets certain preset verbal requirements put on the statute books without awareness or coverage of the infinity of special factors the real world can produce." Opponents contend that the new laws are a charade, an attempt to put a false front on a decision that is inherently arbitrary and capricious.

The Florida and Georgia laws, with their lists of circumstances and mitigating factors, have plenty of fuzzy language and opportunities for debatable judgments. But the heaviest criticism has been directed toward the Texas statute.

Most of the Texas law is cut-and-dried, almost absurdly so. If a defendant has been found guilty of one of the types of murder eligible for the death penalty, then the jury must answer three questions affirmatively to impose a death sentence:

1. "whether the conduct of the defendant that caused the death of the deceased was committed deliberately and with the reasonable expectation that the death of the deceased or another would result;

2. "whether there is a probability that the defendant would commit criminal acts of violence that would constitute a continuing threat to society; and

3. "if raised by the evidence, whether the conduct of the defendant in killing the deceased was unreasonable in response to the provocation, if any, by the deceased."

Since the defendant will already have been convicted of first-degree murder, it is hard to see how any jury could answer the first and third questions with anything but yes.

This leaves the second as the only real decision, and this is the question of dangerousness. It is a delicate topic among professionals, for criminologists have been searching for hundreds of years to find a way to foretell future crimes. Most modern psychiatrists admit that they cannot. Police chiefs, judges, and parole board members may believe that their steely gaze can penetrate the hidden motives of the criminal mind. But numerous studies have shown that the prediction of future behavior is an illusion. In controlled experiments, no one—psychiatrist or warden, police officer or taxi driver—has been able to accurately predict future dangerousness. The trend is always to overpredict, to say some people (particularly those who are ugly or different) will be dangerous when, in fact, they will not be.

Of this provision, Professor Black commented, "People are then to live or die, in Texas, on a jury's guess as to their *future* conduct. . . . This is really enough to stamp this section as outside the bounds of civilized law."

But the Supreme Court has upheld this law. Wrote Justice Stewart: "It is, of course, not easy to predict future behavior. The fact that such determination is difficult, however, does not mean that it cannot be made."

One unresolved paradox is that mental instability serves as a mitigating circumstance in Florida, but in Texas an inability to control one's actions would be seen as proof of dangerousness. Defense lawyers in Miami often try to introduce psychiatric testimony that, in Dallas, they would fight to exclude. It is curious that what could save a man's life in one state would serve to condemn him in another—and curious that the Supreme Court would countenance such a conflict.

When one looks at the thrust of prosecutors' closing arguments in Florida and Georgia, it appears that Texas is perhaps more honest about the reason jurors decide to execute someone. Danger seems to weigh more heavily on jurors' minds than aggravating or mitigating circumstances. It is fine to be able to point to detailed phrases in statute books, but after all, what the laws are trying to do is define in the abstract the people we hate and fear in the flesh. And hate and fear, being emotions, are elusive concepts to pin down.

CHAPTER THREE

● The Road To Glory Row

Profile: Richard Hager

Bob Allen didn't make the two-and-one-half-hour drive from Oklahoma City to the Oklahoma State Penitentiary in September 1977 in order to be anybody's salvation. He just wanted a story.

Allen, a veteran reporter for *The Daily Oklahoman*, had received a letter from a Death Row inmate named Richard Lawrence Hager saying it would be worth his while to interview him. So Allen did, and got his story. "KILL ME, STATE SLAYER URGES," the headline read. The article began with a blunt warning from Hager: "If they'd cut me loose, I'd probably just try to go over the walls and pull the trigger on somebody else." The inmate went on to say, "While a bunch of kids are going unclothed and hungry, Rich Hager is sitting here eating and flushing the food he doesn't want down the toilet. What Oklahoma taxpayers are paying for me could furnish clothing to a bunch of little kids. It could also send a lot of them to college so they could become something besides a criminal."

After three months on Death Row, Richard Hager had had enough. "I'm ready to be executed just like they said I should," he said. "I don't care how they do it. If they'll just go ahead and get it over with they can even use me as a pin cushion."

Deep inside the cavernous Oklahoma state prison, a black and white sign hangs conspicuously over one of the barred gates: DEATH ROW. Behind the gate is a corridor of 5-by-7½-foot cells. Inside each cell is a man sentenced to death. The condemned live here for months and years, awaiting the outcome of their appeals. They spend all their time in their cells, whiling away their precious time with books, magazines, and a radio. By law they get fifteen minutes of exercise twice a week, and two showers a week. Breakfast comes at 6:00 A.M., lunch at noon, dinner at 5:00 P.M. Lights go out at eleven o'clock. Every day is the same. Whenever an inmate leaves Death Row, he does so in shackles.

When their time is almost up, they will be moved under heavy escort to another building. In the basement there is a room with another sign: CRIME DOES NOT PAY. Underneath that sign stands the big wooden chair with the straps on the arms. The last person to sit in it was James D. French, on August 10, 1966. French told his executioner, "I'd kill your mother, your father, or your daughter. I love to kill. So you'll be doing society one of the best jobs you ever did." He also said that if they would tie a string to the switch he would pull it himself. But the executioner pulled it for him.

Hager's story in the newspaper attracted a lot of attention. Hager had said he wasn't emulating Gary Gilmore, wasn't seeking publicity. But those who knew him—both those who liked him and those who feared him, not to mention the sizeable number who did both at the same time—wondered. It wouldn't have been the first bizarre stunt he'd pulled to get attention. Hager's mouth had got him in more trouble than his gun. It was easy to believe that his death wish was just another con job, or at least the last flamboyant trump by a man so addicted to manipulating other people that he was reduced to playing the last card in his hand, his own life.

A few months later, Hager came off Death Row, dangling his chains, for another interview. He lounged in a chair in the office of the chief of security, with the chief listening in. He accepted the fact that the handcuffs had to stay on his wrists even during the interview; they did not interrupt his smoking or his fidgeting, not to mention the restless darting of his eyes.

No, he hadn't changed his mind. "Well, like I've said, I've got a lot of time," he began in a gruff voice. "I've got the death sentence plus thirty-five years, plus another kidnapping charge. There's just not much hope of seeing daylight, you know what I mean? I'd really rather get it over with, you know?" He chuckled with exaggerated bravado. "That's what it comes down to, in a nutshell."

But the fire of the earlier interview was gone. The spirit here was resignation, not defiance. "It's my life, you know what I mean? I've got to handle it the best way I can. If they're going to try you on murder, and they find you guilty of murder [here his voice became clear and insistent]—and you *are* guilty, you *know* you're guilty—I can't see the state leaving a guy on Death Row. It's hard on your people. I've got a mother who's aged thirty years over this thing. It's just not worth it. I'll put it to you this way: If they come up here in the morning and say, 'Hey, it's your time,' I'd say to 'em, 'Hey, let's go!' "

Do you think you might change your mind?

"No," he replied instantly, confidently. "No. I sure don't."

Throughout this exchange, Hager had been talking like the early Humphrey Bogart of *The Petrified Forest*, a cardboard tough guy in a black hat. But then his tone modulated and he began to grope for words and thoughts.

"You know, before I made that statement to the newspaper, I could really have cared less." His tone indicated that he could not have. "Up to that point I could have cared less."

He sucked in his breath. "But after I made this statement,

I began to get a lot of letters. And I found out there's a lot of people out there that really are concerned. What was really bad—I had a little gal from California write me. She had been the victim of a rape and beating—and *she* was really concerned about people on Death Row. . . . I don't know, it really got to me. When you've got a victim of one hell of a crime that writes you and really, really cares—well, it tells me one thing: There's one hell of a power on this earth somewhere."

Shyly, almost humbly, he continued. "I got a lot out of that. I just don't know how to put it . . . a lot that I never in my life dreamed of." The strength returned to his voice momentarily. "I'm not crying, sitting here jumping behind a Bible, 'cause I'm not a Bible-thumper. But I tell you what"—he took a deep breath, then plunged—"I believe in Jesus Christ. In the last two, two and a half months, I've found something that's beyond words. It's brought a real peace to me. And it's brought a lot of peace to the other four men on Death Row. We've had something real fantastic happen back there. We're all pretty well behind it now. I tell you, Jesus Christ walked Death Row."

The slender, blond, middle-aged woman showed up for the appointment holding a large pink teddy bear. She herself was dressed in matching pink.

"Hi, I'm Lilly," she said in a lilting voice. "And this"—turning to the bear—"is Candy. Candy goes everywhere I go." She noted a puzzled response. "Richard sent me Candy. I use him to symbolize all the boys on Glory Row." Another puzzled look. "Other people call it Death Row, but we call it Glory Row because the boys are so close to the glory of Jesus."

Lilly is the crime victim whose letter so affected Hager. They struck up a correspondence and she set about showing him the road to salvation. She corresponded with the other condemned men in Oklahoma, and with hundreds of prisoners across the country, but Hager was a special project. She brought some of his letters with her.

"The Lord's walking Glory Row, and you'd be surprised at

the changes here," Hager exulted in one letter. In another: "I've got to learn, and learn some more, and I sure want to turn someone else on to Jesus!" From another: "Can you even dream of a day without pain or hassles? That in itself is worth anything. I wish we were all in heaven now! I used to think death was the end. But it's really the beginning of forever. Hallelujah, praise to Jesus!"

Lilly began writing to prisoners after a low point in her life. It was a couple of years after she had been the victim of a brutal crime, she says. "I was alone—nobody cared if I lived or died," she said in a tremulous voice. "So I said, 'Jesus, please take me home. I don't want to live any more.'" But a few days later she had a vision which inspired her to take up the cause of the lowest rank in society. "Can you imagine how lonely those men are?" she asked. "How much they need to know that somebody cares—really, really cares? Each one of those men is so special to me. They're my family for Jesus."

Now she was devoting her full time to proselytizing via letters and tapes, and was about to set out on the lecture circuit. Her ministry was to be called "Love Is the Key," and she herself planned to take up the title "The Death Row Angel." She said she was hesitant about the nickname, but Katherine Kuhlman's agent told her to go ahead, a sure sign from God. Another vision showed her that she was to build a city for prisoners to live in when they are released on parole, to be called "God's City of Love." She had brought with her a drawing for yet another project revealed in a vision, a Christian shopping center to be run by the handicapped. It looked like a cross between Disneyland and a toy box: one building would be a birthday cake, complete with candles; another was shaped like a teapot; a gigantic drum would house a toy store; a long thermometer was to be a doctor's clinic. "I do what Jesus wants me to do," she said. "I never question it, no matter how ridiculous it might seem. If you don't understand what I'm saying you probably think I'm some kind of a kook. Well"—she giggled—"if I am, I'm a kook for Jesus!"

Lilly was planning to drive from California to Oklahoma to see her boys. The prison authorities said she couldn't come in, but she said she had no worries because a vision showed her praying with them. And for the past several months they had been conducting a prayer and Bible study group together on Saturday nights. From 10:00 to 11:00 P.M. every week, she said, the men knelt down to pray at the same time (yes, an allowance was made for time zones) she and a California congregation were praying for them. "They give a call down the row," she said. "They say, 'Hey, everybody get ready. We're going to California to be with Lilly.'" Her voice was close to breaking as she described the scene. "Just to think that they're sitting on Glory Row, praying, reading their Bibles, and saying 'I love you, Jesus.' It's a beautiful thing."

Are you afraid of anything?

"Yeah," Hager replied, shrugging so his chains rattled. "I'll tell you something. At one point I wasn't afraid of anything. I'm being very honest with you. But I'll guarantee you, I fear God now."

He burst out with a laugh, nervous and loud. "I mean, they can kill this ol' body, but hey—there's something a lot worse coming."

In the summer of 1976, Tom Hughes was nineteen. He was a smallish, stocky boy, and people recalled him as a "simple kid" or "immature." Local authorities in Enid, Oklahoma—a farming community of twenty-eight thousand located some eighty-five miles northwest of Oklahoma City—remembered him as a CB radio thief, but he was never convicted of anything. He did hang around the edges of a rough crowd. And the person at the center of the crowd was twenty-seven-year-old Rich Hager.

Hager was Tom's boss on a crew in the oil fields where they worked. But everybody knew that wasn't where Hager got his money. He frequently bragged that he was a member of the "Dixie Mafia," a loosely organized group of thieves, robbers, and drug dealers. He was involved in oil field thefts, some of them involving expensive equipment, and he hinted that there were darker activities involved. Hager had done two stretches in the penitentiary, and was separating from his wife. They had already divorced once, but then remarried. Now Hager had moved out of the house to hang out with a twenty-one-year-old go-go dancer named Tammy Peters. He left his wife, Kathy, alone with their two children. But he felt some responsibility toward them, and sometimes he would send Tom Hughes to run errands and do household chores for Kathy. She was lonely, and Tom was lonely, and soon they began having an affair. He would come by late at night to see her.

The Labor Day weekend was just beginning when Hager came home. He had driven into town from a motel about forty miles away, where he was staying with Tammy Peters and his cousin, Jim Jones. He and Tammy and Jim had been driving around the Midwest for several days together.

Hager arrived at his wife's home at about two o'clock Saturday morning and she let him in. They talked for quite a while. Kathy later said he threatened her, but whatever happened, they made up after a heated spat about their marital infidelities. They ended up making love. It was just getting light outside when Hager left to drive back to the motel where Tammy and Jim were.

Hager came back to Kathy's house about midnight the next night; this time he had Tammy and Jim with him. After a couple of hours together he drove his companions back to the motel. He left them there and drove straight back to Kathy's. This time there wasn't any fighting. Kathy made coffee and they drifted together into the den. This room was a converted garage a couple of steps below the level of the kitchen. The window faced directly toward the driveway; there were no curtains. Hager and Kathy lay down on the sofa together and started to make love.

Suddenly a blaze of light burst in through the window. A pickup truck had pulled into the driveway and stopped. Hager stayed in the den and pulled out a pistol. Kathy went up into the kitchen and answered the knock on the side door. It was Tom Hughes, clad in blue jeans with a western belt with "Tom" engraved on the back; he wore a blue shirt and was barefoot. Kathy let him in.

Kathy paced the kitchen trying to make small talk as she made coffee. From the den Hager motioned to her to bring Tom down there but she shook her head.

"What's wrong with you?" Tom asked her. "You're acting strange."

Kathy said she was tired, hoping he would take the hint and leave. But instead Tom went into the living room and lay down on the sofa.

Kathy went down into the den. "Just get him down here," Hager whispered to her. But she went over and stood by a wall. He marched out of the den, through the kitchen, and into the living room. He pointed the gun at Tom and began to berate him. Kathy stayed down in the den with her hands over her ears, but she could hear her husband yelling and Tom crying. Finally she went up and saw Tom on his hands and knees, being yanked around the living room by his hair. Hager pushed Tom with his foot and kept the gun pointed at his head. He wanted to know how many times Tom had been to bed with Kathy; he threatened to kill him. Then Hager told Tom to stop crying and sit up, which he did. Hager put aside his firearm and tried to get Tom to fight him, but Tom wouldn't. He begged Hager to leave him alone—even offered to give him his pickup truck. "I'm sorry," he sobbed, over and over. Finally, in exasperation, Hager said, "Look, Hughes, I'll tell you what. I'm not going to shoot you here. I don't even know if I'm going to kill you. I really don't know. So don't worry about it."

Hager alternated yelling at Kathy and Tom. For a while there was a roundhouse argument, and then Hager decided he and Kathy should finish what they had been doing when Tom interrupted. He looked around for a place to lock Tom up but couldn't find one, so he led Tom down to the den. There he told him to sit down on the sofa and not try to escape. Tom agreed. Hager and Kathy lay down in the living room and made love, with Hager raising his head every few minutes to call out to Tom. Tom always answered.

Finally Hager got up, pulled on his jeans, and told Tom it was time to leave. Kathy went out to the pickup and fetched Tom's boots. They all had a cup of coffee together, and then the two men left at about 5:00 A.M. They walked down the street and got into Hager's car.

Hager drove the forty miles back to the motel at Perry. When his cousin finally answered the door Hager pulled Tom in by his hair. "Guess who this is?" Hager asked. "This is my wife's lover boy." The four people talked a while, then they piled into a car and drove back to Kathy's house, where they found Tom's pickup and drove it back to the motel. Hager lay down on one bed, Tom on the other, and they slept for several hours. When they woke up, Tammy went out and brought back some hamburgers. Tom didn't eat anything. It was mid-afternoon when Hager announced, "Let's take a ride. It's time to take a ride." As Tom went out the door, Hager whispered into Jim's ear, "It's time to take him out someplace and blow his brains out." Jim picked up the handgun and followed. Tammy remained behind, reading a paperback book.

The men got in the pickup truck and drove onto the interstate. After traveling north for twenty-five miles they pulled off for gas; Hager bought some beer, which the three of them drank in the truck. They got back on the interstate and drove a few miles to the Lamont exit. They headed west, then turned off onto a dirt road. It led down to the tree-lined banks of the Salt Fork River.

The truck slid to a halt and all three got out. Jim looked meaningfully at Hager, declared that he was going to the bathroom, and handed the gun to him. He walked off into the bushes, to return a few minutes later. Hager walked over to the embankment, chatting with Tom, and they went down the slope together. "Hell, just squat down there and relax a little,

Tom," Hager said. Tom did, and Hager walked around him, stopping about twenty feet away. Then he pointed the gun at Tom and pulled the trigger. Tom grabbed for his groin and let out a screech, long and loud. He bolted upright and clambered up the embankment. Hager ran after him, firing several shots, and Tom collapsed. Hager ran up to the body and fired three more bullets into it. Then he turned and ran back toward Jim, who had been staring at what was happening. He jammed bullets into the gun as he ran. "Let's go!" he yelled to Jim. "Let's go!"

It took a week for the police to catch up with Richard Hager, Tammy Peters, and Jim Jones. They had abandoned Tom's truck, smashing the headlights to make it appear stolen. They drove around Oklahoma and Kansas—to Jim's home, to Tammy's parents, to Hager's parents. They even dropped in on Kathy Hager, and Hager told her Tom was dead. She didn't tell the police about the visit for several days. The three ended up in a cousin's apartment in Perry when an informant's tip sent the police there *en masse* early Sunday morning.

At that time, the authorities did not know what had happened to Tom Hughes. Hager said he would talk to only one person, John Peterson, an Enid police officer who had been friendly with Hager and his parents for twenty years. Peterson arrived and soon Hager agreed to show them where Tom Hughes's body was. He led a caravan of police cars to the site, directing the officers to the grassy ridge where the body would be. When the body was discovered—decomposed—Hager wouldn't get within thirty feet of it.

That's the picture of the crime that emerged from the court testimony, from statements by Jim Jones, Kathy Hager, Tammy Peters, and Hager himself. From the time he was arrested, Hager described the crime to almost anyone who would listen, over the strenuous objections of his attorneys. "He said he'd talk to whoever he wanted to, whenever he wanted to," recalled one of the men who guarded Hager during this period.

This picture may not be entirely accurate. A deputy described Jim Jones as "a frightened dopie"; in return for his testimony he was given a suspended sentence on a kidnapping charge. Tammy Peters was given immunity for her cooperation with the authorities. Kathy Hager told the police several different stories.

Almost from the time he was arrested, Hager proclaimed that there was more to the killing of Tom Hughes than jealousy. Although his statement to the police confirmed most of the details described above, he hinted darkly that it was all a setup. He told Jim Jones and several other people that the killing was actually a rub-out; he said he had received an eighty-five-hundred-dollar contract to kill Hughes a day or two before the crime. During his time in jail he struck up a friendship with Kenny Willerton, a deputy sheriff, and he repeatedly told Willerton that Hughes had been "hit," apparently because he was about to blow the whistle on a ring of oil field thieves. In a letter to Willerton he pointed the finger at one man, his employer, but said that he dared not tell everything he knew. Detectives turned up evidence that indeed Hager *was* involved in oil field thefts, and that he had made a number of freewheeling trips with the employer (who said he wanted company after a divorce), but they were unable to get any solid evidence of a "contract." Southwestern law enforcement officials were familiar with the Dixie Mafia, but there was no way of knowing if Hager was involved or not. They did find that Hager had made a number of mysterious telephone calls from different pay telephones in the weeks before the murder, and they were sure these were tied to some kind of clandestine activity. But Hager also sent sheriffs' deputies scurrying around the area on dozens of wild goose chases trying to dig up buried bodies in one place, stashes of money in another. One lead almost checked out: Hager said he once accompanied a man who murdered a barmaid, and the police in the town confirmed that she was missing, but no body turned up where Hager said it would be. "He was extremely believable," recalled the local district attorney, Joe Wideman. "He had a way of whetting stories with things we could actually confirm;

he had some old law enforcement officers and myself believing him." But finally the authorities concluded that Hager was, in the words of one deputy, "full of bullshit."

If the law enforcement people were disappointed in Hager, the inmates of the jail were not. They listened enraptured to Hager's tales of the Dixie Mafia, contract murders, high stakes, and powerful buddies. "They thought he was the greatest thing to walk the earth," said deputy Willerton. They brought Hager towels and cigarettes, bought him goodies.

Hager's power of persuasion over the malleable was given dramatic proof in November, after he had been in jail for two months. He began to fantasize different escape plans—overpowering a jailer, sneaking a gun in through a window. But his most grandiose scheme involved kidnapping a VIP and demanding his own release as ransom. "He tried to talk everybody in that jail into doing it," recalled Willerton. "He didn't know which one would be stupid enough."

Finally he found two eighteen-year-olds who were. Tommy Summers and Billy Park were being held on a burglary charge, and Hager convinced them that forty thousand dollars was waiting for them as soon as they got out—if they would carry out his plan.

On Friday morning, November 12, Summers and Park drove up to Ponca City High School. The son of the district attorney, Joe Wideman, Jr., was walking to a counselor's office between classes when one of the young men approached him and summoned him outside. When Wideman complied, he was confronted with a shotgun inside a car and forced to get in. Summers and Park drove south to Perry and telephoned the district attorney to tell him his son had been kidnapped. A few hours later they called back with the ransom demand: one deputy sheriff was to drive Hager south into Oklahoma City in a vehicle the kidnappers would recognize. They would eventually signal it to stop and the youth would be exchanged for Hager.

The authorities decided to pretend to go along with it. Hager was put into a car driven by Willerton and driven south into Oklahoma City. Behind the car followed a parade of un-

marked vehicles full of plainclothes officers—all late-model se-
dans with little antennas sticking up in the rear, driven by
well-groomed men in sunglasses. The parade snaked through
Oklahoma City but the kidnappers never signaled it to stop.

Summers and Park recognized the car, but even as gullible as
they were they could not help but recognize the armada behind
it. They let the convoy pass and took young Wideman to a small
apartment in Ponca City. Several hours later the police received
a tip and converged on the scene. The kidnappers were captured
and Wideman released unharmed.

Hager was soon sent away for a psychiatric examination. Security was placed around several officials and witnesses connected
with the case because of telephoned threats. The two young kidnappers were eventually given sentences of ten years in prison,
with three years suspended.

"It kinda happened on the spur of the moment," Hager explained, sitting in the office at the prison. This was his current
version of the crime. "I was sitting in my wife's house that
night. My son, seven years old, had some stitches over his eye. I
asked her about it. She said him and one of the neighbor boys
had got into it, which they had done before. Then I find out
from the boy that this old thing [Hughes] got all drunked up,
come out there to get him a piece of that ol' tail, and went upside that boy of mine's head. Now I think I busted my boy's
butt maybe twice in his life—they got a butt to bust, you know.
But I felt, like, if he wanted to go upside somebody's head,
there's a world full of them suckers out there. You don't have to
do it on kids. I was really upset about it. Very upset about it. I
just . . . I lost my cool.

"And he walked in the house just about the time I walked out
of the boy's bedroom. And it was Katy bar the door. It was Katy
bar the door." Hager clucked his tongue. "From that point on,
it was Katy bar the door. . . ."

"Lost my cool . . . Katy bar the door." Those were the
phrases the defense lawyers tried to work with (although the

story about the boy's stitches apparently was never offered to them by Hager). Their slim hope was to convince the jury that Hager killed Hughes in a jealous rage, and that the crime was only first-degree manslaughter.

Not the least of their problems was their client himself. He would talk to any law enforcement officer who would listen to him; in the courtroom Hager joked with reporters and the prosecutors, and willingly posed for photographs, putting his arm around beefy deputies and grinning at the camera. Hager spent most of his time writing letters to his girlfriend Tammy; apparently he didn't care that she was going to be a witness against him. While in jail, he was divorced by Kathy.

The defense presented the story this way: Hager—"a rubber mouth, always has to talk, build himself up to something bigger than life"—was seeking a reconciliation with his wife when Hughes walked in. Hager, challenged by the threat of cuckoldom, kidnapped Hughes to demonstrate his manhood for his wife. He then drove around with Hughes for many hours trying to find a face-saving way out. But he popped off to his cousin, and when Jones handed him the pistol by the riverbank he felt another challenge to his manhood—and fired. "Shot out of the heat of passion, out of rage built up in him," his attorney said.

Because of the kidnapping, the state attorney general sent in two top assistants to handle the prosecution. They brought up the purported organized crime connection whenever they could, hinting that while they could not prove this, it was probably true. Of Hager's claimed Dixie Mafia membership, one prosecutor declared, "If he is not, he darn sure would like to be. And they are just as dangerous as the ones that are." Hager was called "a hired gun, a paid killer, a coward." But they did not have to prove this connection for first-degree murder; they only had to prove that the murder was committed with "malice aforethought," and they rested their case with ample evidence to show this.

If the motive had to be decided, the jury would probably have deliberated longer than three hours. But it did not, and Hager was found guilty.

A few hours later, the same jury took four hours to decide that Hager should be sentenced to death. The jurors declined to find as an aggravating circumstance that the murder was committed for remuneration; they did find that the murder was "especially heinous, atrocious or cruel" and a "probability that the defendant would commit criminal acts of violence that would constitute a continuing threat to society." The judge set formal sentencing for April 15.

Early in the afternoon of April 15, Hager was taken to the courthouse. But before he went to the courtroom, he was taken to the judge's chambers. There he met his girlfriend, Tammy, dressed in white and obviously pregnant. (Several people reported that the child was not Hager's, because he had undergone a vasectomy some time before.) A woman minister conducted a short marriage ceremony, and Hager kissed his new wife.

Ten minutes later he went into the courtroom and was sentenced to death. Hager thanked the judge.

On his way out of the courtroom, Hager was handed a copy of his new marriage certificate. "How about that?" he burbled. "Two death sentences in one day!"

"Well, I'll tell you something," Hager said in the interview. "The day I pulled the trigger on that old boy, I looked at it just one way: If you can pull it you can take it."

New-found religion or not, Hager still seemed determined to give himself an air of danger.

"If I'm messed with, if I'm provoked, the first thing that comes to my mind is just—kill. You know, I hate to say that."

Would you do it again?

"If I were in that position again, I'd probably do the same thing. There's no way to justify it, I know. You can't justify killing. But when I make a decision on something I follow through on it. Hard-headed. Ignorant. And it's got me in a whole lot of problems. Let's say if I had the chance to escape, knowing me I'd probably take the best shot I could. I'd end up getting killed, which is very likely, or I'd be in the position where I'd kill again. You know? There's no need to be cat and mouse about it. That's the way it is."

If you can't justify killing, why should the state be able to kill you?

"Hey, there's a price to be paid for everything you do in this world. You go out here and you kill, you rape some ol' gal, you maim somebody—you gonna pay a price. Sooner or later you gonna pay a price. You gonna pay it here, or you gonna pay it up yonder. And"—a burst of nervous laughter—"I'm hoping I got mine covered up yonder. I really do.

"But as far as it being a deterrent, it's about as much deterrent as that door over there. They been killing for hundreds of years. I don't care if you took four hundred of 'em out there tomorrow and strung 'em up, electrocuted 'em, gave 'em lethal injections—they're still gonna kill people. Just one deterrent to any of it that I can see; I believe in Jesus Christ, and we need a whole lot more of it."

Just how much of Hager was hype and how much was substance?

This question bothered even those who liked him. Kenny Willerton, the deputy who befriended Hager in jail, recalled, "His whole problem was that he felt he had to prove he was a big man to everybody. He had to show his wife he was a big, mean ass." Willerton thought if Hager hadn't had his cousin with him he wouldn't have killed Hughes. John Peterson, the Enid policeman and family friend, said, "I always liked him. He was a bullshitter but he was sharp."

In his school years Hager had been involved in athletics—he was captain of the junior high school football team—until a change came over him. "Around fourteen or so he quit sports and kind of drifted away," said Peterson. "He ran with older boys and became interested in people involved in crime." He began riding a motorcycle to school and took on the image of a hoodlum. He quit school and got married, but after a son was born the marriage broke up.

In 1967 he went to prison for a year after pleading guilty to grand larceny and forgery. "Boy, I seen the mad dogs there," Hager recalled. Apparently he was impressed by them—"You know, everybody drives a Cadillac in the penitentiary"—and wanted to emulate them. "My way of thinking changed," he said. "If I wanted something, I got it, one way or another. And if somebody got in my face . . ."

Shortly after his release Hager married Kathy, but they were divorced in September 1969. He joined the army but then went AWOL. In 1971 he passed a bogus check for sixty-five dollars to Radio Shack, pleaded guilty without a lawyer, and told the judge all he wanted to do was see his wife. He was sentenced to five years in prison but was paroled after two. He and Kathy remarried and stayed together for three years.

Hager expressed little public remorse over killing Hughes. The psychiatric report (not presented at the trial) said Hager had an "antisocial personality," which meant he was "unable to feel guilt or to learn from experience and punishment." But showing remorse also would violate his tough-guy image. He did tell Willerton once that "he hated that the kid had to be killed for nothing."

Almost no one connected with Hager believed that he really wanted to be executed. "I don't know what got into his head when he put out that B.S. about wanting to die," said Willerton.

Does it make any difference to you how they execute you?

"Well, why should it? I've never been electrocuted, so I really can't tell you. But it really doesn't make any difference. If they fry me, hit me with that old needle, whatever—hell, I'm gone. I know I wouldn't want to be hung, though."

Hager was in line to become the first person in Oklahoma to die by the administration of lethal drugs. In 1977, the state legislature passed a bill making Oklahoma the first state in the nation to adopt this new method of execution. Texas followed a few weeks later. Idaho adopted the drug method in 1978.

"We've made many a joke about it," Hager said. " 'Ain't nothing like going out high' and that sort of thing. I don't think there's gonna be too much of a high to that. But then again"— he brightened—"there may be one hell of a high to it."

Do you have any idea what it would feel like?

"Well, I don't imagine it's too pleasant. But you're not going to feel too much. The feeling's not what gets you. If they throw that old switch on you, you ain't gonna feel too much."

Hager stretched in apparent boredom.

"We've talked about [drugs] back there, we believe it's really a more humane act. It's a lot cheaper for the state and I think it's a lot easier on these people here. I don't think they really get any kicks out of watching an old boy fry. It's for the public outside, not for the people inside. The people outside call it humane. I call it dying."

A few months after the interview with Hager, Lilly—the Death Row Angel—called to say that Hager had changed his mind. He didn't want to be executed anymore and had told his attorneys he would cooperate in an appeal. (His attorney agreed that Hager no longer sought execution.) "They're under so much pressure there on Glory Row," Lilly said. "We can never know what it's like."

When Hager had been asked how he would feel if someone commuted his sentence to life, even against his will, he was, for once, at a loss for words.

"Maybe . . . maybe," he groped, "maybe I can stick around and . . ." His voice lowered. "Maybe in some way help somebody."

It seemed to strike him as a novel proposition.

"But I don't know how," he sighed. "It's pretty hard to do in prison. I do know one thing that's changed about me, though. Now I'm gonna try to do the *best* I can with *what* I can for the *time* I got."

Waiting for the Needle

"We plan to use a wheeled bed with a raisable mattress, like you'd use in a recovery room. It'll have restraints for the arms and legs—we don't know what these people will do."

The speaker is a doctor; he is describing not a life-saving procedure, but the way the death penalty will be administered in Texas. He helped design the method.

"We hope it will encompass a maximum of three to five minutes from the time the IV is started. We'll start the IV at one minute after midnight. We'll probably put it into an arm, although we could use a leg. We'll insert a polyethylene tube four to six inches into the vein. That will be hooked up to a rubber tube leading to an IV bottle. It's the same procedure used in pre-operative anesthesia. The patient can thrash around considerably and not move it. I've had people fall off the operating table and it didn't come out.

"Then we'll wheel him into the execution room. The man would be allowed a last say unless he has requested sedation in advance. If he did, we'd probably give him a big shot of Valium or something. No worry about whether he'll get hooked on it.

"We'll have a neutral saline solution flowing from the IV bottle. Once we can see it's running, we'll inject the three lethal solutions into the flow using small syringes. The first syringe will have one gram of sodium thiopental. It's an everyday anesthetic used in surgery. It has a nice smooth induction phase—he'll just fall asleep. We chose the dosages by taking the maximum safe dosage for an average individual—five-foot-seven, one hundred and fifty pounds—and going ten times that dose. The second syringe will have fifty milligrams of pancuronium bromide—Pavulon—a muscle-relaxant. This will paralyze the muscles. Finally, a third syringe will have two hundred milliequivalents of potassium chloride to stop the heart. Otherwise it's possible the heart would keep beating for up to twenty minutes.

"That's it—the man's dead. And he hasn't involuntarily defecated or urinated, hasn't been burned or damaged. If I've ever seen a calm, pleasant death it's an anesthesic death."

This is the latest innovation in execution methods: lethal injection (the "death needle," headline-writers call it). It is the first advance in execution technology since 1921, when the Nevada legislature passed a law creating the gas chamber. Texas and Oklahoma were the first jurisdictions in the world to adopt this method officially, although the *Guinness Book of World Records* noted that the greatest mass murderer of the twentieth century (excluding political criminals), Bruno Lüdke—he confessed to killing eighty-five women—"was executed by injection without trial in a hospital in Vienna on April 8, 1944."

In the early 1950s, the British Royal Commission on Capital Punishment considered the use of drugs in executions, but rejected the idea. No medical personnel could participate in taking away life, it concluded. A few years later, Albert Camus—an adamant opponent of the death penalty—complained that "the technology used for execution today is, to say the least, far below our technological capability." Drugs, he said—preferably self-administered—"would put a little decency into what is at present but a sordid and obscene exhibition." The same idea came to California's Governor Ronald Reagan in 1973: "Maybe we should review and see if there aren't even more humane methods now—the simple shot of tranquilizer."

But no one did anything about it until 1976, when an Oklahoma legislator (like Camus, an opponent of capital punishment) introduced a bill calling for a survey of methods of execution. This struck a responsive chord in the Oklahoma legislature, largely because the state's electric chair was in disrepair and it would cost sixty-two thousand dollars to fix it. Estimates for a gas chamber exceeded three hundred thousand dollars. The survey quickly focused on drugs, and an official change in execution methods was proposed. Many legislators opposed the new method because it was too "soft on criminals," but the bill passed.

The state's chief medical examiner, Dr. Jay Chapman, suggested that a lethal overdose of drugs be given by intravenous injection, rather than by hypodermic syringe or pills. "The same procedure is carried out in hospitals thousands and thousands of times every day—sometimes to people who are in such pain that they fight desperately," he said. Dr. Chapman himself was once sedated with sodium thiopental for an operation. "It was just like somebody pulled a curtain down," he recalled. "There was no sensation at all. Everything just goes dark." His clinching argument was that intravenous injection is the method of choice for suicidal doctors. "About a year ago one of my assistants committed suicide and this is how he chose to do it. Doctors and nurses do it frequently. They hook themselves up to an IV, start a drip, and then let go with an overdose."

Americans seem to be both attracted and repelled by the mechanics of execution. The process of turning a living being into a corpse transforms a "criminal" into a "victim"—"someone injured, destroyed or sacrificed."

"The man who enjoys his coffee while reading that justice has been done would spit it out at the least detail," Albert Camus wrote. Perhaps, but it was not that long ago that huge crowds would gather to celebrate a public execution. At the same time, however, we are repulsed by the act, reserving a special horror for the executioner.

Most states take precautions to protect his identity. Florida, for example, garbs him in a medieval black cloak and hood. Other states sometimes diffuse responsibility so even the participants need not take the blame: three guards press buttons to activate the electric chair, but two buttons are dummies. In Utah, one of the rifles fired at Gary Gilmore contained a blank, and each member of the firing squad could believe that his weapon had fired it.

Americans are particularly fastidious about official killing. The French began the search for "humane" methods of execution in 1789 with the invention of the guillotine, but America preempted the field with the electric chair (1888) and the gas chamber (1921). (Neither of these methods has caught on else-where in the world.) A number of criteria govern our selection: We want a quick loss of consciousness or sensation, little damage to the body, a minimum of horror for the spectators, low cost, physical distance between the executioner and his subject, and the smallest possibility of bungling.

It was not always so. In the past, men have often used their ingenuity in the opposite direction, devising torturous deaths: burning at the stake, impaling on spikes, slicing away the flesh with knives. Sometimes people were stuffed with gunpowder and blown to smithereens, or tied to a stake and smeared with honey to attract insects. Ceremonial elephants were trained in India to crush the heads of victims at a given signal. For the crime of parricide, the Romans would sew a man up in a cloth bag with a monkey, a poisonous snake, a fighting cock, and a wild dog and then toss the bag into the sea. The English cus-tom of drawing and quartering was described in this sentence handed down in 1812:

That you and each of you, be taken to the place from whence you came, and from thence be drawn on a hurdle to the place of execu-tion, where you shall be hanged by the neck not till you are dead; that you be severally taken down, while yet alive, and your bowels be taken out and burned before your faces—that your heads be then cut off, and your bodies cut into four quarters, to be at the king's disposal. And God have mercy on your souls.

By the mid-nineteenth century, however, hanging was gener-ally accepted as the best method of execution. When done cor-rectly, death is instantaneous: the fall snaps the spinal cord and sensation ceases; the twitching and dancing that follow are involuntary muscle spasms. (Or so they say. As Professor Black has said of attempts to determine the least painful death: "Here we knock at a door that never opens.")

Unfortunately, hangings do not always go so smoothly. If there is too much of a fall, the rope will break. If not enough, he strangles to death, slowly. The official execution log of the state of Colorado, for instance, records that the last twelve men hanged there died by strangulation, with the process taking from ten to twenty-six minutes.

If there is an American way of execution, it is to die while seated, masked and strapped into a wooden chair with electrical contacts fastened to the top of the head and one leg. The electric chair was a by-product of the war for control of the early electric industry. Advocates of direct current (who included Thomas Edison) set up demonstrations to show the dangers of alternating current at which animals were electrocuted. In 1888, the New York legislature decided that the lethal nature of alternating current was a boon, and passed a law calling for electrocution of criminals. (Legend has it that Thomas Edison wanted this procedure called "Westinghousing" to discredit his rival.)

The first electrocution was not an auspicious start. William Kemmler, an ax murderer, was the subject on August 6, 1890. The first jolt failed to kill him, and he had to be strapped back into the chair for more shocks. In succeeding years other victims showed signs of life hours after being pronounced dead. A New York prison guard reported that this prompted the legislature to pass a law requiring immediate autopsies for electrocuted men, on the grounds that no one shows signs of life after an autopsy. Whatever truth there is to this story, it does seem curious that autopsies are required in most states when the cause of death is so obvious.

Standard electrocution procedure now calls for the administration of three shocks of varying voltage over a period of about two minutes. No one has survived an electrocution since Willie Francis, a Louisiana inmate, got a reprieve when the state's traveling electric chair could not deliver enough current in 1946. (Francis's case went to the U.S. Supreme Court for a determination of whether a second attempt at execution was "double jeopardy" or "cruel and unusual punishment"; the Court ruled that it was not, and the chair worked on the second attempt.) Those who support electrocution say that the first shock in-

stantly destroys the functioning of the brain, and there is no
sensation.

What happens to the body during electrocution, conscious or
not, is not a pretty sight. Here is an eyewitness account by Don
Reid, a Texas newspaperman who witnessed 189 executions between 1938 and 1964:

> The man is pale. His arms are lashed to arm rests, his legs to the
> chair legs, his body to the chair with a broad strap so taut that it
> straightens his spine to the chair back.
> He smiles—but he tries to cringe away as a guard stuffs cotton in
> his nostrils to trap blood that might gush from ruptured veins in his
> brain.
> A mask is placed across his face. The guard steps back quickly.
> The warden glances around once more; every man is in his place. He
> turns and nods in the direction of the one-way mirror behind which
> [the executioner] is waiting.
> The *crunch*. The mounting whine and snarl of the generator. The
> man's lips peel back, the throat strains for a last desperate cry, the
> body arches against the restraining straps as the generator whines
> and snarls again, the features purple, steam and smoke rise from the
> bald spots on head and leg while the sick-sweet smell of burned
> flesh permeates the little room.

There are even more gruesome occurrences occasionally. Reid
said he once saw a flame shoot out of the top of a man's head;
other accounts have spoken of eyeballs popping out of their
sockets.

Such reports bring a rueful smile to the leathered face of a
Texas man with almost as much experience as Reid. Let's call
him Joe. As a prison guard he participated in the execution of
125 men from 1948 to 1964, working his way up to the head of
the crew.

"I never seen one caught fire," Joe recalled. "They claim their
eyeballs pop out, but I never seen any eyeballs pop out. The
only place marred was the top of the head. You could look right
in a man's face and you didn't see no marks." It left, he admitted, an unpleasant odor in the room. "When you burn skin,
you'll have a smell. It's like branding cattle."

Unlike Reid, Joe was not turned against capital punishment by his experience. He thought it was an unpleasant necessity. But, he said, "I don't know if you ever get used to it. We have a heart just like every human being. I hate to know all this stuff. It's no honor. But it was my job, and I tried to learn to do it the best I could."

When the Nevada legislature proposed execution by lethal gas in 1921, it envisioned a painless and dignified procedure. The law called for gas to be piped into the condemned man's cell "without warning and while asleep." But the logistics were impossible, and by the time the first convict was executed three years later a special tank had to be constructed.

Clinton Duffy, who, as warden of California's San Quentin prison, supervised the executions of eighty-eight men and two women, described the procedure:

He is dressed in blue jeans and a white shirt. He is accompanied the ten or twelve steps by two officers, quickly strapped in the metal chair, the stethoscope applied, and the door sealed. The Warden gives the executioner the signal, and out of sight of the witnesses, the executioner presses the lever that allows the cyanide eggs to mix with the distilled water and sulphuric acid. In a matter of seconds the prisoner is unconscious. At first there is extreme evidence of horror, pain, strangling. The eyes pop, they turn purple, they drool. It is a horrible sight; witnesses faint. It is finally as though he has gone to sleep. The body, however, is not disfigured or mutilated in any way.

Ten states have adopted asphyxiation as the legal method of execution, including three that had previously used the electric chair. There is debate, however, over how quickly the convict loses sensation. Caryl Chessman supposedly sent a prearranged signal to his lawyer six minutes after the gas reached him.

The people most affected by these methods, the condemned inmates, generally say that it makes no difference to them how they die. "This injection thing is irrelevant," said one Texas inmate. "It doesn't make a damn whether they hang you, choke you, or cut your throat. Once you are dead, you are dead."

Another inmate agreed: "Maybe the injection will be a more peaceful death than the electric chair but it all adds up to the same total. I'm going to give up something I can never have again—my life. A man isn't afraid of the way he's going to die; he is afraid of dying."

Life on the Row is a blending of the real and the unreal; it's a clash of internal and external tension, the tension of everyday living magnified a hundred times. You're a prisoner in a strange land. You are and you aren't a part of the larger whole around you. You form friendships and your friends die. You dream and your dreams die. . . . On Death Row life not only copies art, it creates a grotesque art form all its own that makes life its slave, death its master.

Caryl Chessman knew what he was talking about when he wrote those words in his book, *Trial by Ordeal*. He spent almost twelve years, from 1948 to 1960, on Death Row in California while he tried to avoid the executioner.

Physically, the Death Rows of most prisons are no better and no worse than conditions for other inmates. Death Row prisoners sometimes are allowed some special amenities—hot plates or individual radios—but these comforts are more than offset by tight security, restricted movement, and total idleness.

In Florida, for instance, inmates spend virtually every hour of every day in their six-by-nine-foot cells. Three walls are concrete; the front is barred. Across the corridor, windows let in some sunlight. The inmates are let out once a week for an hour's exercise in the yard, weather permitting; there they play basketball or volleyball. Every other day each inmate is allowed to walk down the hallway and take a five-minute shower. While in their cells, many inmates do not bother to wear more than their underwear. Inmates cannot see each other, but they can communicate by shouting. Each inmate has a small hand-held mirror than can be poked through the bars, and whenever a visitor enters the Row a dozen mirrors thrust out like oars on a slave galley.

Diversions are precious. Most inmates read and write letters. Some play cards by placing the deck between cells and reaching through the bars to pass cards. Many try to cultivate an insatiable capacity for sleep. But most immerse themselves in television and radio, even though, as anthropologist Colin Turnbull noted after studying Death Rows in four states, "A man about to die surely has something better to do with his time than watch 'I Love Lucy.' "

Security precautions are extraordinarily tight—to protect the staff but principally to keep the inmates from "cheating the hangman" by committing suicide. Authorities try to keep away from inmates any implement that could be used to cut or suspend. Thus inmates are allowed only wide-mouthed spoons or plastic utensils to eat with, and they are collected and counted after every meal. Belts are taken away. Some states will not allow inmates to light their own cigarettes.

Despite all precautions suicides do occur. One Florida inmate calmly described how he made a lasso out of his shoelaces and tied it to the bars of his cell to hang himself. But at six-feet-seven-inches, he was too tall. So then he found an old razor blade and sliced his wrists. The guards were alerted and he was rescued. Four condemned inmates committed suicide in the two years following the 1976 Supreme Court decision.

This suggests the central fact of life on Death Row: the intense psychological stress. It overshadows both the physical conditions and the method of execution. Shakespeare might have been describing Death Row when he wrote of "that nest of death, contagion and unnatural sleep." Condemned men may live with the knowledge of the precise moment of their deaths, however, this moment is not immutable. It changes with every appeal. Thus there is always hope—right up to the moment the door to the execution chamber swings shut. The combination of meager hope alternating with black despair, plus a lack of outlets for physical or mental energy, produces over the years a tension that is unknowable to those in the outside world.

Psychiatrists who have studied Death Row prisoners have found that many of them undergo marked psychological changes, sometimes succumbing to delusions, withdrawal, and paranoia. Dr. Louis J. West, a psychiatrist who examined condemned prisoners, called Death Row a "grisly laboratory . . . the ultimate experimental stress, in which the condemned prisoner's personality is incredibly brutalized."

This brings up a grim irony. A man who goes insane on Death Row cannot be executed. When this happens—and it is not infrequent—he is given psychiatric treatment; sometimes he must be sent to a mental hospital. When the treatment succeeds and the man is again sane, he can be returned to the prison and executed. The reason for this is that the inmate must be able to appreciate what is being done to him—an indication that executions are rooted not in the protection of the public, but in revenge.

Inmates have a number of ways to cope with the pressure. Some fake insanity. (Don Reid, the Texas newsman, knows of one inmate who acted his part so well that he won a commutation of sentence.) But others respond valiantly. Some even grow with the experience. When someone arrives on Death Row he has surely scraped the very bottom of society, and some touch bottom and bounce upward. As Dr. Johnson put it, an execution date concentrates the mind wonderfully. A New York prison chaplain, impressed by the development of two young men who spent three years on Death Row before their sentences were commuted, commented, "They gazed at the human condition from a perspective almost nobody's had the opportunity to experience." A few men have been transformed by the experience and, when given reprieves, made contributions to society. Lloyd McClendon, for instance, spent two years on Death Row in New Mexico for murder in the 1960s. At a new trial he was given a life sentence, and after spending almost five years in segregation for being an "agitator," he started to take college courses. He earned his degree, made parole in 1974, and went to work as the administrative assistant to the head of the New Mexico prison system. Later he directed a home for juvenile delinquents in Ohio.

But one of the most common ways of "coping" with the situation is to give up. Gary Gilmore was far from the first condemned man to conclude that it would be better to be executed quickly. "Why should the law be permitted to play with my life like a yo-yo by subjecting me to continuous dates of execution?" asked Robert Massie, a condemned California inmate when he wrote an article in *Esquire* in 1971 demanding the right to be executed. "Is life on earth such a blessing or so precious that I should be desirous of spending it in a dehumanized hellhole of steel and concrete where the law of the jungle and degeneracy reign supreme, where all human and moral values are considered a weakness?"

Sometimes the desire to get it over with becomes so strong that it overwhelms even innocent men. Isidore Zimmerman, a New Yorker who came within a few minutes of being electrocuted, has described how he welcomed the news that he was finally going to be executed. When, at the last hour, he was given a reprieve (and eventually a commutation), he was intensely disappointed. "That was the hardest moment of my life," he recalled later—after he had been exonerated by the courts and declared innocent of the crime. In another instance, a Florida man fought his conviction for five years without success and then wrote to his attorney in 1965 to give up all appeals and arrange for his execution. "I have come to the conclusion that I prefer to die rather than to live," he said. The lawyer did not give up, and seven years later it was proven that the incriminating plaster molds of the man's footprints had been made not at the scene of the crime but in the backyard of a deputy sheriff. The conviction was overturned and the man went free.

Then there is the "Jesus Route," as Don Reid called it. He saw it often. Inmates frequently become intensely religious on Death Row. Sometimes they become so caught up in visions of the life to come that they are in a hurry to get there. This is unwittingly encouraged by Death Row chaplains, whose job it is to prepare men to die rather than to live.

Dr. George Beto, former head of the Texas Department of Corrections, recalled in an interview how one man took the Jesus Route to prepare himself to meet his Creator. Beto was standing in the execution chamber awaiting the arrival of the condemned inmate when he heard singing down the hallway. It grew louder and louder until the inmate appeared, walking deliberately, eyes closed, singing "Swing Low, Sweet Chariot." The man continued chanting even as he was strapped in the electric chair and the mask was pulled over his face. Someone whispered to Beto to see if the man should be interrupted for any last words and Beto shook his head. "He was entrancing himself," Beto explained. The man died in mid-song. "To this day, I can't listen to that song without a shiver."

A few of the prisoners interviewed for this book took the position that death was preferable to spending the rest of their lives in prison. Said one California inmate: "I would rather go downstairs to that gas chamber than have to spend the rest of my life here. Being free is being alive. If a person goes down to the gas chamber he's escaped. It is going to cost him his life, but he's escaped." The great majority, however, echoed the sentiments of Robert Sullivan, a thoughtful Florida inmate: "Naturally, I would prefer to have some hope of re-entering society eventually. But even if there was not that chance I would still prefer life to death and the unknown."

When the years and months of waiting have turned to minutes and seconds, most inmates try to retain their dignity and walk to their doom under their own power. But some struggle to the end. California's last execution, in 1967, involved a man named Aaron Mitchell. In his last hours, he slashed his arms with a razor blade. While blood streamed down, he stood against the wall of his cell in a crucifixion stance. "I am Jesus —I am Jesus Christ!" he screamed repeatedly. Mitchell was dragged, babbling and moaning, down the corridor to the gas chamber. When, lashed into the chair, he heard the cyanide pellets plop into the vat of acid beneath him, tears streamed down his cheeks.

Whether the condemned man is dragged to the execution chamber kicking and screaming, or rushes there to kiss the electric chair, as one Florida inmate did, makes little difference in the end. Almost everything will proceed exactly the same in either case. His last moments will be orchestrated according to a routine as rigid as that surrounding the election of a Pope. Executions are highly stylized rituals, full of quasi-religious symbols and a prescribed liturgy.

Rituals mark important events in our lives and help us muddle through difficult situations. The execution ritual is different in each state but, once adopted, it seldom changes. It is designed both to lend an air of dignity to the proceedings for the witnesses and to minimize the chance of mistake in what is frequently a complicated process. "Only the ritual of an execution makes it possible to endure," commented Byron Eshelman, Death Row chaplain at San Quentin for many years. "Without it, the condemned could not give the expected measure of cooperation to the etiquette of dying."

The ritual is played out before an audience, and particular attention is paid to the witnesses. Most states are careful to shield the dying man's eyes with a mask—although Oklahoma's newly designed procedure for lethal drug injections calls for propping the prone inmate's head up so he is looking directly at the audience. Prison authorities usually provide medical personnel to assist those who faint or vomit.

James McClendon, author of the novel *Deathwork* (and, incidentally, a believer in capital punishment), did a great deal of research on the execution ritual of Florida, where his father had been chief prison inspector. Here is his description, as excerpted from an article he wrote for a Florida newspaper in 1973:

Finally there was the "Death Routine." The condemned feared that most of all. When it began you had to get ready to die, and nobody knew how to do that.

The Death Routine began on Saturday morning, forty-eight hours prior to your execution. You were moved to the end of the Death Row corridor to the Death Cell. The death warrant had already been read to you during the week, and your relatives had been notified. You could visit them all day Saturday and Sunday, but nobody ever knew what to say.

If you slept that last night, you were awakened by the watch guard at 5:30 A.M. on Monday. For your last meal you could have anything you wanted. You could also have a few shots of cheap blended whiskey, or a few pills from the hospital. Nobody wanted any more trouble than there had to be.

You finished eating just after six o'clock. Four guards escorted you from your cell down the Row to a small room just off the Death Row showers. The Preparation Room, it was called. Your hair was clipped to a short crewcut. A small spot on the top of your skull and another above your right ankle were shaved clean with a safety razor. Then you were hustled next door to the shower. You showered and put on the cheap suit they gave you.

On your way back to the Death Cell you could say good-bye to others on the Row. You shook hands with those who came to the bars of their cells, and walked back to the Death Cell, where the prison chaplain would be with you.

The executioner, who had been waiting in the hospital canteen drinking coffee, would have already come over to the Death House. He would have dressed in his black robe and hood, and he would be waiting now just outside the Death Chamber, out of sight of the witnesses.

Suddenly it was eight o'clock, and the deputy warden would be sending the four guards onto Death Row for you. "It's time to go," the head guard would say. Two guards would put "iron claw" manacles on your wrists.

You were only eight steps from the electric chair. You were there before you realized it, your manacled arms held onto the chair's armrests, straps buckled around you. Your arms and legs were strapped down lightly to the chair. You were pinned to the seat of the chair by a waist strap.

Sometimes witnesses gasped when they saw the hooded, black-robed executioner—he was something out of the Middle Ages, out of horror. But there was no time for reactions now; everything would be moving swiftly.

Now you could see the witnesses, you could see the black-robed executioner, you could see a room full of strange faces. You knew only the chaplain who was standing by you reading from the Bible in a mumble.

Now the electrician comes into view on your right. He attaches one of the electrical jacks to the metal plate inside the leather strap holding your right ankle. Behind you he retrieves the sponge-covered death implement from the saline solution. He slips the screw post of the death implement into the octagon-shaped death cap. You hear him step up behind you, and then you feel the cold sponge as it touches the bald spot on your head. The electrician moves into your field of vision for a second as he fastens the death cap's leather strap under your chin.

The deputy warden steps in front of you. He asks if you have any last words. Maybe you can form words, maybe you can't. Then he reaches down to you and pulls the black leather mask on the death cap down over your face. The last thing you see is a human hand.

CHAPTER FOUR

● *"I never stopped to think"*

Profile: James David Raulerson

Now it was the prosecutor's turn to question the psychiatrist. "Doctor," he said, "you mentioned the phrase 'defective conscience.' What do you mean by that?"

Leaning forward in the witness box, the psychiatrist replied gravely, "Conscience is the part of the personality that mainly has to do with deterring human beings from doing things which are against certain codes set up by society. It also has the secondary function of providing feelings of guilt when the codes are broken."

Nodding toward the table where the defendant sat impassively, he continued. "In an individual who suffers a character disorder like Mr. Raulerson, this personality function is defective. It's explicable in terms of his thought patterns, the exposures he had growing up, the moral climate of his growth period. The conscience doesn't work as it should, in the primary function of preventing something from happening, something which is wrong. It *can* continue to function in terms of making one feel guilty after the fact."

A short while later, in an impassioned appeal to the twelve Florida citizens in the jury box, the prosecutor wondered aloud if even that vestigial function of conscience was still alive in the defendant. "Raulerson took the stand this morning and he cried. He might have been crying for Officer Warner, or his widow, or the rape victim, or all the people he terrorized. But I don't think so. I think he was crying for himself."

Then the prosecutor made his own appeal to conscience, to "the conscience of Jacksonville," represented by the jury. "You've got to get the word out to people like Raulerson to let them know they can't come to Jacksonville and rape and rob and murder a police officer," he thundered.

"Get the word out": not a bad working definition of deterrence.

David Allen Sweat was born in Detroit on November 24, 1951. His father and mother didn't get along too well. The father (a widower with six daughters from his previous marriage) drank—drank a lot. David's mother couldn't take care of him, so he and a brother were raised by their grandparents in a small Georgia town. Two older brothers were given up for adoption.

David's grandparents were not able to offer many material comforts. They had no indoor plumbing and drinking water was brought from town. David wasn't very close to his grandparents. His taciturn, reserved grandfather didn't have much to say to the talkative grandson. As a boy, David recalled, he wanted to grow up to be a policeman or a schoolteacher. But those dreams faded away, especially when he dropped out of school after the ninth grade. In 1967, convicted of larceny, he was sent to a juvenile institution.

David ran away from the institution, and traveled to Jacksonville, Florida. There he met a man who took a liking to him: Dennis Raulerson. Raulerson ran a restaurant in Ohio, and

when he left Florida he took David back with him. There was
no formal adoption, but from then on David considered Raulerson his father. "That was the first father I ever had who would
sit and talk to me like I was somebody," he later said. He took
on Raulerson's last name and added "James" to his own.

David lived in Raulerson's house and worked in the restaurant. This lasted for four years. In that time, he had taken a
liking to the cook's daughter, Kate. But she was too young, five
years younger than he. This life, probably the happiest he had
known, came to an end one day when a man walked into the
restaurant looking for his wife, who worked there as a waitress.
The woman didn't want to go with her husband, but he dragged
her out. A customer tried to stop the abduction. The man
pulled out a gun and shot him. Dennis Raulerson, with David
behind, ran after the man and his wife. Dennis moved after
him; the man fired and Dennis tumbled to the ground, bleeding. "Get inside!" he gasped to the boy. Then he died.

The man with the gun put it to his wife's head and pulled the
trigger. She slumped into a heap. Soon the man was captured.
David found himself holding a gun and walking over to the
man. "I was going to kill him," David said later, describing the
incident, "just kill him dead, because he had killed the one
man that had ever been my father and that I really loved."

Why didn't he? Why didn't he fire? "I couldn't kill him,"
David said. "Just because he was a human being. I couldn't
kill a man."

That, however, was not the last time James David Raulerson
pointed a pistol at someone.

David went down to Jacksonville to settle Raulerson's affairs.
When he came back to Ohio to open the restaurant he found
that too much was owed in back taxes, so he moved back to
Georgia. This time he brought a wife with him—Kate, his
young sweetheart, whom he married when she was sixteen.

Living in Georgia, Raulerson had a friend who taught him
welding. He earned about four dollars an hour welding, but the

job didn't last for long. He got another job helping to explore for natural gas, but quit because it was too dangerous. He got a job in a gas station but it didn't pay very well. One depressing night he came home to find that all there was to eat was a can of beans and a can of applesauce. And his wife was pregnant.

In February 1974, the baby was born. Kate was in so much pain that she couldn't talk. Raulerson had to choose the name from those they had discussed. He couldn't decide, so he used all of them: Phyllis (for his grandmother), Acacia (Kate thought it was pretty), Freedom ("because David thinks everybody should be free," Kate said)—Phyllis Acacia Freedom Raulerson.

David's friends had as much trouble as he did finding work in the middle of a recession; in fact, it was even tougher for them because they were ex-convicts. But when things got bad enough they knew how to get money.

David didn't tell his wife where he was going when he took those little trips out of town with his friends. To her, it just seemed that he liked to take trips. Interstate highways were great; in just a few hours you could be in another state, spend a little time there, and be right home. A couple of times David went away with his cousin, Jerry Falk. Jerry was a moose of a man, six-feet-six-inches tall and 250 pounds. He dwarfed Raulerson, who stood a little less than six feet.

One of the little trips David and Jerry took was to Alabama, to a little town called Hokes Bluff, about fifty miles west of where they lived.

On the morning of March 12, 1975, the manager of the Hokes Bluff grocery store was accosted by a man wearing a ski mask and carrying a revolver. He ordered all the employees into a cooler at the back of the store. Another man with a gun and a ski mask appeared. He was huge. The manager, on orders from the gunman, called up the cashier at home and told her to bring down the keys. She did and, at the direction of the gunmen, opened the safe. The men grabbed the money and fled. The Etowah County sheriff's deputies couldn't catch the men.

Back in Georgia, James David Raulerson bought a service

station. He bought it for his brother, who was a pretty good mechanic. David's brother never asked where he got the money.

Later the next month, David and Kate got into a little spat. They had been planning to go to Ohio to visit her family. But David suddenly announced that he and Jerry were going to take a little trip—down to Jacksonville to soak up some sun and see Jerry's relatives. Kate didn't like it, but David and his cousin left on April 26. David, hoping for nice weather, took along his tennis racket.

Like Raulerson, when he was young, Douglas Brian Warner wanted to grow up to be a policeman. Unlike Raulerson, Warner finished high school and junior college. Then he fulfilled his ambition: he became a police officer in his home town of Jacksonville, Florida.

Warner married his fiancée, Lydia, and set out to be a good cop. He was enthusiastic about his work. Sometimes, on free afternoons, he and his buddy from the force, Jim English, would spend their own time sitting near school crossings to catch speeders. English and Warner, with their wives, sometimes went hunting together, or water-skiing. English loved to kid his friend about his scrawny mustache, the butt of many jokes around the station house. Warner wasn't very big—five-feet-nine-inches, 150 pounds—but his brother officers knew he had a lot of heart. Lydia made him order a bullet-proof vest for protection.

The vest hadn't arrived yet when Warner and English went out on patrol on the night of April 27, 1975. It was a Sunday. They were cruising Atlantic Boulevard, a busy divided highway, when a call crackled over the radio at 11:15 P.M. It alerted them to a robbery in progress at the Sailmaker Restaurant, a few blocks away.

The Sailmaker was an on-the-town restaurant, but not one where you'd feel uncomfortable wearing a leisure suit. Outside, a few life preservers hung from the weatherbeaten gray wood. Inside, the decor dripped with hanging fishnets and nautical memorabilia. There were several dining rooms and a dimly lit bar.

At the time the patrol car containing Warner and English was rushing to the scene, the eight employees of the restaurant were lying, face down, on the floor of the kitchen. Over them stood two men holding handguns. One was averaged-sized, wearing crepe-soled shoes. The other was very large; he wore boots. They both had ski hats pulled down over their faces, with holes cut in them for their eyes. In the restaurant office the manager and his wife were also lying down. The man in the rubber-soled shoes had already come in, taken twenty-five hundred dollars in receipts, and ordered them to lie down. He had also cut the telephone lines.

One of the waitresses, lying on the kitchen floor, felt someone's foot nudging her. It was a rubber-soled shoe. The waitress, Suzi Watson, was a teacher, twenty-nine, and very pretty, who worked there at night to earn extra money. Her boyfriend tended bar at the restaurant.

"Get up," ordered the man standing over her. She did. He led her into one of the deserted dining rooms. There he told her to take off her clothes. She did. He told her to lie down on the floor. She did, covering her eyes with her hands. She was crying. He stood over her. "You have a nice body," he said. She kept on crying. The man sat down and unzipped his pants. He ordered her to kneel and kiss him. She did what he told her to do. Then he told her to lie down again. By this time she was almost in convulsions, but she did what she was told. The man, still wearing the ski mask, lay down on top of her.

When the patrol car sped into the parking lot behind the restaurant, English and Warner found two off-duty officers already there, covering the back door. Nobody knew what was going on inside. It might be a robbery, or it might be a false alarm—"not bona fide," in radio-code language.

They waited for five or ten minutes to see if anything developed. The door stayed shut. The officers approached. English pounded on the door and rang the bell. Someone opened the door a crack. "Police!" English barked. "Is everything all right?" The door slammed shut. English lunged for the knob and yanked it open. He found himself facing "this giant" with a green mask pulled over his face. The man was pointing an automatic pistol at him.

English drew his own revolver and, at the same time, shouted a warning to Warner behind him: "It's bona fide!" Then he fired at the giant.

The masked man twisted slightly and collapsed on the floor. English climbed in after him. The man was moaning. English kicked the automatic out of his hand and knelt to handcuff him. Warner stood behind, holding the door open.

English caught a glimpse of movement out of the corner of his eye. Then something hit him in the chest, like a huge fist slamming him as hard as it could, and he tumbled backward as he heard the report of a gun. "I'm hit!" he yelled.

Warner heard the shot as well. Apparently thinking that the man on the ground had fired, Warner pumped five bullets into him. But the gunfire kept up, and one of the shots flung Warner to the ground in the doorway.

English, wounded, managed to raise his pistol and fire two shots at the man in the green shirt and ski-hat mask who had appeared around the corner. Then he tumbled out the doorway, rolling over Warner as he did. Somehow he knew Warner didn't care.

Only a minute or two had elapsed since English had pulled open the back door. He found himself on the ground, clutching his chest, while other officers rushed to his aid. "I'm dying," he moaned. "No, you're not," one of them replied after taking a look.

Raulerson, meanwhile, in crepe-soled shoes and green shirt, had crawled out of the restaurant holding his stomach, where he had been shot. He was thrown to the ground and hand-cuffed. English found that he could stand and he plodded over

to where Raulerson lay. English straddled him, and his own
blood dripped down to join the crimson stain that covered
Raulerson's shirt. "Why did you do it?" English demanded.
"Why did you kill my buddy?"

Raulerson didn't reply.

Few crimes can so outrage the public as the murder of a
police officer, and Jacksonville responded. The story was front-
page news for weeks. It was kept there in part because of a
newspaper-sponsored "Invest in a Vest" campaign started after
it was known that Doug Warner had ordered a bulletproof vest
that might have saved his life. The "Invest" drive aimed to
raise $63,000 to buy vests for the 900-officer Jacksonville police
force. Within several weeks the fund had surpassed $56,000,
with Doug Warner's widow contributing $2,000. Newspaper
articles promoting the campaign detailed the Sailmaker shoot-
out as an example of why the vests were needed. The newspapers also noted that the woman judge who would preside
over Raulerson's trial had never before sentenced anyone to
death.

Despite the extensive publicity, Raulerson's attorney (hired
with money raised by relatives) did not ask for a change of
venue (relocation of the trial to another city). The trial itself
was a somewhat perfunctory affair. The main prosecution witnesses were Suzi Watson and Officer English. Asked if he could
identify the person who had fired the shots at him and Warner,
English walked over to the defense table, pointed his left hand
at Raulerson's face, about a foot away, and said, "This gentle-
man right here is the man who killed my partner."

Raulerson's attorney, facing a hopeless task, called no witnesses and presented no evidence. His only defense, a slender
straw indeed, was presented in the closing arguments. "We've
admitted my client went to the Sailmaker to rob," the attorney
said. "He went there with the worst motives possible. But the
law demands perfection." The attorney argued that the state
had failed to prove an essential element of the crime: that the

"Douglas Brian Warner" mentioned in the indictment was the same person as the "Officer Doug Warner" referred to throughout the trial. The attorney maintained that, despite its seeming triviality, this was a fatal error and that an acquittal was necessary. "My client is not innocent," he declared. "But he is not guilty of the allegations in the indictment."

It took the jury little time to reject this argument. Raulerson stood mute as the guilty verdict was announced.

The sentencing hearing began the same day, August 7. The prosecution called witnesses who identified Raulerson as the perpetrator of the March 12 robbery in Hokes Bluff, Alabama.

The defense attorney made a stronger effort at this stage. He called two psychiatrists who had examined Raulerson several times. The first psychiatrist testified that Raulerson exhibited a loss of memory concerning the incident which could be genuine, although he had a strong suspicion that Raulerson was only pretending. Raulerson, he testified, "suffers a deep-seated characterological disturbance; he suffers defective conscience." Pent-up hostilities, he said, could easily be released under the influence of drugs or alcohol. The defense attorney was trying to establish mental instability as a mitigating factor, but this testimony would hardly convince the jury that Raulerson presented no danger to the public. In cross-examination, the prosecutor led the psychiatrist to characterize Raulerson as a "sociopath." This term has been abandoned as meaningless by many psychiatrists, but juries find it powerful. The other psychiatrist said Raulerson had a "passive-aggressive personality," very similar to an "antisocial" personality. Neither doctor would characterize Raulerson as insane at the time of the crime.

Then Raulerson himself took the stand. Haltingly, in short answers to the prompting of his attorney, he mentioned details of his early life and his marriage. He admitted robbing the store in Alabama. He said he did not drink much because "my father had been a drunk." He had only taken illegal drugs once or twice, he said.

Raulerson said he could remember nothing of the robbery

or the shoot-out; the only thing he could recall was walking outside with his hands over his head. Tears ran down his cheeks as, over and over, the prosecutor pressed him for details. He just couldn't remember much. "I have lain awake, trying to think," he mumbled. "I couldn't remember."

In his argument for the death penalty, the prosecutor commented on the tears. "Oh, he's sorry now, but that's because he's sitting in this courtroom convicted of first-degree murder. He's shown utter indifference about his acts and all he can say is, 'I don't remember.' " But the people of Jacksonville remembered, the prosecutor said, and he was sure the jury would "get the word out" that robbers were not welcome in Jacksonville.

Forty minutes later, the jury returned and announced that it recommended the death penalty by a vote of eight to four. Afterward, outside the courtroom, Officer English said the recommendation was "like an answer to a prayer."

Later that month the judge did what the newspapers had forecast. She told Raulerson, "Your crime can never be erased, but your participation in society can be permanently erased. And it will be." She sentenced Raulerson to die.

So James David Raulerson, the little boy who wanted to grow up to be a policeman or a teacher, awaited execution for killing a policeman and raping a schoolteacher. The irony was not lost on him.

"It wouldn't go over too good with some of the guys up here," he said while sitting in an office a few yards away from his Death Row cell. "When you're with a bunch of convicts you don't tell them you wanted to be a cop at one time. But I grew up thinking I would like to do something good for people—for this country. Because I love America. The country is terrific—it's just the people in it."

The strain showed. Another time, interviewed a day after the U.S. Supreme Court approved capital punishment, he was visibly angry as he described a news reporter's comment that some Death Row inmates were crying when they heard the news. "I ain't baby-crying *nothing*," he barked. "But this is my life. And I don't want to die."

Bitterness, frustration, and anger came through many of Raulerson's statements. He had a long list of complaints about the case and his attorney's handling of it. He hinted that perhaps he was framed; he had been told, he said, that his cousin had done the killing and the rape. "But there was no one left to prosecute but me." Since he had no memory of the incident, however, there was no way to prove this. What seemed to anger him as much as anything was that he was "brutalized at the scene" by the police. The police denied this allegation, although doctors testified that there were bruises on Raulerson's face and hands in the hospital. Raulerson contended that he was beaten in the ambulance. How, in Raulerson's mind, the beating mitigated the killing was not made clear.

Raulerson agreed to be interviewed partly out of curiosity, partly to get out of his cell and into an air-conditioned office. While he seemed bitter, he could be engaging. His blue eyes, which several trial witnesses said they noticed, were indeed vivid. He was not without charm, even as he wandered and rambled in answering questions. He sometimes felt, he said, that he was grappling with his mind in the long months alone in his cell. "I try to keep my mind busy, but when you are in a six-by-nine-foot cell twenty-four hours a day, it isn't very easy. It never gets off my mind. I can never forget it. It's like going to your bathroom. Lock yourself in there. Sit there for twenty-four hours. Don't eat. See how easy it is to forget about eating."

Were his sentence to be commuted to life imprisonment, Raulerson said, "I would be a very happy person. Because at least then I would know that they are not going to put a date on my life and say, 'We're going to kill you in thirty days.' "

Discussing robbery and deterrence, Raulerson attributed his activities to his early life and to hard times. "I didn't turn to stealing until I almost didn't have no other way to go. I wasn't going to let my wife go hungry, and her pregnant and almost time to have her child.

"But I never stole from anybody when it would take food

out of their children's mouths. If I robbed a place, they had insurance to cover their loss. They really didn't lose money.

"There ain't nothing they accuse me of [before the Sailmaker incident] where anyone was ever hurt, injured, raped. They were robbed. But no person was ever harmed."

Did he ever think about the risks of getting caught?

"I never really thought about it a lot. The only thing I thought about was that we needed money to live. I never stopped to think, 'Well, I am going to hurt somebody.' I never thought of hurting nobody, nobody. Because when you point a gun at somebody, they usually ain't going to do nothing anyway."

Did he see any evidence that people up here on Death Row could have been deterred?

Raulerson answered elliptically. "I see men up here who have committed a crime because they were scared that the police were going to kill them. They were as scared as the cop was." That seemed to be how Raulerson reconstructed the fatal moment, either from memory or from descriptions he had read. "If you get scared," he said, "then a lot of people are going to do something just out of reflex. They are not going to do it because they want to kill someone, but because they are scared."

In March 1978 the Florida Supreme Court upheld Raulerson's death sentence.

Scared? Kate Raulerson sounded scared. They're trying to kill her husband. And despite his problems, she still thought he was "a wonderful man." His troubles, she said, came about because "he just had a messed-up life."

The evening of the Sailmaker robbery, Kate recalled, she got a call from her husband saying that he'd be home the next morning. Afterward, she couldn't get to sleep. "Something kept me awake. Then about two in the morning I got a call from his brother. He told me what had happened. I thought, 'Oh, wow!' "

Oh, wow. That's how she came across in a telephone interview. Only nineteen, with a baby to take care of, and her husband waiting to be executed, she was perky, feisty, ready to fight for Raulerson's life. She told of writing to the governor of Florida: "I told him to stop and think. One of these days he might catch his wife with another man, or see his daughter raped, or need food for his family—and he might kill somebody. I asked him if he'd ever committed any sins. I said one sin's no greater than another. I told him if he lets them go ahead he might as well pull the switch himself. I asked him to please reconsider." An aide to the governor wrote back. "A real nice letter," she said. "He said they were sorry for the pain the families go through, and if it did go to the governor they would take my letter into consideration."

If things do move close to an execution, she said, she would move to Florida. "If they're going to kill him, then naturally I'm going to move down there," she said. He would need someone to help him get through it.

Officer Jim English considered himself a liberal on the issue of capital punishment. "If there's one iota of doubt, some other penalty should be used," he said. "In those cases, justice is not best served. And I don't think rape should have capital punishment. I think there have been misuses in the past." In Florida, that probably did make English a liberal. But to him, Raulerson's case didn't present that iota of doubt.

During an interview, English lifted the shirt of his dark blue uniform to show a scar. He said that a pen in his shirt pocket had deflected the bullet from his heart and saved his life.

He thought about the fatal night often, he said. He kept in touch with Doug Warner's widow, who was having a very hard time. And the waitress, Suzi, had problems readjusting, he said. But it was Doug's parents who suffered most. "His father is very emotional about it and cries a lot. For me, it's very painful to see them. They must be asking themselves why I was spared and Doug was killed. For a long time they couldn't bring themselves to accept the fact that he was dead. They're so bitter about it. I think we all are.

"How do I feel about Raulerson?" English asked. "I don't hate the man. But I think he should be punished to the limit of the law. The Bible says 'an eye for an eye.' He killed my partner in cold blood. He could have come around the corner and given up."

Doug's family, English said, "only hopes that the court will see that it's carried out." Doug's father, he said, "would like to pull the switch himself."

"Raulerson showed no remorse," English reflected. "If he had, I would have felt there was a chance for his soul. But when I looked down at him [after the shooting] he just looked up at me with all the hate in the world."

If the execution ever comes about, English said he would willingly attend, "so I could see this man and see if he was sorry."

The Social Issue: Protection

In view of the crime situation in recent years, Americans certainly deserve whatever protection the laws can offer them. For many people, debate over the revival of the death penalty need go no further than a glance at what happened during the ten-year moratorium on executions: murders went from twelve thousand in 1967 to eighteen thousand in 1976. To a frightened public, it was time to declare war—war on crime. Societies, no less than individuals, have the right to kill in self-defense. If the death penalty was a potent weapon, this was no time to keep it sheathed.

The bulwark of American support for capital punishment has always been the notion that, unpleasant as executions might be, they prevent future murders. We are a practical people, more interested in utilitarian considerations than philosophical ones. And in view of the fear that enveloped the streets in the early 1970s, Americans began to call for drastic action against criminals.

But it would be a cruel and dangerous deceit to give the

public a false sense of security if, in fact, capital punishment offers no real protection.

We must keep in mind that both the 1870s and the 1930s suffered from crime rates comparable to today's—and those decades featured high rates of execution. The proposition that capital punishment is necessary for the safety of the public must be examined in some detail.

The debate over whether capital punishment is socially useful centers on these topics:

Deterrence: Will the execution of some murderers frighten other potential killers away from committing crimes? Will it do so better than the threat of life imprisonment?

Incapacitation: Is it necessary to execute a murderer to keep him from killing again?

Expense: Does execution save the taxpayers a significant amount of money?

Let's address the least important issue first.

Without a doubt, it is frightfully expensive to incarcerate any criminal. In 1978 it was reported to cost twenty-six thousand dollars to keep an inmate in a New York City jail for a year. Other places may spend somewhat less, but even so it will cost a half-million dollars to keep a convicted murderer in prison for, say, thirty years. That is a significant expense, and of less apparent benefit than the textbooks or traffic lights it would buy.

On the other hand, execution is not the bargain it might seem. The price of a dose of lethal drugs or a few jolts of electricity is negligible, but the hidden costs are enormous. Death Row, with its constant security and isolated cells, is expensive to maintain. Richard McGee, former head of the California prison system, estimated that this alone could equal the cost of imprisoning an inmate for the rest of his life.

But the major area of expense is the legal work involved in getting an inmate on Death Row and keeping him there. Capital trials are much more complicated than those where life is not at stake. Guilty pleas are seldom entered; insanity defenses are more frequently raised; sentencing hearings are required. One capital trial in Georgia cost three quarters of the county's tax revenues for the year. When the state of Iowa recently had to hire a special prosecutor to conduct a capital trial, it cost $210,000. Even if the original trial is a perfunctory affair, subsequent appeals will be long and costly. A case that goes all the way to execution will probably have a dozen lengthy court hearings after conviction. In almost every case the state must foot the bill for the defense attorneys, not to mention the time required of prosecutors, court reporters, and judges. For every case that results in an execution, a dozen others will have been dropped after several rounds of expensive litigation. Judged strictly on an actuarial basis, life imprisonment begins to look like a bargain.

Incapacitation is a more substantial issue. A murderer who has been executed obviously will commit no crimes in the future. Will a murderer sentenced to life imprisonment ever kill again?

Advocates of capital punishment can point to shocking cases where they have. There is, for example, the case of a man who was sentenced to death in New Mexico in 1958 but won a commutation. After fourteen and a half years in prison he was paroled. Two years later he murdered two people in California. A highly publicized case involved Edgar Smith, sentenced to death in New Jersey for the 1957 slaying of a cheerleader. Once on Death Row he became an excellent jailhouse lawyer and author, writing several best sellers, and gaining reprieve after reprieve. He eventually won the support of columnist William F. Buckley, Jr., in his efforts to get a new trial. In 1971 he was granted the new trial and, still maintaining his innocence, pleaded guilty to a reduced charge in exchange for an immediate release from prison. The judge, after listening to psychiatric testimony, pronounced him thoroughly rehabilitated. But in 1976, Smith was arrested in California for kidnapping and attempted murder. He pleaded guilty to this crime and at the same time confessed that he had, after all, committed the 1957 murder. Then there is Robert Massie, the California inmate who wrote an article in 1971 demanding execution. Saved by the 1972 Supreme Court decision, he was paroled in 1978. In 1979 he was charged with killing a man in a robbery.

The finality of capital punishment, of course, could have prevented these crimes. Historian Jacques Barzun made this the bedrock of his support for the death penalty: "If a person of adult body has not been endowed with adequate controls against irrationally taking the life of another, that person must be judicially, painlessly, regretfully killed before that mindless body's horrible automaton repeats."

But from society's standpoint, we must ask whether repeat murders occur frequently enough to justify the execution of hundreds of people.

Despite the popular image of the murderer as a drooling beast (or "automaton") who, having once tasted blood, is addicted to killing, statistics indicate that murder is a once-in-a-lifetime crime. Several studies have been done of those convicted of first-degree murder who were spared execution and later released from prison. Surprisingly, they do much better on parole than any other type of ex-convict. A nine-state study of 1,293 first-degree murderers who were paroled showed that only nine subsequently committed new felonies. One of these was murder. The execution of 1,293 people to prevent one death seems hard to justify. More recent figures from California are less dramatic, but they still belie the image of the habitual killer. Of 2,076 men paroled from first-degree murder convictions between 1945 and 1977, only four percent returned to prison with new offenses. Less than one percent (nineteen) had second convictions for any degree of homicide.

In sum: The death penalty does do a better job of incapacitation than imprisonment. But it is a touchy moral question as to the point at which the benefits outweigh the costs. Statistically, once a capital offender is caught and convicted his criminal career is over, whether his sentence is life or death. And, as the abolitionists point out, adoption of a *true* life sentence would go a long way toward increasing incapacitation.

However, the chief social justification for the death penalty is deterrence. As a formula for controlling human behavior, deterrence (or threat) is one of the oldest and most successful approaches. It lies at the base of our system of laws and punishments, and plays an important role in educational processes.

As an explanation for how capital punishment protects society, deterrence at first glance has logic and experience going for it. We can see deterrence at work in our daily lives: If the penalty for double-parking is tripled, fewer people will take the chance of being caught. The swiftness and predictability of punishment are as important as its severity, however.

The debate is whether a slight chance of being executed will be a significantly better deterrent than the threat of life imprisonment. Keep in mind that we are looking for a *marginal* difference. After all, most of us need no threat to refrain from violent behavior. At the other end of the spectrum, many murders (perhaps most) seem clearly undeterrable—those committed by the insane, the suicidal, the uncontrollably angry who would kill even if they knew for certain that it would cost them their own lives. In between, there are many for whom the threat of imprisonment is enough of a deterrent. This leaves us looking for those for whom the threat of prison is not enough, but for whom the threat of execution would be effective. Are there such people? Are they numerous enough to offset the drawbacks of capital punishment?

Police and prosecutors assert that there are such people, and that during the moratorium on executions they arose in considerable numbers to strike down innocent victims. Most detectives with experience before 1967 can tell stories of criminals who refrained from killing witnesses because they feared the electric chair. One frequently cited case occurred in 1959, when an escaping convict commandeered several hostages but released them at the state line because, he said later, he knew the neighboring state provided the death penalty for kidnapping. In 1971 the Los Angeles Police Department questioned ninety-nine robbers who had been armed with fake guns or who did not use their weapons; half of them, police officials reported, said that it was fear of the gas chamber that kept them from hurting anyone. The near-unanimity of law enforcement officials on the deterrent value of the death penalty is not to be ignored.

There are, however, some startling failures of deterrence— cases where any rational person would have been deterred and yet seemingly rational people were not. In the first part of the century, an Ohio inmate who designed and installed the straps for the state's electric chair was paroled and then proceeded to commit a murder. In 1961 a Delaware highway patrolman, who had spoken out in favor of capital punishment, killed his wife only ten days after the state's new death penalty law was passed.

And if we blame the moratorium on executions for the rise in murder, then we now would expect to find dozens of people on various Death Rows who would not have committed murder had there been no moratorium. But looking at the cases in this book, or talking to a cross-section of condemned inmates in any state, it is hard to believe that any potential punishment could have prevented their crimes.

In recent years, criminologists and statisticians have combed through execution records and murder statistics trying to discover whether capital punishment makes a discernible difference in murder rates. Many experts who have studied the question have concluded that it does not. In 1970, Professors Morris and Hawkins, in their book *The Honest Politician's Guide to Crime Control*, stated: "The existence or nonexistence of capital punishment is irrelevant to the murder, or attempted murder, rate. This is as well established as any other proposition in social science." Hans Zeisel, professor emeritus of law and sociology at the University of Chicago, said in a monograph that "the evidence we have is quite sufficient if we ask the right question; and the request for more proof is but the expression of an unwillingness to abandon an ancient prejudice." The right question, for Zeisel, is "whether an effect that is at best so small that nobody has been able to detect it, justifies the awesome moral costs of the death penalty." Even a supporter of capital punishment on moral grounds, former director of the U.S. Bureau of Prisons James V. Bennett, called the belief in deterrence "a snare and a delusion."

But it must be admitted that the evidence is not conclusive. If the death penalty were the only factor influencing murder rates, research would be simple. But it is not. Too many social conditions vary from state to state and from time to time for simple comparisons to be valid. The most comprehensive review of evidence on deterrence, sponsored in 1978 by the National Research Council of the National Academy of Sciences, concluded that "the deterrent effect of capital punishment is definitely not a settled matter." Moreover, the report doubted whether "the death penalty, so long as it is used relatively rarely, can ever be subjected to the kind of statistical analysis that would validly establish the presence or absence of a deterrent effect."

The earliest and most influential studies of the problem were conducted by Thorsten Sellin, a criminologist at the University of Pennsylvania. In one of his studies he tried to compensate for demographic differences between states that had abolished the death penalty and those that retained it, by grouping them according to geography and size. Thus, homicide rates in Maine, without capital punishment, were compared with the rates of retentionist neighbors Vermont and New Hampshire. Michigan, abolitionist, was compared with Indiana and Ohio. The result: In most comparisons, abolitionist states fared as well as (or better than) their retentionist neighbors. No deterrent effect was found.

Another type of study looked at the homicide rates of states before and after abolition (or reinstatement) of the death penalty. To be sure that any changes were not due to other factors, the rates were plotted on graphs next to graphs of neighboring states which made no changes. The result: Rates followed the same patterns regardless of whether a state abolished or imposed capital punishment.

Several other studies looked at homicides during execution weeks, to see if publicized executions scared potential murderers, at least for a while. No significant pattern was found.

Two studies by Sellin focused on specific crimes for which capital punishment was considered particularly appropriate. One concerned the murder of police officers. In a widely quoted article on capital punishment, a California police chief, Edward Allen, had called abolition "almost an invitation for murderous thugs to kill more police officers." But Sellin's study showed that police faced no greater risk of murder in abolitionist states than in states retaining the death penalty.

The other study concerned prison assaults and homicides. Sellin found that the level of prison violence did not seem to be associated with the presence or absence of capital punishment.

All of these studies had shortcomings, but the implications were clearly against deterrence. More recent studies, compiled with better data, produced similar results. Retentionists were forced to speculate that if abolitionist states had kept the death penalty they would have had even fewer murders or that a saving of lives too small to show up in the statistics still could be worthwhile.

In 1975, however, a new study sent students of the death penalty question scrambling for their computers. Using the most sophisticated statistical techniques employed so far, Isaac Ehrlich, a University of Chicago economist, announced that he had found the elusive deterrent effect. In his most dramatic pronouncement, Ehrlich asserted that "an additional execution per year over the period in question may have resulted, on average, in seven or eight fewer murders."

Ehrlich's study was seized upon by defenders of the death penalty; at last someone had been able to prove what they had known all along. Even before the Ehrlich paper was officially published, the U.S. Solicitor General, Robert Bork, trumpeted the findings to the U.S. Supreme Court.

Since then, however, Ehrlich's conclusions have been largely discredited. He had used a statistical technique called regression analysis, which attempted to separate the effects of the death penalty on murder rates from the effects of other factors such as unemployment rates, age groups, racial disparity, and probability of arrest and conviction. Ehrlich had gathered data in these areas for the years between 1933 and 1969. The technique was valid—indeed, it was a major step forward in capital punishment research. But when other scholars tried to duplicate Ehrlich's study they found that the deterrent effect disappeared when other equally valid mathematical models were used. Ehrlich also neglected some factors that might have contributed to the increase in murder, such as shorter prison sentences, increased drug usage, and the rise in handgun possession. Most importantly, the deterrent effect disappeared entirely when the years 1960 to 1969—years with very few executions—were excluded.

But the Ehrlich study did inspire some important new research. Two recent studies using the regression analysis technique found that changing the risk of execution did *not* affect murder rates. They went on to identify factors that did: poverty, youth, migration from rural to urban areas, conviction rates, average prison sentences, and racial tension.

The most interesting study inspired by Ehrlich was conducted by Brian Forst, director of research at the Institute for Law and Social Research, Washington, D.C. He used an advanced regression analysis technique to analyze the years 1960 to 1969, the most controversial period in Ehrlich's data. His conclusion was that the moratorium on executions was not responsible for the rise in murder. He wrote: "The 53 percent increase in the homicide rate from 1960 to 1970 appears to be the product of factors other than the elimination of capital punishment. Foremost among these are a decline in the rate at which homicide offenses resulted in imprisonment (from 41.3 percent in 1960 to 34.7 percent in 1970, for the states that reported in both years) and the increasing affluence during the 1960s."

But these studies have changed few minds, pro or con. "The policy recommendations of scholars are often used in political debates on crime, but more as intellectual ballast than as the rudder or sail of public policy," one influential scholar noted. This is largely due to the technical cast of the recent research. Here, for example is a pithy quote from Ehrlich:

"It can easily be demonstrated that:

$$\epsilon_{Pa} = -\frac{\partial U_{om}^*}{\partial Pa}\frac{Pa}{U_o^*} = \frac{1}{U_o^*}\{Pa(1 - Pc\,|\,a)$$
$$\cdot[U(C_a) - U(C_b)] + PaPc\,|\,a(1 - Pe\,|\,c)$$
$$\cdot[U(C_a) - U(C_c)] + PaPc\,|\,aPe\,|\,c$$
$$\cdot[U(C_a) - U(C_d)]\} > 0$$

$$\epsilon_{Pc|a} = -\frac{\partial U_{om}^*}{\partial Pc\,|\,a}\frac{Pc\,|\,a}{U_o^*} = \frac{1}{U_o^*}\{PaPc\,|\,a(1 - Pe\,|\,c)$$
$$\cdot[U(C_b) - U(C_c)] + PaPc\,|\,aPe\,|\,c$$
$$\cdot[U(C_b) - U(C_d)]\} > 0$$

$$\epsilon_{Pe|c} = -\frac{\partial U_{om}^*}{\partial Pe\,|\,c}\frac{Pe\,|\,c}{U_o^*} = \frac{1}{U_o^*}\{PaPc\,|\,aPe\,|\,c$$
$$\cdot[U(C_c) - U(C_d)] > 0$$

Clearly, $\epsilon_{Pa} > \epsilon_{Pc|a} > \epsilon_{Pe|c} > 0$.

Easily, indeed. This can be intimidating to even as learned a body as the U.S. Supreme Court. In 1978 the Court curtly dismissed the social science studies as "inconclusive." Technically, the Court was right, for "conclusive" proof is beyond the reach of current research methods. But the weight of the evidence was clearly against the deterrent value of the death penalty.

One question worth asking is *why* the death penalty does not seem to deter. Logic tell us that it ought to, but no reliable study has been able to find any significant protective value, and dozens have tried. For a proposition that is supposed to be intuitively obvious, this is disturbing. We can imagine how

Copernicus felt when he began to question whether the sun revolved around the earth.

It is ridiculous to argue that the death penalty deters *no one*. People sometimes commit (or refrain from) murder for what seem to us the most frivolous of reasons; surely there are some who consider the odds of being punished.

But why don't they show up in the statistics?

One explanation is that at the same time the death penalty *deters* a few murders, it *inspires* others. Perhaps the two influences cancel each other out.

This may sound fantastic. But consider the case of James French. In 1958 he was convicted of murder in Oklahoma. At his trial he stated that he had killed in hopes of being executed; he begged for a death sentence. This attitude was taken to be evidence of mental instability and he was given a life sentence. Three years later he strangled his cellmate for no discernible reason. When tried for this crime, he sent letters to the judge and jury demanding a death sentence. This time they obliged him; in 1966 he was executed.

Then there is the case of the California man who tortured and killed three women, hoping each time to be caught and executed. He later told a psychiatrist, "When I was planning the first killing, I was planning at the same time what I was going to order for my last meal before the gas chamber." His wishes were fulfilled.

Such bizarre cases are, unfortunately, not rare enough. Psychiatrists and criminologists assert that for some twisted mentalities, the thought of execution is an attraction rather than a threat. These include suicidal types who lack the will to kill themselves, glory-seekers who want to bow out of the world in a blaze of notoriety, and those who feel they have as much right as the state to execute their enemies. Dr. Louis J. West has collected a number of these cases, and has come to the conclusion that capital punishment is, on balance, counterproductive. Capital punishment, he wrote, "becomes a promise, a contract, a covenant between society and certain (by no means rare) warped mentalities who are moved to kill as part of a self-destructive urge." This position seems more credible if we keep in mind that we are talking about people already walking a fine line between rationality and psychosis.

But this argument is not enough for many people. They demand a higher standard of proof before abandoning the ultimate penalty. The most eloquent exposition of this view was set forth by Ernest van den Haag, a psychoanalyst and social critic. At a time when we cannot be absolutely sure of the death penalty's effects, van den Haag wrote in *Punishing Criminals*, we should abandon the ancient practice only if substantial benefits can be demonstrated. He put it this way:

In the absence of conclusive statistical proof of either its effectiveness or ineffectiveness, the case for or against the death penalty as a deterrent rests on one's preference for one of two risks:

1. If the death penalty does not add deterrence and we carry out death sentences, we lose the life of the executed convict without adding deterrence.

2. If the death penalty does add deterrence, and we fail to pronounce and carry out death sentences for murder, we fail to deter murderers who could have been deterred had the death sentence been pronounced and carried out.

Clearly, van den Haag would argue, it is preferable to gamble with the lives of convicted murderers than with unsuspecting potential victims.

In the end, the outcome of the argument over the protective value of the death penalty is determined by how the question is framed. If one accepts capital punishment as the norm, validated by centuries of human experience, then the question is whether we should take the risk of doing away with it. This places the burden of proof on the abolitionists. They face a difficult challenge, for failing to find a deterrent effect is not the same thing as proving that it does not exist. If, on the other hand, one is writing on a blank slate of social policy (or, as at the present, trying to decide whether to *resume* executions), then the burden of proof shifts to the advocates of capital punishment. And so far they have not been able to scientifically demonstrate any advantages to a policy of executions.

It could well be that the effects of capital punishment run too deep to be measured. Supporters of capital punishment can argue that the true value of the death penalty is its psychological impact in branding murder as taboo, and that this impact is felt most strongly in childhood. Any deterrent value from this would not show up for a full generation. But the abolitionists have an equally valid argument: that the lesson capital punishment teaches children is that killing can be acceptable, and that the way to get rid of serious problems is to get rid of the people who manifest them. Here we are confronting a moral judgment, not a scientific one.

As we resume executions in this country, their impact will be scrutinized by legions of social scientists. But for the foreseeable future they will be so rare, and our tools for measurement so imprecise, that it would be naive to expect a conclusive demonstration of the effects of the death penalty. A prestigious panel of experts assembled by the National Academy of Sciences in 1978 went so far as to say that "research on this topic is not likely to produce findings that will or should have much influence on policy matters." The evidence available to us now, however, indicates that fear of the electric chair comes too late, only when one is living next door to it.

CHAPTER FIVE

The Youngest Person
on Death Row

Profile: George Vasil

On April 2, 1974, George Vasil had a birthday party. His parents invited relatives to their suburban tract home in Fort Pierce, Florida, for a birthday dinner. George blew out the candles on a chocolate cake (his favorite) and opened his presents—new clothes and a wristwatch. He had turned fifteen.

George was now old enough to get a learner's permit, but not a full driver's license. He was still too young to drop out of school, or to attend the jai-alai fronton in Fort Pierce. State law protected him from holding jobs operating power machinery or wrestling alligators. He was too young to buy cigarettes, serve on a jury, donate blood, or write his own will.

But, as far as the state of Florida was concerned, George was not too young to die in the electric chair.

In Florida, youth is no automatic barrier to execution. Four sixteen-year-olds have been electrocuted there since 1924. In

1976 a twelve-year-old was tried for murder in Miami, although the prosecution declined to seek the death penalty.

The youngest person executed in recent times in the United States was a fourteen-year-old black youth, George Stinney, who was electrocuted in South Carolina in 1944. Since the turn of the century, at least 239 teen-agers have been executed. In common law, a child under the age of seven cannot be tried for a crime. Between seven and fourteen, children are presumed to be incapable of forming criminal intent, but it is legally possible to prove otherwise. In the last century, children as young as ten were hanged in this country. Most states deal with youngsters under sixteen or eighteen in special juvenile courts, but exceptions can be made for the most serious offenses.

Neither is youth a barrier to crime. In 1975, 184 people fifteen years of age or younger were arrested on homicide charges, about one percent of the total. Murder victims that year included 840 children under fifteen.

In the fall of 1974, George began tenth grade at the public high school in Fort Pierce, Florida, a quiet coastal town located a hundred miles north of Miami. He was a pretty good student, getting A's in most subjects. Sports were his passion, however. He played tennis, was the best miniature golfer in town, and belonged to the YMCA football team. On Sundays, George went to the Greek Orthodox Church with his parents; often he served as an altar boy.

"An average kid—kind of quiet," his classmates said of George. Wilma Vasil sometimes thought her son was too quiet. "Getting George to tell you something was like pulling teeth," she said. George didn't talk much with other kids; he was a loner. As an only child, he had learned to entertain himself. George also seemed very aware that he had been adopted. Wilma Vasil tried several times to see if her son needed profession help, but everyone told her that some boys were just that way. But more often than not, George seemed content, a dutiful son.

A few blocks away from George's house, the quiet suburban life was shared by twelve-year-old Peggy Pitzer. She lived with her parents and her older brother in a house somewhat smaller than the Vasils'.

Peg was a bright girl, always reading. In the fall of 1974 she was in the seventh grade at Dan McCarty Middle School. She joined the yearbook staff and had many friends. Her ambition for the year was to win the state spelling bee. She wanted to be a schoolteacher when she grew up.

Sometimes, for fun, Peggy would go down to the miniature golf course that Ted Vasil ran. It was called the Putt-Putt, and it was one of the few things for young people to do in Fort Pierce.

Peg had two fears. One was of "snaky things" such as spiders and lizards. Because of this, she wouldn't play in Oleander Park, an overgrown vacant lot located behind the Searstown shopping center, about a hundred yards from her home. Peg's other fear was of missing a meal. This fear had been instilled by her mother because Peg had diabetes. In addition to the insulin shots she took, she had to eat six times a day. Her mother was strict about the meal regimen, and Peg had adjusted her life to it. She was never late for a meal or a snack.

That's why, on Thursday, September 19, 1974, Peg's mother was worried when her little girl hadn't shown up by suppertime. Vera Pitzer began to telephone Peg's friends to see if she was with them. One girl, Sandra, had walked home from school with Peg, but they had split up at the Searstown shopping center at about four o'clock. None of the other girls had seen her since. Vera Pitzer got in her car and drove around the shopping center. No sign of Peg. At 7:45 Vera called the police.

That same Thursday evening, George Vasil ate supper with his parents as usual. Then he and his father went to watch an intramural football game. The game was boring, so they left early. On the way home, they stopped at Sambo's for a snack.

On Friday afternoon, George rode his bike to the Searstown shopping center. He went to Dipper Dan's Ice Cream Parlor and bought himself a treat.

Outside the store, George was approached by a policeman. Would George mind telling what he had done on Thursday afternoon? George said he rode his bicycle to Oleander Park. It started to rain, he said, so he stayed there, crawling into a culvert pipe to read a hot-rod magazine until the rain stopped. Then he went home. Had George heard about the Pitzer girl? Of course, George said; everybody had. Did George know anything about it? No, George said, he didn't. The policeman thanked George and let him go.

That evening, George and his parents ate dinner with their relatives. But later that night George got sick, racing to the bathroom and not quite making it to the toilet. Wilma Vasil got up to clean the floor and put the rug in the wash. The next day George seemed fine; he mowed the lawn while his father worked.

Sunday morning Wilma Vasil took George to church, where he assisted at Mass as an altar boy. When they came back Wilma fixed dinner. After the meal George and his father stretched out in the den to watch a football game. Wilma cleaned up the kitchen.

At about two-thirty Wilma heard a knock and went to the front door. Outside were two men in ordinary clothes. They flipped open their wallets to show badges; they were investigators from the state attorney's (prosecutor's) office. The chief investigator, Lt. Lem Brumley, told Mrs. Vasil that they were canvassing the neighborhood, questioning everyone about the Pitzer case. "Yes," she replied, "I was just reading about it in the papers." She invited the men in.

"Do you have a son named George?" Brumley asked.

"Yes," Wilma replied. "He's in the other room."

Brumley looked surprised. "Would you ask him to come in?"

When Wilma brought George and his father, Ted, out from their football game, she neglected to tell them what the detectives wanted to talk about. Ted wondered whether his son had broken a window. Ted had always supported the police, had great respect for them. If something was wrong, he wanted to get to the bottom of it.

Brumley conducted the interview in the living room. Before he asked any questions, he made sure that Ted and George signed "Miranda" forms acknowledging that they had been informed of their rights. "Just like on TV, eh?" Ted joked as he glanced at the forms.

Asked what he had done on Thursday, George gave the same account as he had given to the policeman at the shopping center.

Brumley was not satisfied with the explanation. If George had been in Oleander Park between 4:00 and 5:45 P.M., as he said, then he must have seen something going on, something involving Peggy Pitzer. To see if George's story checked out, Brumley asked whether George and his father would return to the park and point out exactly where he had been. Ted and George both consented. Ted wasn't worried; he trusted his son, and besides, Brumley was gentle and fatherly in his questioning, not at all like the Torquemadas of the television cop shows.

The two investigators drove to the park in their car; Ted and George used the Vasil family car. At the area, Ted, plagued by a bum knee, lagged behind. George and Brumley went ahead. First they went to the culvert pipe, and George pointed out where he had read his magazine. Brumley took George some distance away to a ditch and asked if George had ever been there before. George replied that he had not. Brumley asked if his partner could take some photographs for identification purposes. George agreed, and so did his father.

While the pictures were being taken, Brumley called Ted aside. Several things in George's account did not add up, Brumley said. Either George had seen what happened to Peg Pitzer—or he had something to do with it himself, Brumley said. Whatever his thoughts, Ted kept them to himself as he drove home with George.

When they all returned Mrs. Vasil stayed in the kitchen. In the living room, Brumley confronted George: If he had been in that park at that time, he had either seen something or been a part of it. George denied knowing anything about it. Brumley mentioned a footprint that had been found. Ted, ever helpful, volunteered to get George's shoes. First, Brumley said, they would have to sign a form waiving the need for a search warrant. Fine, said Ted; he signed.

The shoes were produced. Brumley examined them, and announced that the sole looked like the same design as a footprint he had seen at the site.

Brumley then asked if he could see the clothes George had been wearing on Thursday afternoon. George went out and got a pair of cut-off jeans. They had been washed the previous day, but Brumley examined them and declared that he saw a stain on the fly area. It might be blood, he said. Then Brumley asked George if he owned a knife.

As Wilma Vasil nervously paced the kitchen, George passed her on his way to the utility room. This time he was after his fishing tackle box, the one his grandfather had given him. He got down the box, took out a fishing knife, and started back to the living room. This time his mother followed him; she wasn't going to stay on the fringes any longer.

Brumley examined the knife. "This may be a bloodstain on the handle—do you know why it's there?" Brumley asked. George replied that the stain came from a fish.

Brumley asked if George could leave the room for a moment, and the boy did.

Brumley pointed to George's shoes, his pants, his fishing knife. They had blood on them, he said. Disturbed, Mrs. Vasil looked at the jeans; she couldn't see any stain, and she hadn't seen anything when she put them into the washing machine. But she kept silent.

Brumley solemnly told the shocked parents that he thought their son had killed Peggy Pitzer. Ted and Wilma were too shaken to say anything. They remembered how understanding Brumley seemed to be. "These things happen," Brumley said, as Ted recalled later—"the boy obviously has mental problems, and he can be helped."

The way to get help, Ted remembered being told, was to get

everything out in the open. Turning to Ted, Brumley asked, "Do you want to talk to the kid first, or do you want me to talk to him?"

Grim-faced, Ted marched into George's room—where his son now was—and shut the door behind him. Mrs. Vasil shrunk into her bedroom to weep.

Inside George's bedroom, Ted confronted him. Had he killed that little girl? George said that he had not. Sternly, Ted said that the police had evidence, that they were going to get help for him, and that George should tell everything.

Yes, George muttered, he was very sick; he had killed her.

Ted went out and brought Brumley back to the bedroom. George and the detective sat on the bed and talked. Ted slumped in a chair nearby. He did not hear what George said.

That Thursday evening, the police had responded quickly to Vera Pitzer's call. Soon, the police and the county sheriffs were hunting; they were joined by the Sunrise City Citizen's Band Radio Club. Outside the Pitzer home, cars were parked bumper-to-bumper as friends and radio clubbers tried to ease the time and keep the family informed of the progress of the search.

The search continued all night. Shortly after 5:00 A.M., a policeman was looking in Oleander Park, near the Pitzer home. In a ditch covered with trash, he found something that made him recoil.

There lay a little girl. She was naked. Her head was covered with blood. So was the area between her legs. Cloth had been stuffed into her mouth. She was dead.

Beside the body was a brown paper bag that held candy and gum wrappers. Nearby were her clothes, including blue sneakers with "Peg P." lettered on them.

An autopsy established that Peggy Pitzer had suffocated on the cloth, her own panties, stuffed in her mouth. Her funeral was held on Monday in Athens, Alabama, where her grandparents lived.

In some states, no matter what the crime, any juvenile must be tried in juvenile court. These courts can usually order only treatment or confinement within the juvenile corrections system. In New York, for instance, the maximum punishment at that time for George would have been to confine him for up to three years in an institution for youthful offenders.

Florida has a highly developed juvenile corrections system, but there are no strict age limits when a youth is charged with a serious crime. If a grand jury, at the behest of a prosecutor, returns an indictment, then the case must be tried in adult court, with adult penalties, no matter what the age of the defendant. Theoretically, a ten-year-old could be tried for murder.

The local prosecutor, Robert Stone, had some misgivings about George's case. The age of the defendant bothered him. But the brutality of the killing shocked him, and he had reservations about the ability of the juvenile courts to deal severely with a crime as serious as this one. Stone called a minister and prayed with him over the telephone. He decided to take the case to the grand jury, and on October 17, George Vasil was charged with the premeditated first-degree murder of Peggy Pitzer. A conviction would bring either life imprisonment or death in the electric chair.

George's parents were totally bewildered by the indictment, for they thought that George was going to be given help. George's attorney, a public defender, told them he would try to keep the case from going to trial, by offering a guilty plea to a reduced charge if necessary.

In the meantime, George was being held in the St. Lucie County Jail. There he was examined by two psychiatrists. When Ted and Wilma Vasil came to visit George, he wouldn't talk about the incident, on orders from the attorney. The braces were removed from George's teeth while he was in jail.

In the midst of the legal maneuverings, a dramatic scene took place at a church in Fort Pierce. There, the Vasils had arranged a meeting with Peggy Pitzer's parents, through their minister. When they met, there was not much to say. The Pitzers asked a few questions; the Vasils tried to answer them. The Pitzers said they didn't blame the other parents for the crime. The two women wept together. But there was nothing that either couple could say to help the other.

Early in December, despite the defense attorney's expectation that the state would offer a plea bargain, the case went to trial. Psychiatrists had pronounced George sane. The day before the trial, a hearing was held to determine whether the statements George had made to Lieutenant Brumley could be admitted as evidence. George's attorney argued that the confession had not been given voluntarily, because the Vasils had thought the information would be used to help George, not to put him on trial for his life. Ted and Wilma testified that they had not read the forms they had signed, and had not been aware that the evidence could be used in an adult court proceeding.

The defense lawyer had an interesting argument. Most of the time when an alleged confession is challenged, the defense argues that the police exerted pressure through threats of physical force. Here, the argument was that the police had not been too threatening, but rather that they had been too friendly. The talk of psychiatric help, the attorney argued, had seduced the Vasils into producing evidence.

The defense lost the point. Brumley testified that he had warned the Vasils of their rights numerous times, and that he had made no promises of psychiatric help. The judge ruled that the confession, as related by Brumley, could be used in the trial.

What was in that confession?

Here is Brumley's account of what George told him:

George was at the edge of Oleander Park on Thursday afternoon when he saw two little girls (Peggy and Sandra) walk by. He wanted to have sex with them at any cost, Brumley testified. George followed them but became frightened, so he gave up and returned to the park. A short time later, as he was standing by a post, Peggy came walking back, alone. George waited until she had passed him by. Then he ran up behind her and grabbed her. Peg started to scream. "If you scream, I will kill you," George said.

George took Peggy to a wooded area. There, he made her take off her clothes. He started to fondle her. Peg continued to scream. To quiet her, he picked up a rock and struck her on the head. She fell to the ground in a daze.

As she lay on the ground, George tried to rape her. But he could not get an erection. At this, he became overwrought. He picked up her panties and ripped them apart—"to let out my anger." At this point, Peggy became conscious. She looked as if she would scream again, so George stuffed the panties into her mouth as a gag. He hit her again with a rock. Then he stabbed her between the legs several times.

At some point, Peggy suffocated.

George dragged her body to a nearby hollow and covered her with grass and leaves. He gathered her clothing and the rocks. He threw the clothing into a culvert, tossed the rocks into a water-filled canal, got on his bicycle, and rode home. Friday night, George tried to commit suicide by taking an overdose of aspirin, but it only made him sick.

That was Brumley's version.

The trial began on Tuesday morning. Twice during the questioning of prospective jurors, prosecutor Stone made a point of saying that the state would not actively seek the death penalty. He was corrected by the judge, who pointed out that the determination of the penalty, in the event of a conviction, was up to the judge and the jury.

It took several hours to choose the jury. The final panel consisted of five women and seven men. One juror was black. Most were parents. All were over fifty; one woman was in her eighties.

The first evidence was presented at 3:45 P.M. Peggy's friend Sandra testified that she had walked to Woolworth's with Peggy and left her at the shopping center. Someone else testified that she had seen Peggy buying candy there. Mrs. Pitzer testified.

The policeman who found the body took the stand. That was all there was time for that day.

The rest of the evidence was presented on Wednesday. The jurors stared in horror at the color photographs of Peggy's body they were asked to examine. The only evidence against George was presented by Brumley, who related George's confession. The tennis shoes, fishing knife, and pants obtained from his home were not presented.

The defense presented no evidence or testimony. In closing arguments, George's lawyer pointed out alleged discrepancies in the prosecution's accounts. The lawyer argued that George had not actually raped Peggy (there had been conflicting testimony on this point), and that her death had been the result of an effort to silence her, not to kill her. The lawyer argued that a verdict of second-degree or third-degree murder would be more appropriate than first-degree murder. (The jury had the power to reduce the charge.)

The jury took about forty-five minutes to reach a decision. The verdict: guilty of first-degree murder.

After the judge and jury had left the court room, Jake Pitzer, Peggy's father, approached the prosecutor. "I'm satisfied," he told Stone quietly.

The next day the sentencing hearing was held. The choice for the jury was between death in the electric chair and the twenty-five-year-minimum life sentence. The prosecution could be expected to emphasize two aggravating circumstances enumerated in Florida's law: that the crime occurred during the commission of a rape, and that it was "especially heinous, atrocious or cruel." The defense would point to mitigating circumstances: a mental disorder, lack of a prior record, and, especially, age. All these were set forth in the law as justifications for the lesser sentence.

Stone, the prosecutor, called no witnesses. Wilma Vasil took the stand for the defense. Often in tears, she told of the problems she had with George—what a loner he was, how hard it was to talk to him. "Many times he would just put his hands over his ears," she said. She also told of seeking help from counselors, doctors, and ministers. In 1970 she went to a local mental clinic, she said. "I was more or less laughed at," she testified. "The young woman I spoke to said, 'Oh, that is nothing—you should know what I go through with my stepdaughter.' She suggested that my husband and I come to group therapy sessions once a week. If we heard what other parents went through with their children we would feel much better."

Ted Vasil took the stand to tell of George's home life. He supported his wife's account of George's difficult childhood. He also said that while he did not have a lot of money, he would find some way to provide psychiatric help for George. "The cost is of no concern," he said. "It will be done."

Then the defense called to the stand a court-appointed psychiatrist who had interviewed George for an hour and a half in jail. After much prodding, the psychiatrist said, he had gotten George to discuss the crime with him. The psychiatrist testified that George had not realized the consequences of some of his acts. When he gagged Peggy, for instance, George was only trying to silence her. The cuts made in the girl's genital area were not an attempt to cause pain, the psychiatrist testified; they were symbolic attempts to enlarge the opening that had frustrated him.

George suffered from a severe personality disorder, the psychiatrist said—"a pathological type of immaturity" marked by "aggressiveness and impulsiveness." But, he said, with intensive psychiatric care, the chances were good that George could be cured.

Upon cross-examination, the prosecutor asked how much treatment would be required. At least two hundred hours of individual psychotherapy, over a couple of years, the psychiatrist replied. The prosecutor asked what the chances were that George would get that kind of help in the state prison system. The psychiatrist admitted that they were very slim.

In his final plea to the jury, Stone, who had announced two

days earlier that he would not seek the death penalty, argued for the most severe sentence. "He is a fifteen-year-old boy and his parents are here and very nice people, but you can't consider that," he told the jury. "Don't consider sympathy. Consider the aggravating circumstances. Consider that he jabbed a knife. . . ."

After the jury retired to consider its recommendation, things got loud inside the jury room. One juror shouted that nothing was severe enough for someone who had committed such a crime. Several others clamored to talk. The noise was such that the judge sent someone to rap on the door and ask that the deliberations be quieted.

Several jurors announced that no amount of arguing would convince them to vote for the death penalty. Soon the fore-woman sensed that positions were not going to change. Also, everyone wanted to get it over with that afternoon. So she took a vote. It was nine to three in favor of the death penalty.

The jury filed back into the courtroom twenty minutes after it had left. Her hand shaking, the forewoman handed the verdict slip to the court bailiff. The bailiff handed the slip to the judge, who read it and handed it to the clerk. The clerk read the decision for all to hear: "A majority of the jury impose and recommend to the court that it impose the death penalty upon the defendant."

George had one last hope. The judge could reject the recommendation. If he wasn't sure what to do, he could call for a pre-sentence investigation.

The judge did not wait. He called George and his attorney before him immediately. He asked if George had anything to say. George looked down, and in a low voice he said, "If you give me life I will try to help myself and with the help of God try to mend my ways."

The judge spoke. "It is the sentence of the court that you be committed to the custody of the Division of Corrections and put to death according to law. May God have mercy on your soul."

"Oh, no!" gasped Wilma Vasil. Ted Vasil muttered something to the effect that "they're trying to crucify the kid!"

George, as ever, showed no emotion.

Fifteen years is not much time to prepare for the electric chair. But George's anguished parents thought his problems may have started before they met him. George was eleven months old when he joined the Vasil family. Until March 1960 he lived in a state-run adoption center in Ohio. The officials who ran the home told Wilma, at the time of the adoption, that George had never seen his natural mother. They said he hadn't been put up for adoption at six months, the usual age, because his development was slow. At the age when other infants were beginning to roll around in their cribs, George didn't. He just lay there.

It seemed to Wilma that "no one had ever talked to him or cuddled him."

"And when they get a little bit tired or fretful, most kids want to be cuddled and loved," she said in an interview a year and a half after George was sentenced. "But not George. He was just the opposite. When you picked him up he would start crying; when you put him in his crib he'd be satisfied and stop crying."

Wilma sighed. "It seemed like he wanted to be left alone from the time we got him."

As he grew older, George became a very fussy eater. "Mealtimes were hell in our home," Wilma recalled. Ted, sitting near his wife in the living room of their home, chimed in, "All you had to do was put plates on the table and he would start crying, because he knew what was coming."

When George was three, the family left Ohio for Florida. They wanted to be near Wilma's parents, who had moved to the warmer climate, and they could see how Florida was booming. Ted purchased a franchise from the Putt-Putt miniature golf chain. They lived with Wilma's mother for a while, until their home was ready. The Vasils had thought of adopting more children, but there were always too many things un-settled. By the time they moved into their own house, it was clear that George was going to be an only child.

As single children do, George learned to play by himself. He liked to read, and often went to the public library by himself to get books. When he found a book he liked, he would read it again and again. He had board games, like Monopoly, which he would play by himself when he couldn't get his parents to join him. George often had to play alone, since his father could not take much time off from the golf course, especially in the evenings and on weekends. When George did play with his parents, however, he was a very poor loser. "He really liked sports and he never cheated," recalled a playmate. "But when he got mad, he got mad."

But there was a sentimental side to George, too. When he was eight or nine he sneaked out to Sears and used all his savings, about eight dollars, to buy a locket to give his mother on Mother's Day.

In early 1972, when George was thirteen, a poor family moved into the neighborhood. They came in a bus and they lived in it, parked on a vacant lot in the subdivision. George felt sorry for the kids in the family because they didn't have much. He tried, Mrs. Vasil recalls, to give them his own clothes and toys, but she stopped that.

One summer, George's mother hurt her shoulder. To work it back into shape required painful exercises. For a while, George helped her go through the routine, but he finally re-fused. "I can't, Mother," she remembers him saying. "I can't stand to hurt you."

When he was about ten, George ran away from home a few times. Once, he got as far as the edge of town. That time, the police who found him showed him the town jail. They told him to be careful or he would end up there. The sight scared him, George recalled, and he quit running away.

George joined the Boy Scouts, but after a year he wanted to quit. His mother found out that George had started to make a few friends among the kids—but when they began to do things together George would find an excuse to break it off.

George would occasionally play with the neighborhood boys. Often there were fights, or other kinds of mischief. George was often accused of starting the fights. He would deny it, but Mr. Vasil wasn't one to brook disobedience. George would take his punishment silently. Much later, Ted found out that his son had not really done some of the things for which he was blamed. But George would never tattle on the other kids.

For two seasons George played with the YMCA football team. He was the center. George got along fine with the other kids on the team. His coach said that during George's two years with the team he was conscientious, and not particularly aggressive.

As George grew into adolescence, his parents felt uncomfortable about discussing sex with him. When he was little, they had waited for him to ask normal questions. Part of the problem was that they wanted to be honest about his adoption. So when he would ask where he came from, they would say he came from a children's home. They expected him to ask more questions; George, however, always seemed satisfied with that explanation.

It is interesting that the psychiatrist who examined George did not even mention the fact that George was adopted. His parents said that he had always wanted to know who his "real" parents were—a concern that hurt the Vasils, who always explained that they were his real parents, since they had loved and wanted him enough to adopt him. But some psychiatrists who have studied adoptees say that George's interest was normal, and that the implied rejection of having been given up for adoption can be a very threatening thing—particularly to adolescent boys. It can lead to a terrific rage, they say—particularly against females.

Ted and Wilma eventually began to worry about their quiet son. "He does not show his emotions," Wilma said. "Even if he is frightened or angry, he just holds everything in." But they weren't sure if they were being overprotective; neither Ted nor Wilma had grown up with brothers. When Wilma expressed her fears to her friends, "everyone told me, 'Oh, you're not used to boys. They're different. You should hear how my kids carry on.'"

Finally, however, Wilma went for help. She tried a counselor at school, who assured her that George was perfectly normal. Then there was the episode at the mental health clinic. Her last attempt to get help came when George had an appointment with a doctor for a physical examination. Without telling her son, Wilma went to the doctor beforehand and told him of her worries: how withdrawn and argumentative George was, how he suffered from frequent headaches. After the examination, she remembered the doctor telling her, "Well, George is shy, he's at that age now. He has acne, and wears braces and glasses. He's got an inferiority complex—but that's perfectly normal. He'll grow out of it."

A few of George's classmates said, after the crime, that they had always thought him "weird." But most acquaintances say he seemed normal, if quiet. The man who coached him in football for two years said, "When this first happened, I said to myself, 'Anyone is capable of this, if George is capable of it.' That's how I felt about George."

Do you think he was crazy?

The question was directed at two people sitting on a couch. They were Peggy Pitzer's parents: Jake, a large man with short hair whose every move was as slow and deliberate as his speech; and Vera, a small woman, a reed, stripped down to whip-like strength. Her eyes were a deep well of pain.

Jake spoke first, softly, with a drawl.

"No. He wasn't crazy."

Vera blurted out, "It would be easier if I could convince myself that he *was* crazy. 'Cause then you could say, well, he didn't know what he was doing."

The interview took place in a city to which the Pitzers moved some time after their daughter's death. Also present was their surviving child, Gary, nineteen years old, and in college.

"I don't ever forget about it," said Gary somberly. "I think about it every day. I don't imagine that there has been a day gone by since it happened that I haven't thought about it. I don't guess there ever will be."

Silence.

Has it changed your life a lot?

"Yes, it has changed mine, a lot," answered Vera.

Changed your outlook on life?

"Yes, to a great extent."

How about your faith?

"No, it has not changed my faith. Without God, we would be insane today."

Was there anything you could have done to prevent it?

"I have thought and thought, and I cannot think of a thing. You cannot keep a twelve-year-old kid at home all the time. She was just in the wrong place at the wrong time. Just because you live in a nice quiet neighborhood—well, things can still happen."

Jake said that he had no objections when the prosecutor told him before the trial he was going to push for the maximum prison sentence, rather than the death sentence. But now, Jake said, "He was sentenced to death, and it should be carried out. The jury saw fit to recommend it, the judge—who didn't have to take their recommendation—took it. That was what the sentence was, and that is what it should be."

The Pitzers thought capital punishment "a necessary evil." They didn't want revenge, they said, but they were tormented by the thought that if George were ever to walk free, someone else might have to suffer as they have suffered.

"The doctors testified that he would commit the same crime, or a crime even worse, if he was let out," Vera said. "So why take the chance of letting him out?"

"Twenty-five years from now, he'll be forty," said Jake. "Well, I'm older than forty. . . ."

So mostly your feelings are based on not ever wanting to see him out in the streets?

Vera answered. "Listen, we have suffered. To put other parents through what we went through?" Her eyes brimmed and her voice cracked. "My child suffered. I know she had to suffer. No, I wouldn't want to take the chance of another little girl having to go through that."

"Well, to me he don't have a right to live," said Jake. "Twelve people on the jury decided it that way. I didn't have nothing to do with it."

"He showed no mercy whatsoever," added Vera. "And she had never done anything to hurt him. Peg was a lovely little girl. She loved people. And everybody loved her."

"I've never had any more sympathy for any family than I did for Mr. and Mrs. Vasil," said Judge Wallace Sample, who conducted the trial. "When the verdict was announced, she just went to pieces," he recalled in an interview almost two years after the trial. "It's a nerve-wracking thing. I've never seen anything sadder."

Still, Sample said, he had to do his duty. In all his capital cases, he has followed the jury's recommendation. In written findings, required by the Florida statute, Sample had said George's sentence was justified because the crime occurred during a rape, because George planned the crime, and because it was, in the words of the statute's listing of aggravating circumstances, "especially heinous, atrocious and cruel."

Sample didn't see any need for a presentence investigation following the testimony taken at the second phase of the trial. "I don't believe there's going to be anything in a presentence report that has any material bearing on whether a man should be given a life sentence or death."

Sample supported capital punishment, acknowledging that contradictory statistics could be cited by advocates and abolitionists. For him, it boiled down to a simple choice. "Some like vanilla, some like chocolate; I believe in the death penalty," he said. "I used to have my doubts. But a person's life is not worth two cents anymore."

Robert Stone, the prosecutor, recalled the case as "a very emotional thing." The age of the defendant bothered him, but so did the brutality of the crime. "I was there when they found that girl," he said. "If some of the bleeding-hearts could have seen that, they might have a different attitude."

Stone maintained that he didn't "actively" seek the death penalty. But, he said, he felt obliged to oppose "purely emotional" appeals for George's life. "Age is only one factor," he recalled. "I don't think it's an overriding circumstance." Neither, he said, should the lack of a prior criminal record always mean that a person was capable of being rehabilitated.

However, Stone said, the case "still left me kind of empty and cold."

But the nervousness of George and other Death Row inmates, as they squirmed through months of legal proceedings to decide their ultimate fate, did not bother Stone. "That's a luxury their victims didn't enjoy," he said.

"It was pitiful—you could wish you were a hundred miles on the other side of anywhere and not be where you were," recalled one of the jurors in the Vasil case. "I hated that it had to be. But if I had it to do over again, I'd do the same thing."

Several jurors contacted about the case refused to discuss it. But two would, provided that their identities were shielded.

"It was a hurtful thing," said the first juror, "to think that right there was a young man that had probably never even—well, he wasn't a man, hadn't been able to prove his manhood. And yet it was up to us to snuff his life out." This juror remembers watching George at the moment he was sentenced and thinking: "I'm sorry to be a part of taking your life away from you. But I don't think you deserve to live."

The other juror also had no second thoughts. "Sometimes you just can't help people," the juror said. "What's within you is going to come out and you can't stop it. He was evidently a child you can't stop. I never at any time had any mercy or sympathy within my soul for him. He tortured that girl. I have sympathy for his people, of course. We all know that death is much worse on those left behind. What his parents are going through now, that's torture. That's cruel. I think they should just take him out and kill him, get it over with. When his parents open their eyes the next morning, it will be a new day for them. Some people are better off dead than out in the world. I can truthfully say I had rather seen my son dead than to know he would commit a crime like that, and be likely to do it again."

The interviews with these jurors made it clear that, at least in some cases, the new capital punishment laws do not operate very differently than the old ones in the jury room.

For example, neither juror recognized the terms "mitigating circumstances" or "aggravating circumstances." The overriding questions in the jurors' minds were what punishment was "deserved" and, most importantly, was there a chance that George would commit another crime if ever released from prison—not the considerations enumerated in the law.

In the light of the second question, the jurors turned two of the law's "mitigating circumstances"—George's age and his mental problem—into liabilities, factors that justified a harsher, not a more lenient, punishment. As the first juror put it, after the minimum sentence of twenty-five years, "That would have made him forty, still very much a young man. Our question was, well, do we want somebody to get out that might do it again?" The doctor's testimony that George needed help, plus the inability of the prison system to provide that help, made up her mind. "The only way we could avoid him getting out at age forty was to put him in the electric chair."

Another interesting point was that the jurors took full responsibility for their decision. They did not pretend that they were just answering abstract questions, or that someone else— the judge or the governor—would make the real decision whether George lived or died. "It never once occurred to me that there would be any other decision once we made ours," said one juror. "I had it in my hands to snuff out his life or let him live. And it's a horrible feeling to have."

This wasn't George Vasil's first time away from home; he once went on a camping trip with the Boy Scouts. George didn't have much to say about growing up on Death Row.

"It's not the same as home, but—got to make do," he shrugged in an interview after a year and a half in his cell. "The same routine every day gets kinda boring."

The same routine every day, for George, was to sleep late; breakfast wasn't worth getting up for. He turned on the radio or the television. Both were provided for Death Row prisoners. Sometimes he would work a jigsaw puzzle. He read. He smoked a pack a day of the rough prison-issue cigarettes given to all inmates—even though, under Florida law, he wasn't old enough to buy them. Every day or two someone brought around a cart from the prison canteen; he bought candy, potato chips, cakes. On Thursdays he got ice cream. He went to bed late.

George's cell was six feet wide, nine feel long and eight feet high. Every other day he got a five-minute shower. Once a week there was recreation in the yard. There, he played basketball or volleyball for an hour or two. In his cell, he had some exercises to do, sent by his YMCA football coach. From age fifteen to age seventeen, he grew four inches, but his skin was pale from the long hours away from sunlight.

For a while, George had a companion on Death Row, a pigeon that couldn't fly. George named it Chris, and fed it scraps as it roosted in his cell. But one day a lieutenant saw the bird, and it had to go. Pets are not allowed on Death Row.

George learned how to get along with the older men on Death Row, and even made some friends. Some of the other inmates worried about him. "I'll tell you, that kid's getting worse," confided one of them. "If they don't get him out of here pretty soon, or get some help for him, they might as well execute him."

For his strength, George had become very religious, changing —with his parents—from his Greek Orthodox faith to a more salvation-oriented, fundamental evangelism. He spent a good bit of his time studying his Bible.

Had he learned anything in the last couple of years?

"I understand things more clearly now by being here," George said. "I just got to learn to control myself—watch out for things."

When, on July 2, 1976, the U.S. Supreme Court ruled that it was constitutional for Florida to execute people like him, George didn't feel like eating lunch. That afternoon, a television reporter came back and asked how he felt. "Got me scared now," George replied. His face, for a few seconds, flashed on television screens across the nation.

When interviewed in his cell the next day, "scared" was still the word George used. He had slept all right, he said. But when he was asked for his opinion of the constitutionality of the death penalty, he showed a rare burst of emotion and verbosity. "It is unconstitutional—it's got to be," he blazed. "They tell me, and the others, a month or so ahead of when we are going to die. And we see other people going to get killed in that chair. I mean, that is cruel."

Pointing through the bars of his cell toward the death house, which can be seen through a window, he continued, "They have been keeping the light on in there all night lately. I think they keep it on to try and bother us."

George has seen the electric chair. In the death house, the window shades are kept open, and when the light is right, prisoners can peer across a walkway from their exercise yard and glimpse the chair.

"I really don't know much what they do before you go up there. But from what I've heard you got to sit down here and wait, wait. And you have seen other people go by. I don't think it's right."

What if he were to get his sentence reduced to life imprisonment? That would mean a minimum of twenty-five years in prison. Some people might prefer death. Would a life sentence really be better?

George replied instantly. "Sure it would be a relief to me. Life is"—he swallowed—"a lot easier to handle than"—another pause—"going to the chair."

George did not expect to die in the electric chair. He put his faith in his appeal, which was prepared by Tobias (Toby) Simon—a crusading, maverick Miami lawyer, perhaps the best-known civil rights attorney in the state. Simon had been involved in much of the civil rights, labor, and antiwar litigation of the previous decade. And he was an expert on the death penalty, having played an important role in bringing about the nationwide moratorium on executions after 1967.

Simon's appeal raised several major points:

• That the judge's instructions to the jury were wrong, since they made it difficult for the jury to consider a lesser degree of murder.

• That George's statements to Lieutenant Brumley should not have been admitted at trial because neither he nor his parents were aware that they could be used in an adult, rather than a juvenile, court proceeding.

• That the death penalty was always a cruel and unusual punishment when applied to a fifteen-year-old.

• That Florida's death penalty statute was being applied unequally and unfairly.

To support the last two contentions, Simon and his associates compiled a list of death sentences handed out since Florida's new death penalty law went into effect in 1972. They were compared to cases in which murders were committed but the defendants were given life sentences. In one of these cases, four teen-age boys older than George brutally killed and mutilated a woman for a fee of twenty-five hundred dollars. The defendants were given life sentences. The attorneys also point to a Kentucky case where two fourteen-year-olds, convicted of a brutal rape-robbery, were sentenced to life in prison. The Kentucky Court of Appeals overturned the sentence, saying:

We are of the opinion that life imprisonment without benefit of parole for two fourteen-year-old youths under all circumstances shocks the general conscience of society today and is intolerable to rudimental fairness. . . . We believe that incorrigibility is inconsistent with youth; that it is impossible to make a judgment that a fourteen-year-old youth, no matter how bad, will remain incorrigible for the rest of his life.

The Florida Attorney General's office, which rebuts all appeals in capital cases, contested all these points. The reply was particularly vehement in rebutting the assertion that merely because George was a juvenile, his confession should be excluded and he should not face execution.

Does one of "tender years" attack a girl of twelve threatening death if she screams? Does one of "tender years" force this girl to undress before smashing her head with a rock? Does one of "tender years" rape this girl and then cruelly ram a sharp object into her vagina *several* times with sufficient force to puncture both rectum and bladder? Does one of "tender years" in an effort to silence this pitiful girl then shove her torn panties into her mouth and thereby suffocate her?

Indeed.

After their son was sentenced and taken away, the first word Ted and Wilma Vasil had of George came when the prison authorities called for parental permission for emergency treatment, if it should be needed.

"Now, isn't that ironic?" Wilma asked bitterly. "He's old enough to be put to death, but he's not old enough to get an aspirin without our consent."

The cruelest irony to the Vasils was that they cooperated with the authorities in hopes that their son would be helped, but their actions helped to condemn him. "Tricked" was a word they often used. Wilma thought back to the agony of those moments immediately after Brumley told her that her son had killed Peggy Pitzer. As her husband was persuading George to tell what happened, she sat in her bedroom with her head in her hands. "I was thinking of doctors and the hospital," she said with a breaking voice. "I wasn't thinking of the courtroom."

Their cooperation with the detective caused the Vasils many anguished second thoughts. Once an unquestioning law-and-order advocate, Ted seemed particularly embittered: "We were stupid, naive fools. I was brought up, from day one, to feel that the law is something that you respect at all times, and cooperate with. But I was wrong. With today's modern justice, that's the worst thing you can do."

The parents were troubled, too, by doubts and recriminations about the way they raised George. Should they have let him remain an only child? Could they not have seen his sexual problems? Why didn't they insist on professional help before it was too late?

They still tried to act as parents. They didn't let George see local newspaper articles that might upset him. One Christmas, what George wanted in his package was fruit. Prison regulations allowed only six apples, so Wilma searched long and hard for the biggest, juiciest ones in Florida. The Vasils made the 530-mile round trip to the prison every other weekend, to see George from 9:00 A.M. to 3:00 P.M. on Sunday. George didn't talk with them about the future; he mostly dwelt on the good times he had with his parents in the past. He had never spoken of the crime to them.

The Vasils put their faith in the Lord. They also tried to have faith in George's appeal. They hoped for a new trial, one where he might be charged with only second-degree or third-degree murder. There seemed to be no hope that, at this late date, the system would treat George as a juvenile. At this point, however, a life sentence looked good to them, and to George. If the court appeals fail, their last hope is that the governor of Florida, and his cabinet, will commute George's sentence to life imprisonment.

Do they have faith in that? Are they sure that George will
not be executed?

Wilma answered the question in a quavering voice. "Everyone said it would never come to trial. So it came to trial.

"Everyone said he would never be convicted of first-degree
murder—never, never.

"Then they were saying that he would never get the death
penalty.

"They are telling us now, 'No, no, he will never be executed.'

"So now you ask me—do I think he will ever be executed?"

The Moral Issue: The Value of Life

There's nothing that can be done for the person who is dead, but
you must realize that the families of these people who have been
murdered have to live with this year after year. Have the victims
in this crime become so obscure that we forget what the criminal
has done? Gentlemen, my family and the millions of other people
like them around this country cannot really come to peace with
themselves until this matter is concluded, when Charles Proffitt
dies. Perhaps that will relieve some of the burden that my family
carries for the loss of their child.

—Brother of a murdered man

My wife, Jane Williams, was murdered by Jimmie Smith. She was
a good and beautiful person, and I loved her very much. Her life
was precious, as is all life. Jane's death was a real tragedy to all of
those who loved her so dearly. Her life as a person and as a
psychologist represented an attempt to create better interpersonal
relations among people and to promote understanding. Therefore,
it is even more tragic that her death will, by sentencing Jimmie
Smith to his death, reinforce and perpetrate feelings of vengeance,
hate and further human evil. Despite my feelings of anger, disgust,
pity and nausea toward Smith, I do not believe that his life should
be taken. Nobody has the right to take a human life, and this includes the state of Florida. The laws should be changed.

—Husband of a murdered woman

Two eloquent pleas; two clashing concepts of justice. Both appeal to the law to reinforce the value our society attaches to life. To one victim, it is not right that the murderer should continue to live. To the other, it is not right that society should kill him.

This moral dilemma lies at the heart of the capital punishment issue. Does the death penalty enhance the value of life, or demean it?

All other arguments are secondary to this one. Deterrence is irrelevant if you believe that the murderer *deserves* to die, and that only death will suffice. But if one believes that life is an inalienable right not subject to the judgment of men, then the death penalty cannot be justified under any circumstances.

Our moral sense of proper punishment lies at the heart of the word *justice.* "The argument on grounds of justice is certainly the most profound and to me the most interesting," James Q. Wilson, professor of government at Harvard, observed. "It may be the *only* proper basis for a decision." Unfortunately, in recent years (in this country, at least) the moral dimensions of capital punishment have been largely ignored, taking a back seat to arguments over deterrence, racial prejudice, and legal procedures.

But these arguments are often only rationalizations for what is at bottom a moral choice. This was demonstrated by a poll in which two thirds of the supporters of capital punishment said they would cling to their beliefs even if it could be proven to their satisfaction that the death penalty did not deter crime. Half would continue to support capital punishment even if they were shown that it increased crime. Among those who opposed capital punishment, less than a quarter said they would change their minds if capital punishment proved to be a strong deterrent to crime. This is evidence not of closed minds, but of people concerned with the moral order regardless of short-term advantages.

First, it must be acknowledged that when we talk of deliberate killing, none of us is Galahad-pure. Rare indeed is the pacifist who would sacrifice his life rather than defend himself. Killing is an evil, but one that can be justified under extreme circumstances.

Often we are not even consistent in our views. Many resolute opponents of capital punishment refuse to recognize anything disturbing about the casual use of abortions. And those who zealously proclaim the right to life of any fertilized ovum (even if a child will be born with the most severe abnormalities and even if a pregnancy threatens the life of the mother) have no trouble supporting the execution of adults. Our defense budgets proclaim the importance we place on being prepared to kill at a moment's notice. As Jacques Barzun wrote in defense of the death penalty in 1962, "The West today does not seem to be the time or place to invoke the absolute sanctity of human life."

One can make a decision on the morality of our current laws without going to extremes. To oppose the death penalty here and now for common murderers, it is not necessary to defend Adolf Hitler's right to life. To support it, one need not be prepared to execute everyone who points a pistol at another person.

On a moral issue of this magnitude, we might hope to proceed with cautious humility. Unfortunately, debaters frequently hide behind a smokescreen of righteous indignation, accusing the other side of moral obtuseness, if not downright barbarity. Thus we have Frank Carrington, in a book defending capital punishment, asserting this dubious moral principle:

You cannot have it both ways. If you go to bat for the "sanctity" of the life of the murderer, you are by definition taking a stance completely opposed to his victim or victims.

At the other extreme we have Clarence Darrow, perhaps overcome by the fervor of his opposition to the death penalty, declaring:

Every human being that believes in capital punishment loves killing, and the only reason they believe in capital punishment is because they get a kick out of it.

Rhetoric of this sort, so common in political campaigns, is a good indication that a little soul-searching might be in order.

To cut through moral issues such as this, many of us look to our religious teachings. But here again there is no easy solution.

For Christians and Jews the Scriptures are the codification of religious wisdom. No justification for capital punishment is cited more frequently than the biblical phrase, "an eye for an eye, a tooth for a tooth, a life for a life." The Old Testament is filled with commands to kill murderers. From Genesis: "Whoever sheds the blood of man, by man shall his blood be shed." From Leviticus: "He who kills a man shall be put to death." From Numbers: "If any one kills a person, the murderer shall be put to death on the evidence of witnessess."

But opponents of capital punishment can also cite Scripture. The Old Testament precepts cited above have today the same irrelevance as those justifying slavery, they say. After all, even at the time of Christ rabbinical courts had ceased to give out death sentences because of the limitations of human judgments. But opponents usually base their case on the New Testament, where there are two direct references to capital punishment. One was the warning Christ issued when an adulteress was about to be killed: "Let he who is without sin cast the first stone." The other came when Christ, as He laid down the Beatitudes, confronted the principle of talion: "You have heard that it was said, 'An eye for an eye and a tooth for a tooth.' But I say to you, 'Do not resist one who is evil. But if any one strikes you on the right cheek, turn to him the other also.'" It is difficult to view this as anything other than a reversal of the earlier law.

For many centuries, churchmen were among the leading exponents of execution, especially when trying to crush religious heresy. But recently many major religious groups have taken positions against capital punishment. Among these are bodies representing Baptists, Episcopalians, Catholics, Methodists, Presbyterians, Disciples of Christ, Unitarians, and Jews.

Religious conviction seems to grant no immunity from silly

pronouncements on this issue. In 1977, for instance, a New York State legislator offered, as justification for capital punishment, the argument that there would be no Christianity if it were not for the death penalty. "Where would Christianity be if Jesus had gotten eight to fifteen years with time off for good behavior?" he asked. But New York's Governor Hugh Carey had an apt rejoinder to the legislator: "It was the Resurrection of Jesus Christ which began Christianity, not His death. And if the senator can put resurrection in the bill, then I might look at it."

Some people look to the surviving relatives of murder victims as the people best qualified to speak on the subject. The assumption here is that society, represented by the court system, is standing in the place of the victim. (This is not entirely accurate; society is looking out for its own interests.) Even from this standpoint there is no unanimity, as the second letter at the beginning of this section indicates. We have only to look to the Kennedy and King families—each struck twice by assassins—to see that victims do not always demand the life of the murderer.

But without a doubt the first letter comes closer to describing the views of the majority of victims' families. And while we do not give these families the right to take the life of the offender, they do have a special interest in the criminal justice process: seeing that justice is done, the law is upheld, its promise validated by punishment. Punishments can be selected for other reasons (their ability to reform or deter), but the fact that they are given in the first place is central to "doing justice"—best expressed by the term *retribution*.

Retribution is often confused with revenge. Many victims do want revenge, as expressed by the anguished mother of a New York girl who was beaten, raped, and strangled: "Oh, God, the electric chair is too good for them! I want the same thing they did to my beautiful daughter done to them." Albert Camus saw this spirit as the root of the death penalty: "Let us call it by the name which, for lack of any other nobility, will at least give the nobility of truth, and let us recognize it for what it is essentially: a revenge." One state's attorney general went so far as to defend executions on this ground: "Society is entitled to revenge, pure and simple. It's for society's own good health and well-being. It has a cleansing effect."

For many hundreds of years, however, we have rejected revenge, cleansing effect or no. As Sir Francis Bacon put it: "Revenge is a kind of wild justice, which the more man's nature runs to, the more ought law to weed it out." Revenge seeks only pain; it is self-serving, not limited by rules, proportional not to the offense but to the hatred of those seeking satisfaction. Retribution, as Ernest van den Haag has pointed out, is not the same thing. Retribution is imposed not for the victim's satisfaction, but to assure society that its laws cannot be broken with impunity. Punishment *is* retribution (although we hope it will accomplish other purposes at the same time).

But admitting that retribution is a basis for punishment, however, is not the same as acknowledging the morality of capital punishment. Any punishment can meet the requirement of retribution so long as it is considered proportional to the gravity of the offense. And retribution is a double-edged sword; it places limits on the maximum amount of punishment at the same time it demands a minimum.

The cornerstone of support for capital punishment is that death is the *only* punishment equal to murder, or at least to certain kinds of murder. As Justice Stewart put it in the *Gregg* decision:

In part, capital punishment is an expression of society's moral outrage at particularly offensive conduct. . . . [Retribution is neither] a forbidden objective nor one inconsistent with our respect for the dignity of men. Indeed, the decision that capital punishment may be the appropriate sanction in extreme cases is an expression of the community's belief that certain crimes are themselves so grievous an affront to humanity that the only adequate response may be the penalty of death.

Here, advocates of capital punishment agree with their opponents that death *is* different—it is a greater punishment than any term of imprisonment, and therefore is required because murder is greater than any other crime (except, perhaps, treason). A radical penalty is needed, they say, to mark murder as taboo. In the words of one supporter, capital punishment "places an inestimable value on human life—the forfeiture of the despoiler." It would be wrong if the stiffest punishment for murder were the same as the stiffest punishment for robbery or rape, but, given the vicissitudes of our current system, it often is.

Retribution does more than vent outrage. It serves an educational function, alerting the community to the strength of the taboo against different crimes. As a former prosecutor put it, "the death penalty helps to educate the conscience of the whole community, and it arouses among many people a quasi-religious sense of awe." This is the deterrence theory mentioned at the end of the last chapter. As explained by a sociologist, Marlene Lehntinen:

Deterrence is too narrowly defined when it includes the assumption that the threat of punishment produces fear in the populace and that it is this fear that reduces the number of criminal violations. . . . The punishment structure of law may exert its strongest effects morally and pedagogically, in which case the consequences of changes in punishments would not be expected to appear within a single generation.*

Over the generations, murder and execution have been intertwined in our imaginations. It would be dangerous, advocates say, to go further in reducing executions than we already have in this century. We are not writing on a clean slate, but deciding whether to abandon a long-established practice. Ernest van den Haag wrote:

No matter what can be said for abolition of the death penalty, it will be perceived symbolically as a loss of nerve: social authority no

---

* Acceptance of this timetable makes it difficult to blame the recent rise in murder rates on the moratorium of the 1960s.

longer is willing to pass an irrevocable judgment on anyone. Murder is no longer thought grave enough to take the murderer's life, no longer horrendous enough to deserve so fearfully irrevocable a punishment. . . . Life becomes cheaper as we become kinder to those who wantonly take it.

Opponents of the death penalty do not deny that the passion for retribution exists, nor that we have been told for centuries that we can kill murderers. But, they say, these natural reactions cry out for control. To them, the passion for retribution seems outmoded, not worthy of a civilized society. Camus called it "a quasi-arithmetical reply made by society to whoever breaks its primordial law. . . . This is an emotion, and a particularly violent one, not a principle." The English novelist Arthur Koestler, who himself spent three months under a death sentence during the Spanish Civil War, wrote in *Reflections on Hanging*:

Deep inside every civilized being there lurks a little Stone Age man, dangling a club to rob and rape, and screaming an eye for an eye. But we would rather not have that little fur-clad figure dictate the law of the land.

In his dissent to the 1976 decisions, Justice Marshall wrote that "the taking of life 'because the wrongdoer deserves it' surely must fall, for such a punishment has as its very basis the total denial of the wrongdoer's dignity and worth." This is the heart of the abolitionist position: that capital punishment is an affront to human dignity and human rights—a rejection of the offender as a member of the human race. The language used by some advocates of the death penalty—"beasts," and "monsters" —seems to support the contention that we have to treat a person as an "it" in order to send him to the execution chamber. This is morally unacceptable, in view of what theologian Paul Tillich has called "our unconditional imperative to acknowledge every person as a person. The Christian may not treat any person as a thing."

As for the value of capital punishment as a moral lesson, abolitionists say executions have exactly the opposite effect.

"Murder and capital punishment are not opposites that cancel one another, but similars that breed their kind," George Bernard Shaw wrote. The lesson drawn from executions is said to be that it is all right to kill your enemies, to eliminate the people who cause problems for you. As psychiatrist Louis J. West put it:

Philosophers and social scientists have long contended that the legal extermination of human beings in any society generates a profound tendency among the citizens to accept killing as a solution to human problems.

Legal scholars Morris and Hawkins reached the same conclusion:

The question is, will people learn to respect life better by threat or by example? And the uniform answer of history, comparative studies, and experience is that man is an emulative animal.

Society seems to acknowledge this by the way it hides executions behind prison walls, forbids photographs, reviles executioners, and generally tries to pay as little attention as possible to an execution. If we were confident of the deterrent power of an execution, Camus said, "society would give executions the benefit of the publicity it generally uses for national bond issues or new brands of drinks." And if terror was so effective at preventing murders, Clarence Darrow said,

why not do a good job of it? If you want to get rid of killings by hanging people or electrocuting them because they are so terrible, why not boil them in oil, as they used to do? Why not sew them into a bag with serpents and throw them out to sea? Why not stake them out on the sand and let them be eaten by ants?

This leads us to another moral question: whether capital punishment, as administered in this country, is cruel.

The Supreme Court first confronted this issue in 1890, when it had to decide whether the newfangled electric chair was permissible. The Court declared:

Punishments are cruel when they involve torture or lingering death; but the punishment of death is not cruel, within the meaning of

that word as used in the Constitution. It implies something inhuman and barbarous, something more than the mere extinguish-
ment of life.

No method of execution has ever been found unconstitutional by the Supreme Court. When properly administered, all
are considered relatively quick and painless ways of dying,
certainly less painful for the victim than most murders.

But abolitionists argue that the true cruelty of the death
penalty is psychological—"The devastating, degrading fear that
is imposed on the condemned for months or years is a punishment more terrible than death," Camus wrote. "For there to be
equivalence, the death penalty would have to punish a criminal
who had warned his victim of the date at which he would
inflict a horrible death on him and who, from that moment
onward, had confined him at his mercy for months. Such a
monster is not encountered in private life." (However, the 1978
kidnapping and eventual assassination of Aldo Moro, Italy's
former prime minister, proved that private parties could indeed
attain this level.)

Granted, most of the delay is due to the appeals brought
by the condemned themselves. But it is ironic that our attempts
to improve the administration of capital punishment have
rendered execution more cruel, for those few who finally suffer
it, than a century ago.

This brings us to one of the arguments that some people
succumb to: that execution is really less cruel than life imprisonment, and therefore preferable. Jacques Barzun, sensitive
to the horrors of prison life, declared, "for my part, I would
choose death without hesitation." This sounds noble, even
humanitarian. But, as Arthur Koestler observed, it is ridiculous
to reject life imprisonment as a substitute for execution because it is both too cruel and not cruel enough. Few people
suggest that for the most heinous crimes—the extermination of
the Jews in World War II, for example—only life imprisonment will do, while common murderers should be executed.

Retribution is, it must be acknowledged, a sufficient justification for capital punishment. But even if we accept retribution as necessary, we still have moral choices to make. One is where to draw the line. Few people argue any more that *all* murderers must be executed. But the principle of "just deserts" requires that all who are equally culpable receive the same penalty. Legally, we have laws and precedents to decide who shall be executed. But morally, is there really any difference between someone who kills a policeman and someone who kills a derelict? Should we execute mothers? Fathers? There seems something profoundly immoral about strapping a fifteen-year-old in the electric chair. What about an eighteen-year-old?

Even if we can draw acceptable boundaries around the death penalty, we have to question whether human judgments can apply these standards. In the words of Professor Charles L. Black, Jr.: "Though the justice of God may indeed ordain that some should die, the justice of man is altogether and always insufficient for saying who these may be."

An elegant rebuttal to this position was provided by Richard Rovere in a review of Arthur Koestler's book, *Reflections on Hanging,* in *The New Yorker:*

Man must play God, for he has acquired certain Godlike powers, among them a considerable degree of mastery over life and death, and he cannot avoid their exercise. . . . The judge who orders an execution is no more guilty of playing God than the doctor who, having decided that a human being has been summoned to eternity too soon, restores him to the world of time and suffering and sin.

Rovere's analogy, however, loses much of its force if we consider the case of the doctor who takes away life, rather than restoring it. He will likely be tried for manslaughter. There remains a profound moral distinction between the godlike power to prolong life and the godlike power to terminate it.

The problem of administering justice fairly is downplayed by those who subscribe to what is known as the "Social Defense" theory—a school of thought more popular in Europe than here.

A prime example of this approach is Ernest van den Haag's analysis in the previous chapter, where he weighs the safety of potential victims—the great majority—against the risks of injustice faced by a tiny minority of culpable criminals. But—pragmatic though we may be—American philosophy generally holds that an injustice to one is a threat to the liberty of all, not to be outweighed by cost/benefit analysis. This is the theory that underlies the Bill of Rights. We do not care how many guilty defendants go free because of the ban on self-incrimination; the dangers of injustice are greater.

If the burden of deciding questions of life and death were not so awesome, we might see people willing to stand up and take responsibility for deciding that an individual should die. But no one does. It is always "the system." Prosecutors, judges, juries, governors, and prison guards usually disclaim responsibility, saying they were merely deciding points of law or carrying out their duties. "The end result is that somebody's dead, but nobody killed him," Anthony Amsterdam observed. Defense lawyers have called this the "Eddie Slovik Syndrome," after the case of the only soldier executed in World War II for desertion. As described by William Bradford Huie in *The Execution of Private Slovik*, officials at every level evaded responsibility, assuming that someone higher up would stop the execution. But no one did.

Public policy on moral issues is supposed to be decided by majority rule. And public opinion—whether based on retributive principles or not—has clearly favored capital punishment in recent years. In 1977 the Harris Poll showed sixty-seven percent of the respondents in favor of capital punishment, only twenty-five percent opposed. Public referendums in California, Washington, Illinois, Oregon, and Colorado in recent years have supported the death penalty by landslide proportions, generally two to one.

But we have the right to question how well-informed the public is on this issue, and how accurately broad questions such as "Do you favor or oppose capital punishment?" measure attitudes. More sophisticated polls show that when presented with a broad range of punishments for murder, people are less likely to choose death. In-depth interviews have shown that most people know very little about the issue, and have given it little thought. Other studies have shown that people who support capital punishment are likely to have authoritarian personalities and are more likely to rely on dogmatism than reason, to be less tolerant, and more likely to harbor racial prejudice. Support for the death penalty also seemed to be associated with people reared in a home where violence was a part of daily life, people who themselves believed in violent solutions to complex problems. One particularly interesting study concerned how moral attitudes develop. Researchers interviewed the same group of boys as they grew from age ten to age thirty. It seemed that the balancing principle of "a life for a life" was a characteristic of childhood; as intellect grew, tolerance and social responsibility increased—and support for capital punishment decreased.

But the major problem with relying on polls is that opinions change. In 1936 the Gallup Poll showed that sixty-two percent of the people supported capital punishment; by 1966 that figure had declined to forty-two percent. In 1976 it was back up to sixty-five percent. This is hardly evidence of an immutable conviction.

That, of course, is the problem with all moral judgments: While we would like to believe that they reflect age-old values, the fact is that they fluctuate from time to time. Early in the last century, when it was proposed that England remove the death penalty for shoplifting objects worth less than five shillings, the bill was laughed out of Parliament. One lord declared self-confidently: "Repeal these laws, and see the difference—no man can trust himself for an hour out-of-doors." By these standards—or even by the standards of thirty years ago—it is amazing that we have come even as close as we have to abolishing the death penalty. From this perspective, the trend of history is clearly against capital punishment, and while we may draw the line for a few years at certain extreme types of murder, it seems unlikely that the tide will reverse.

Moral judgments also fluctuate from place to place, and while Americans must be the ones to decide American policies, we should not harbor the illusion that our sense of morality is universal. In countries that follow the Islamic code, a proposal to cease cutting off the hands of thieves would be blasphemy. But all the Western European countries save France and Spain (who use it in rare cases) have done away with capital punishment, and even terrorist rampages have not been enough to bring it back in Northern Ireland, West Germany, Italy, or Israel.

Perhaps no one had a broader view of human customs across both time and place than the late anthropologist Dr. Margaret Mead. She was convinced that the retributive justice embodied by the death penalty is on its way out. In "A Life for a Life," she wrote:

If we do in fact take seriously our chosen role as champions of human rights, then certainly we must also reinterpret drastically the very ancient law of "a life for a life" as it affects human beings in our own society today. . . . "A life for a life" need not mean destructive retribution, but instead the development of new forms of community in which, because all lives are valuable, what is emphasized is the prevention of crime and the protection of all those who are vulnerable.

"A new sense of community"—heady words. Perhaps the moral choice presented by capital punishment boils down to the vision of society one longs for: a restoration of the past, with a strong moral order bolstered by stark demonstrations of what will happen to those who violate it; or evolution of a utopia now unfamiliar to us, with tolerance replacing rules, and hope replacing fear. We will see neither in our lifetimes, but we must choose our direction.

CHAPTER SIX

"It could have gone either way"

Profile: Clifford Hallman

DECISION: *Did Clifford Hallman cut the throat of Roxanne Mary Monroe?*

Not much doubt about it. Hallman himself doesn't question whether he was the one who grabbed the barmaid by her red hair, tilted back her head, and slashed her throat twice with a broken beer bottle.

That was one of 19,640 homicides in the United States in 1973. Unlike the way it happens in detective novels, this case wasn't resolved when Hallman was caught. The courts had more questions to ask: Was it premeditated? Was Hallman robbing her? Did she hit him first? Was he crazy? And, at the end: Should he be executed?

The final answer—from the prosecutor, the jurors, and the judge—was that Clifford Hallman should die at the hands of the state of Florida. The highest courts of the state and the nation endorsed that outcome. The electric chair waited.

But sometimes human beings do not ask all the right questions. And in Hallman's case, one question went unasked until four years after the murder and after he had been condemned at every step. It was a significant question: Did Clifford Hallman, in slashing the throat of Roxanne Mary Monroe, kill her? Or did someone else share responsibility for her death?

In the spring of 1973 things were going pretty well for Hallman, perhaps for the first time in his twenty-three years. The third child of six, Hallman had grown up in a working class neighborhood of Tampa. Hallman's father, a heavy drinker, had been away from home more than he was there. From an early age, Clifford Hallman was partially deaf—and explosive. He bounced in and out of various reform schools, dropping out of school entirely after the tenth grade. He had been arrested three times, and had spent time in jail. But in the spring of 1973 he began to settle down. In March he got married. Three weeks later he was offered a new job, laying tile for a floor-covering company near his home. He quit his old job and looked forward to better times.

On Tuesday, April 10, Hallman reported to work at the flooring company for the first time. When he arrived, however, he was told there wouldn't be any work for him that day. The way things sounded, he couldn't even be sure if he had a job at all. So he sulked. He smoldered. Then he marched down the street to a bar.

They weren't surprised to see the wiry frame, red hair, and mustache of Clifford Hallman come into Danny's Bar, even at nine o'clock in the morning; drinking was something he did often. He ordered a beer.

He had, Hallman figured, plenty of money to drink on, something over twenty dollars. Both Hallman and his wife were on a first-name basis with Wilma Hunt, the waitress and wife of the owner. Another of Hallman's haunts was right across the street, the North Town Tavern. Several times that day Hallman changed his drinking spots: a beer at Danny's, then across to the North Town, then back to Danny's.

Three o'clock found Hallman and one other customer in the North Town, served by the waitress, Roxanne Mary Monroe. Like Hallman, she had red hair and a quick temper. She was forty-five years old, divorced, the mother of a seven-year-old boy who rode his bicycle to the bar every day after school to meet her. Hallman and Mrs. Monroe weren't on the best of terms, but he drank there frequently.

The other customer, a man named Red, had also been drinking heavily. He got into an argument with Mrs. Monroe. Loud words ensued and Mrs. Monroe, no shrinking violet, settled the affair by grabbing the drunk by the scruff of the neck, forcibly escorting him to the door, and shoving him out. That left Hallman and Mrs. Monroe alone in the bar.

At about 3:45, Wilma Hunt looked out of Danny's Bar and noticed Hallman leaving the North Town by the side door, walking quickly. A little later, she glanced across the street again and saw Mrs. Monroe sitting in the front doorway, leaning on the doorpost. She didn't think anything of it.

Just about then, Mary Scranton stopped in at the North Town. She had worked there previously and wanted to pass some time with Mrs. Monroe. Scranton came in through the side entrance but couldn't see anyone in the darkened bar. Then she heard a voice calling weakly, "Someone please help me." She went to the front door. There she found Mrs. Monroe slumped against the door in a pool of blood. Blood covered her hair, gushed from her throat, and streamed from her wrists. "What happened?" Scranton asked. "Clifford tried to kill me over money," Mrs. Monroe replied. Scranton yelled out the door for help and Wilma Hunt rushed over from Danny's Bar. She called for an ambulance. While they were waiting, she asked Mrs. Monroe what had occurred. "Clifford tried to take my money and he cut me," Mrs. Monroe replied. Then she asked Mrs. Hunt to keep an eye out for her little boy coming home from school while she was at the hospital. She was weak, but she walked to the ambulance and talked to the attendants.

The police arrived at the tavern just as the ambulance was

ready to leave. Inside, detectives found pools of blood, a beer glass smashed on the floor, and an empty cash register.

At about that time, Hallman re-entered Danny's through the back door. There were red spots on his shirt and a vacant look on his face. No one said anything. After a few minutes Hallman slid off the bar stool and staggered out the door. He broke into a weaving trot across Nebraska Avenue, entered the North Town Tavern, and stared at the police. They took one look at him—bloodstained clothing, blood-smeared hands, a cut on his index finger—and arrested him. When they searched him, they found $41 in paper money, $11.06 in change, and an identification card in the name of Roxanne Mary Monroe.

Back at the hospital, Mrs. Monroe was admitted to the emergency room at 4:33 P.M. She had an ugly wound: a 5½-inch gash across her throat, deep enough to leave a flap of skin. Next to it was a 1½-inch gash. But the nurses had no trouble stopping the bleeding, and then they stitched up the wounds. A more serious concern was the swelling that was sure to come; it could cut off her breathing.

Mrs. Monroe was conscious throughout the treatment, conversing with a nurse as she was being put into a hospital gown. They treated her for shock with one thousand cc's of glucose from an intravenous drip shortly after she arrived, and another dose a half-hour later, at 5:15.

Shortly before 7:00 P.M., a nurse suddenly noticed that Mrs. Monroe, lying on a cot in a corner of the emergency room, had turned blue in the face. She had stopped breathing. The doctor cut a hole in her throat to allow air into the lungs and she began to breathe again. But it was too late; the loss of oxygen had damaged her brain. She languished for four days and died on April 14. An autopsy stated the cause of death as "brain stem necrosis" (a lack of oxygen to the brain) resulting from "lacerations of the blunt trauma to the neck area."

Hallman, who had been arrested on charges of robbery and assault with intent to murder, at first denied any involvement in the incident, saying he was playing pool elsewhere at the time. The day after his arrest he changed his mind. He gave a statement to the police admitting that he had cut Mrs. Monroe. He said they had argued, she had slapped him, and, in a rage, he slashed back at her. In his panic to get away, he said, he grabbed the money from the cash register and ran.

When Mrs. Monroe died four days later, the case took on a new importance in the legal system. This was no longer assault and robbery; this was murder.

DECISION: *Should Hallman be charged with first-degree or second-degree murder?*

Tampa law enforcement authorities had the following to go on: a woman had died, her throat cut. A suspect in custody admitted doing it. Physical evidence—bloodstained clothing and the victim's identity card—linked him to the crime. Moreover, it looked like robbery—money was missing from the tavern, and witnesses said that Mrs. Monroe talked of Hallman taking her money. On the other hand, Hallman claimed the cutting was impulsive, the result of an argument, and the taking of the money was afterthought. There were no eyewitnesses.

The first round of decision-making was up to the assistant state's attorney (prosecutor) for Tampa, Robert Nutter. Nutter considered the alternatives. If the murder was premeditated—if, at some point, Hallman took a moment to reflect and then proceeded to injure Mrs. Monroe—it would be first-degree murder. If Hallman attacked her in order to get the money, or to get away after taking the money, it would be first-degree murder. But if, as Hallman claimed, his cutting was an instantaneous reaction and the theft of the money an afterthought, second-degree murder would be the proper charge. Second-degree murder carried a life sentence with parole possible after a minimum of seven years. First-degree murder would bring a life sentence with parole possible after twenty-five years, or death.

There was evidence to support the more serious charge. Mrs. Monroe had been cut on the wrists as well as the throat, indicating more than a single slashing motion. And there were her words about "Clifford" and "money." On the other hand, it didn't seem likely that anyone would try to rob a place where he was so well known, especially when he was not desperate for money. And he certainly did not make a very efficient getaway.

On June 11, Nutter filed his charge: murder in the second degree.

DECISION: *Was Hallman a mentally disordered sex offender?*

The next major step in the case was initiated by Hallman's attorney. Since Hallman had virtually no money, a public defender, Thomas Meyers, was appointed. Meyers asked the judge scheduled to hear the case, Robert W. Rawlins, Jr., for a hearing on Hallman's sanity. The judge appointed two psychiatrists to examine Hallman, at the state's expense, concerning several points: whether he was capable of standing trial, whether he was sane at the time of the crime, and whether he was a "mentally disordered sex offender." Florida law section 917.13 established a special class of sex criminal: "a person who is not insane but who has a mental disorder and is considered dangerous to others because of propensity to commit sex offenses." If the judge found that Hallman qualified under this provision, it would not diminish his guilt, but the judge would have the power to send Hallman to a mental institution rather than a prison.

At first glance there seemed no sexual overtones to the crime; Mrs. Monroe had not been molested. But Hallman's version of the incident depicted an overwhelming, irrational response to a slap on the face, and he had previously been involved in several offenses that did include sexual threats. It would not hurt Hallman's cause if the judge started thinking in terms of treatment, rather than of punishment.

Each court-appointed psychiatrist interviewed Hallman for an hour at the Tampa jail. Each wrote back to the court reporting that Hallman was legally sane.

As soon as the psychiatrists had filed their reports, Judge Rawlins held a brief hearing. The psychiatrists were the only witnesses. One testified that "[Hallman] is within the sexual psychopath statute. And I think he would benefit from some treatment of these conditions." The other doctor said he had not examined Hallman on this point because he had misunderstood the judge's instructions. "However," he testified, "during the examination he gave me enough details [of] enough events that I felt that perhaps he would qualify as a mentally disordered sex offender." This condition had existed for several years, he went on, and could be helped by treatment.

The decision was up to the judge. Without comment, he ruled that Hallman would not be treated as a mentally disordered sex offender.

DECISION: *Should the prosecutor let Hallman plead guilty for a life sentence, or take the case to trial? If so, on what charge?*

For three months, Hallman had been jailed on a charge of second-degree murder. But something made Nutter change his mind. He decided to raise the stakes. At his urging, the grand jury indicted Hallman for first-degree murder on September 12. It charged that he, "from a premeditated design to effect the death of Roxanne Mary Monroe did cut the said Roxanne Mary Monroe with a broken glass . . . [and] did then and there inflict divers mortal wounds of which the said Roxanne Mary Monroe did languish and die. . . ."

The prosecutor then made overtures to him and his attorney about a possible plea bargain—a life sentence in exchange for a guilty plea. But Hallman turned down the offer.

Before proceeding to the trial, let's let Hallman, from his prison cell, give us his version of the events of April 10. It is a story that has hardly changed a word since he first told it to the police years before.

"Oh, I admit being there, but when the actual thing happened, that part I can't really remember. Oh, I'm not saying I did do it or I didn't do it, but from the looks of me at the time I guess I did do it.

"Now, when I went in the North Town Tavern I had no intention of hurting this woman. I had no intention of robbing the place. I just went in to drink. This other guy had been drinking real hard, like me. He was talking real loud, cussing. This woman—I heard her use worse language than I do—told the guy to shut up and get out. When he wouldn't get out she walked around the bar and grabbed him. He was a lot bigger, but he was so drunk. I said you shouldn't do that. She said if I didn't like it she would throw me out. I was just drunk enough that I didn't care what I said. I said it would be a cold day in hell when she threw me out. She slapped me.

"The next few seconds I really don't remember. All I know is that when I did realize what was going on, she was lying on the floor, you see. And she's bleeding like hell. And that's when, in my mind, I was going to leave town, and I didn't have any money. That's why I took the money out of the cash register. But when I left, I only went to another bar, ordered another beer, and sat there drinking that. I said, 'What the hell.' I went back to the same bar. I hadn't changed clothes or anything. I knew the cops were there. I knew I would be arrested. I don't even know what I was thinking. But I went back in there."

DECISION: How should the trial be conducted?

Hallman and Meyers decided not to proclaim innocence, but instead chose to try for a verdict on the lesser charge of second-degree murder. They would call no witnesses. Red, the man in the bar who supposedly precipitated the argument between Hallman and Mrs. Monroe, could not be located. Hallman would not take the stand, because if he did the prosecution could have brought up his prior record of assaults on women, and that might well have prejudiced the jurors. Hallman's version of the incident would have to be related by the police detective who had questioned him. Meyers thought there were enough holes in the prosecution's case to convince the jury to bring in the lesser charge.

DECISION: *Was Hallman guilty of first- or second-degree murder?*

This was the only substantive question for the jurors to decide in the first stage of the trial.

The prosecution had to prove beyond a reasonable doubt that Hallman cut Mrs. Monroe as an integral part of a scheme to rob the tavern, or else that he premeditated his act before he cut her. For evidence, the prosecution called the two barmaids who saw Mrs. Monroe, the police detectives, the medical examiner who looked at the body, and the detective who took Hallman's confession.

The defense presented no witnesses.

The case came down to the closing arguments. Nutter cited the cuts on Mrs. Monroe's wrists (as well as her throat) as proof that Hallman fully intended to kill her. The prosecutor noted that the money was taken and that Mrs. Monroe twice said this was why she was cut. While no one except Hallman knew exactly what took place in the bar, Nutter told the jury, "probably what happened was that Roxanne Mary Monroe either went to the rest room or stepped out of that area in the bar there for a minute and he went behind the register because he was the only one there and tried and got into the register to get the money. And when he was coming out she saw him and stopped him, and at that point he struggled with her and fought with her and deliberately cut her."

When his turn came, Meyers tried to blast holes in the prosecution's scenario. A hypothetical "probably" wasn't enough. Was it likely, Meyers asked, that Hallman would try to rob a place where he was so well known? Would he have entered the bar without a weapon if he intended to hurt Mrs. Monroe? Why would he rob the tavern when he had his own money? Why would he return to the scene? Hallman took the money in panic after an impulsive outburst of rage, Meyers said; that was, at worst, larceny, which would make the murder only second-degree.

The trial had taken a day and a half. When the jurors retired to the jury room (as one of them recalled) at first everyone sat silently, afraid to speak. Finally one woman voiced her opinion and the others gradually joined in. At first a few jurors favored the lesser verdict, but it did not take long for the majority to convince them that Hallman should be found guilty of first-degree murder.

DECISION: *Should Hallman be sentenced to life in prison, or death in the electric chair?*

Judge Rawlins recessed the case for six days before calling the jury back for the hearing on punishment.

What the jury had to decide was whether certain aggravating circumstances existed, and if so whether they outweighed the mitigating circumstances. From the Florida law, here are the circumstances relevant to the facts of Hallman's case:

Possible Aggravating Circumstances:
(b) The defendant was previously convicted of another capital felony or of a felony involving the use or threat of violence to the person.
(d) The capital felony was committed while the defendant was engaged, or was an accomplice, in the commission of, or an attempt to commit, or flight after committing or attempting to commit, any robbery. . . .
(f) The capital felony was committed for pecuniary gain.
(h) The capital felony was especially heinous, atrocious, or cruel.

Possible Mitigating Circumstances:
(b) The capital felony was committed while the defendant was under the influence of extreme mental or emotional disturbance.
(c) The capacity of the defendant to appreciate the crimi-

nality of his conduct or to conform his conduct to the requirements of the law was substantially impaired.

(g) The age of the defendant at the time of the crime.

The prosecutor concentrated his efforts on the first circumstance, hoping that the evidence already presented would show
the others. Nutter called several detectives and victims to testify
regarding prior incidents involving Hallman.

The first occurred in September 1969. As a detective described
it, Hallman climbed into a woman's car, displayed a switch-
blade knife, and tried to make sexual advances. Then he demanded money. She finally pretended to give in to his demands,
but was able to flee. The charge was plea bargained down from
attempted robbery and attempted rape to assault and battery.
He was sentenced to the time he had spent in jail waiting for
trial, two and a half months.

Another detective testified that the day after Hallman was released from jail, he accosted another woman in her car, demanding money and sex. He found a screwdriver in the car and
held it to the woman's throat, but she fought him off. Hallman
pleaded guilty to "breaking and entering an automobile with
intent to commit assault and battery." He was sentenced to
eighteen months in prison.

Hallman was arrested again in 1971 for attempted rape, but
only after the detective had already given a detailed account of
the incident at the penalty hearing did he admit that the
charge had been dropped. Judge Rawlins ordered the jury to
disregard the testimony since the law mentions only *convictions*
for violent felonies. But, from the point of view of the defense,
the damage had already been done; the jury had heard the story.
Overlooked at the time was the fact that the first conviction
only constituted a misdemeanor, not a felony. Under the law,
only one incident should have been presented to the jury.

When its turn came, the defense tried to show that Hallman
was not in full control of his actions because of a mental disturbance. Meyers called to the stand the two psychiatrists who

had examined Hallman. Both of them repeated their findings that Hallman, while sane, was a sexual psychopath with a basic behavioral disorder that would make it difficult for him to conform to the law. One of them testified that with Hallman's personality, he would be likely to react impulsively and violently to being slapped by a woman. Meyers also contended that Hallman had been drinking all day and that his state of drunkenness constituted an "impaired capacity."

In his closing arguments, Nutter seemed less concerned with talking about the specific aggravating circumstances than with implanting in the jury's mind the thought that Hallman was dangerous and that if sentenced to imprisonment he could someday get out to prey on the public.

The jury, after an hour of deliberation, reported back to the judge that it recommended death for Hallman.

DECISION: *Should the judge accept or reject the jury recommendation?*

Nine days after the penalty hearing, Hallman stood before Judge Rawlins for sentencing. The judge did not have to accept the jury's recommendation, but he did, and condemned Hallman to die. By law, Judge Rawlins was required to send to the state supreme court for review the reasons for sentencing Hallman to death. The judge found that all four possible aggravating circumstances had been proven—that the murder occurred during a robbery, that it was committed for money (a separate circumstance in the law), that he had been previously convicted of violent offenses ("both involved a threat to the throat of the victim," the judge wrote, even though it appears that only one incident involved such a threat), and that the murder was "especially heinous, atrocious and cruel."

The judge said that there was only one mitigating circumstance, Hallman's age. He specifically rejected the argument that Hallman acted under a diminished mental capacity. He turned the testimony of the psychiatrists upside down, saying that Hallman's "behavioral disorder" made it clear that he "was a menace to society and that he was a person who felt no anxiety or remorse over any of his actions."

DECISION: *Did Hallman get a fair trial?*

That was the question the appeals courts had to decide. In late 1975 the Florida Supreme Court, by a five-to-two vote, affirmed Hallman's conviction and death sentence. An appeal was made to the U.S. Supreme Court. In July 1976—a few days after the Court had ruled Florida's death penalty law constitutional—the Supreme Court declined to review Hallman's case.

That could have been the end of the line for Clifford Hallman. But then, in a curious twist of circumstance, new evidence came to light that brought into question one of the basic premises of the case—one that not even Hallman himself had ever contested. That premise, as stated in the indictment, was that Hallman "did then and there inflict divers mortal wounds of which the said Roxanne Mary Monroe did languish and die. . . ."

DECISION: *Is Clifford Hallman the only one responsible for the death of Roxanne Mary Monroe?*

This startling new aspect of the case stemmed from a lawsuit brought, ironically, on behalf of Hallman's victim. About two years after Mrs. Monroe's death, a suit was filed by the attorney handling her estate. It charged the Tampa hospital that had treated her with "wrongful death." The attorney, William Hapner, charged in the suit that Mrs. Monroe had not been given proper medical care by the hospital—that, as Hapner put it in a later deposition, she died "as a result of their clear malpractice." In effect, the suit charged that Hallman had not really inflicted "mortal wounds" on Mrs. Monroe, and that the hospital was responsible for her death. Hapner sought money damages for Mrs. Monroe's sole beneficiary, her young son (then living with his father in another state).

The hospital hired a prominent local physician, Dr. James Crumbley, to investigate the case and help the hospital defend the lawsuit. After his investigation, Dr. Crumbley advised the hospital that it would be very difficult to win the suit. Mrs. Monroe should not have died, the doctor said; Hallman's wound should not have killed her.

Acting on Dr. Crumbley's advice, the hospital settled out of court with Mrs. Monroe's estate for forty-two thousand dollars —full value, as far as the plaintiffs were concerned.

Hallman's attorney, Thomas Meyers, learned of the lawsuit as soon as it was filed. He let it run its course. As soon as it was settled, he set out to prove that the hospital's actions reduced Hallman's responsibility for the death of Mrs. Monroe.

First, Meyers took depositions from Dr. Crumbley, attorney Hapner, and the nurses who were on duty in the emergency room when Mrs. Monroe was admitted to the hospital. The testimony from Dr. Crumbley, Meyers hoped, would be particularly strong because he had been hired by the hospital to defend its actions and had been forced to conclude that they could not be defended. In his deposition, Dr. Crumbley made it clear that no one could determine exactly what did take place in the emergency room the evening Mrs. Monroe died. The records were incomplete. There was, for example, no record of a doctor ever having looked at Mrs. Monroe before she turned blue. The doctor who was on duty at the time could not be located.

The cause of death, Dr. Crumbley told Meyers, was a "hematoma"—a collarlike swelling underneath the skin that resulted from the wound. Such a hematoma should be expected from any neck wound, Dr. Crumbley said, and it could have been controlled easily by inserting a tube into Mrs. Monroe's throat to keep the air passage open. But apparently, he said, no one thought of this. The swelling cut off her breathing, and by the time the problem was noticed it was too late; severe damage had already been done to the brain.

Meyers: Were any major blood vessels cut in her throat?

Dr. Crumbley: The autopsy report, as I recall, indicated that no major blood vessels were cut.

Meyers: From the description that you have seen of the autopsy report and the hospital records and your general knowledge about the case, was this a mortal wound in and of itself?

Dr. Crumbley: No, sir, people who have this type of a wound and who have the situation recognized and appropriate treatment taken can expect to recover.

Meyers: Would you say that had she been given proper care over there that she would be alive today?

Dr. Crumbley: Well, let's put it this way: I would be most unhappy if a member of my family had been treated that way. We all make mistakes. As the old saying goes, to err is human, but somebody somewhere in the team of people failed to recognize what they had and just did not afford the woman the standard of care that should have been gotten in an up-to-date emergency room.

DECISION: Should the malpractice case affect Hallman's fate?

There are several possible decisions here. The courts could declare that the information regarding the hospital's role should have been brought out at the trial, and it was too late to raise it as an issue. In a case where a man's life is at stake, however, this seems unlikely. The courts also could decide that the new evidence would not have changed the outcome of the trial; in that case the sentence would stand. Or the case could be sent back for a new penalty trial, with the new evidence presented to the jury. Or the courts might conclude that the information might have caused the jury to bring in a lesser verdict of second-degree murder, and require a new trial for the entire case.

Hallman's attorney argued that the evidence justified a retrial of the whole case. The state's attorney replied that several honored legal principles preclude any consideration of Hallman's claims. But for his actions, he argued, Mrs. Monroe would never have had to go to the hospital—and had she not gone to the hospital, she probably would have died from the same condition, the swelling of the neck.

The man who prosecuted Hallman in 1973, Robert Nutter,

publicly declared that he felt the new evidence merited a new trial on the sentence. He did not think it would have affected the jury's decision on the degree of guilt, even though he conceded in an interview that the original trial "could have gone either way." He had little sympathy for Hallman. "He grabbed her by the hair on her head and pulled it back," he said, making a slashing motion with his hand. "After that he cut her wrists. It appeared to me that he was trying to kill her. And even though the hospital may have been negligent, I can't help but think that but for Clifford, she would be alive today."

The local newspaper, in its coverage of the case, found one juror who believed that she would not have voted for the death penalty had she known about the hospital's role. She said she might even have held out for a second-degree murder verdict. (The other jurors would not discuss the case.)

At this writing, it looks as if several years will be required to decide what to do with the new evidence. Even if Hallman loses this battle he has one more hope: clemency. In early 1977 the Florida Parole and Probation Commission investigated Hallman's case, along with those of five other inmates whose appeals had been turned down by the U.S. Supreme Court. Hallman was the only inmate who won a recommendation for mercy. The final decision must be made by the governor and the cabinet of the state.

Clifford Hallman was pale from the years away from sunlight. On Death Row, he slept until noon most days, and frequently declined to eat his food. The fingers on his left hand carried a dark brown nicotine stain that came from chain-smoking the rough prison-made cigarettes given to the inmates.

On Death Row, Hallman's isolation was more complete than that of his comrades. With his poor hearing, he could not join in the banter that echoed up and down the corridor. "I guess sometimes you can get lonely," he said in an interview. "But that's only when you start thinking about home or family. But if I'm not asleep, I usually try to keep my mind on the TV or the radio [he used an earplug] or something. That way, I don't have to think about these things."

Asked if he had learned anything in his years under lock and key next to the electric chair, Hallman replied, "I learned one thing: I'll never touch another drink in my life." He'd keep that vow, he swore, "because I know now what it did to me—and because I made a promise to someone, to a special lady who writes to me and comes to see me." That "special lady" is a Roman Catholic nun who struck up a voluminous correspondence with Hallman, and then began visiting him regularly. She said that knowing Hallman had made her change her mind about capital punishment, and had shown her that anyone can change for the better.

When he first heard about the lawsuit involving the hospital, Hallman said, it was the first ray of hope he had had in quite a while, changing his mood from despair to hope. With an optimism that his past experience with the courts does not seem to warrant, he became convinced that he would avoid execution. When the Supreme Court approved Florida's death penalty law, he said he reacted differently than his cell neighbors. "I'm not going to say that it doesn't scare me," he said. "It scares every man up here. But it doesn't bother me as much as the others because I am convinced that I am not going to go to the chair."

The Legal Issue: Reasonable Doubt

At half-past twelve on the afternoon of September 19, 1975, Freddie Lee Pitts and Wilbert Lee squinted into the bright Florida sunshine, paused, and then began walking. They passed through two sets of chain link gates and into a parking lot, never glancing back at the concrete fortress behind them—the Florida State Prison. "I've had enough of this hotel," Pitts said dryly. "They have very poor accommodations." Then the pair climbed into a waiting car and sped off.

Pitts and Lee were free, free of what they called "the shadow of death." They had spent the years from 1963 to 1972 on Death Row at the prison, waiting to be executed—executed for a crime they did not commit. Their lives had been saved, first by the U.S. Supreme Court's 1972 *Furman* decision, then by an unusual re-examination of their case. Several lawyers, a polygraph operator, and an investigative reporter spent years trying to reopen the case, because they were convinced that Pitts and Lee were innocent. Finally, another man admitted that he had committed the two murders for which Pitts and Lee had been condemned, and the key prosecution witness confessed that she had lied. In 1975, after studying the case for a year and a half, Florida Governor Reubin Askew pardoned the two inmates.

Gene Miller, the newspaper reporter who brought the case to light (and won his second Pulitzer Prize for his efforts), depicted in *Invitation to a Lynching* how coincidence, racial animosity, and shoddy police work could send innocent men to Death Row. It was a dramatic illustration of the shortcomings of our legal system. One can grant the state the abstract right to take a life in retribution for murder and still oppose the death penalty on the grounds that the day-to-day workings of the criminal justice system are not adequate. As the Marquis de Lafayette put it early in the nineteenth century: "I shall continue to demand the abolition of the death penalty until I have the infallibility of human judgments demonstrated to me."

As Pitts and Lee walked out of the Florida State Prison, they left behind them fifty-four men sentenced to death under Florida's revised capital punishment law. Virtually every one of them claimed that he, too, had been framed, or at least that he had been treated unfairly in the courts. However improbable some of their stories might sound, their claims cannot be dismissed out of hand. And sure enough, in 1978 one of those fifty-four, Delbert Tibbs, was proven innocent. In its ruling, the Florida Supreme Court noted that the prosecution could not show that Tibbs was within 150 miles of the crime. It said the testimony of the only witness against him "is so riddled with conflicts and is so inherently unreliable that his conviction and death sentence should be reversed." All charges were later thrown out of court.

In the past, there have been some chillingly close calls. James V. Bennett, former director of the U.S. Bureau of Prisons, once described the panic that ensued in 1933 when President Roosevelt commuted the death sentence of Charles Bernstein only fifteen minutes before his scheduled execution. A cab dispatched to the prison got caught in traffic, and all the telephone lines were tied up. Bennett finally got through to the prison by phone only five minutes before the appointed time. Bernstein was later exonerated of the crime.

At least these mistakes were caught in time. Timothy John Evans was not so lucky. Evans was hanged in England in 1950 for murdering his wife and child. Evans, a man of limited intelligence, had confessed to slaying his wife (but not his child), then had recanted. The bodies were not found, but a witness testified against him. Four years after Evans was executed, the witness, John R. Christie, confessed that he had been the murderer, and had also killed several other women. Horrified police found the bodies of Evans's wife and child among seven corpses hidden in a wall of Christie's home. Evans was pardoned posthumously, for whatever good it did him, and Christie was hanged.

The Evans-Christie case is the best-documented modern example of an execution in error. Hugo Adam Bedau, the leading American scholar of the death penalty, included in one of his books short descriptions of seventy-one twentieth-century cases in which an innocent person was believed to have been wrongfully convicted of murder. Most of these cases resulted in imprisonment, however; only eight went all the way to execution. Compared to thousands of legitimate homicide convictions, such outrages occur extremely rarely. ("But," Albert Camus noted, "the word 'rarely' itself makes one shudder.") Bedau, no advocate of capital punishment, conceded that it was "false sentimentality to argue that the death penalty should be abolished because of the abstract possibility that an innocent person might be executed."

But such dramatic cases are only dark nuggets on the surface of the legal system, indicating a deep vein of imperfection below. The popular image of a "mistake"—"Sam Smith was convicted of the crime, but now it turns out that Joe Jones really did it"—is much too limited. Consider, for instance, the question of self-defense. Someone who kills to protect his own life is innocent of any crime, but if there are no witnesses then the issue can be hard to decide.

A recent case in Texas provides a good example. A girl was shot and killed in the apartment of her boyfriend by a security guard. The district attorney claimed that the boyfriend had hired the security guard to kill the girl; the defendants claimed that the girl, angry at being spurned by her boyfriend, attacked them. The two men were tried separately. The man accused of hiring the guard was convicted and sentenced to death. But another jury believed the security guard's story and acquitted him. One of the verdicts must be mistaken.

In his short and eloquent volume (*Capital Punishment: The Inevitability of Caprice and Mistake*), Charles L. Black, Jr., demonstrates the depth of possible error in our judicial system. An injustice is done, Black points out, whenever a person is deprived of life through an incorrect judgment at *any* stage of the proceedings against him. Such errors are less common with the question "Did he or didn't he?"—but they are no less serious when the question involved is "Was he insane or not?" or "Was this crime 'especially heinous, atrocious or cruel'?"

Granted, all human institutions are fallible. But the law acknowledges that as the stakes rise, so must the reliability of decision-making. Only a rudimentary form of due process is required for those who wish to argue about a parking citation, but when imprisonment can result, the legal procedures must become very protective. When life itself is at stake, we demand something very close to perfection. After-the-fact apologies do no good.

We must recognize that for the past several decades—since long before the moratorium of the 1960s—executions have been unusual in this country, the exception rather than the rule as punishment for murder. Nowadays, the issue is whether the few who are given death sentences are really any different from the majority who are not. Are executions reserved for the worst criminals, or only for the unluckiest ones?

The accusation is that the death penalty has become the grim booby-prize of a macabre lottery—thousands of defendants buy tickets each year by participating in a homicide, and a few unlucky losers are drawn from a hat. Or, even worse, the losers are selected according to the color of their skins or the skill of their attorneys.

This is the heart of the debate over the constitutionality of the death penalty.

The Bill of Rights' declaration that "no person shall be deprived of life, liberty, or property without due process of law" implies that people *may* be deprived of life—but only with due process of law. And it is not due process if the few people sentenced to death are "a capriciously selected random handful," the Supreme Court declared in 1972. The laws enacted after that decision (examined in Chapter Two) attempted to define just who, among thousands of homicide defendants, should be given the death penalty. Here we must consider whether these reforms can work—whether two-stage trials and enumerated standards will yield a uniform result or whether, as the abolitionists claim, the legal system as a whole is so honeycombed with unguided discretion and opportunities for error that the results will still be determined by luck.

One troublesome source of unfairness left untouched by the new laws involves the role of the prosecutor. No one wields more power—discretionary power—than he does. Some prosecutors would have us believe that they are automatons, sorting facts into legal categories the way mail clerks file letters by ZIP codes. But while each prosecutor may be consistent in his policies, there is no coordination between prosecutors. One will seek the death penalty against a fifteen-year-old; dozens of others would not. One offers a life sentence in exchange for a guilty plea; his colleague in the next county would take the case to trial. One treats a case as first-degree murder; another decides it is manslaughter.

The touchiest area is in plea bargaining. A few prosecutors assert that they will never plea bargain in a murder case, but only a few. In many court systems criminal justice would be entirely blocked if all murder cases went to trial. Many defendants indicted on capital murder charges are offered life sentences if they will plead guilty.

The decision on whether to offer a plea bargain does not always depend on the circumstances of the crime or the background of the defendant. Prosecutors usually consider factors such as the number of witnesses; how crowded the court calendar is; pressure from the newspapers or the victim's family; the quality of the defendant's attorney. None of these has any proper place in a life-or-death decision—and these are only the more honorable of the practical considerations. Sometimes the decision on whether to seek the death penalty seems to depend on racial prejudice or the need to have a sensational trial before election time. Some prosecutors play cynical games, offering a reduced sentence to the triggerman in a murder if he will testify against accomplices who refuse to cooperate. Too often it seems that while the criminal justice system pretends to model itself on the ideal of "Truth or Consequences," in practice it can bear a closer resemblance to another television program, "Let's Make a Deal."

This is not to suggest that most prosecutors are venal, biased, or cruel. But hidden judgments leave room for extralegal factors—and they inevitably lead to inconsistent results. There are no standards here. A crime that inspires an impassioned plea for ultimate justice in south Georgia will merit three years imprisonment in Atlanta.

When a trial does take place, there are scores of decisions that depend not on the weight of the evidence, but on arcane points of law. Life often depends on the judge's determination of the admissibility of evidence, for example.

But in many murder cases, the most baffling problems have to do with the state of mind of the defendant. Premeditation is required for a first-degree murder conviction, and we can all think of examples of murder that we would consider "premeditated." But jurists and lawmakers have struggled for centuries to come up with a workable definition of premeditation to apply to the infinite variety of situations that arise in courtrooms—and have failed. "In practice, premeditation means little more than appearing before an unsympathetic jury," Franklin Zimring, one of the leaders of a new generation of statistically sophisticated lawyer-criminologists, commented.

Judging from the frequency with which it is raised in murder cases, the most difficult issue of all is insanity. This is truly an all-or-nothing decision. If a defendant is insane, he is innocent of any crime (although he will be legally confined in a mental institution, where conditions may be as bad as prison and where he may spend more years than if he had been found guilty). If not, then he is liable to the full weight of the law.

At least since the thirteenth century, the question of what to do with murderous lunatics has plagued English and American law. Gradually, we have come to the conclusion that someone who is not responsible for his acts should not be punished for them. But where do we draw the line?

Since 1843 that line has generally been known as the M'Naghten Rule. It comes from a famous English case in which a man named Daniel M'Naghten became obsessed with the idea that the prime minister, Sir Robert Peel, was persecuting him. M'Naghten shot and killed Peel's private secretary, whom he had mistaken for the prime minister. After a sensational trial, the jury found M'Naghten not guilty because of insanity. Soon afterward, a general rule was formulated requiring that, in order to sustain this verdict, "it must be clearly proved that, at the time of the committing of the act, the party accused was labouring under such a defect of reason, from disease of the mind, as not to know the nature and quality of the act he was doing; or, if he did know it, he did not know he was doing what was wrong."

To the layman this may seem reasonable. In the courts, however, this standard has led to chaos. As Black says, "Every word in this rule, except the prepositions and definite articles, has been problematical." There have been two major attempts to refine the rule. One is the "irresistible impulse" standard, which requires that a defendant suffer from a "diseased mental condition" that renders him unable to resist an impulse to perform a criminal act. Another refinement was the Durham Rule, set down in 1954. It held that "an accused is not criminally responsible if his unlawful act was the product of mental disease or mental defect." Neither of these two standards, more protective of defendants than M'Naghten, has been widely accepted. Nor are they much easier to interpret in practice. The majority of states stand by M'Naghten.

To chart their way through the fog of language, modern judges and juries look to psychiatrists for guidance and, frequently, everyone ends up lost. A look at a complicated murder trial, with prominent psychiatrists parading to the stand to give diametrically opposing interpretations of the same situation or personality, should disabuse us from any notion that "the science of the mind" can give us scientifically reliable answers. From the point of view of the jurors, psychiatrists are frequently unintelligible and evasive. From the psychiatrists' standpoint, the very basis of the rule—that there is a definite class of insane persons easily distinguishable from the rest of us—is outmoded. It recognizes no advances in our understanding of the human mind since 1843, including the theories of Freud. Dr. Karl Menninger, one of our most respected psychiatrists, denounced the M'Naghten Rule as "medieval" and "absurd." Black said our techniques for resolving the insanity issue "are about as useful as flamingos for playing croquet." Still the parade of expert testimony continues, with some psychiatrists confidently labeling defendants as "sociopaths" or "psychopaths," ignoring the fact that much of the psychiatric community has abandoned these terms. Dr. Menninger went so far as to urge that psychiatrists be banned from the courtroom, because of the vagueness of the law and the doctors' capacity to mislead.

The issue of mental stability takes on a deadly seriousness when it comes to the second stage of a capital trial, when punishment must be fixed for a defendant found sane and guilty. Once again the psychiatrists troop to the stand—in Texas, to give insights on the future dangerousness of the defendant; in Florida, to offer opinions on whether "the capacity of the defendant to appreciate the criminality of his conduct to the requirements of the law was substantially impaired."

The dangers of overreliance on psychiatric opinion were illustrated in a Texas case involving a man named Ernest Benjamin Smith, Jr. Smith and a companion had entered a store to rob it. Apparently the owner had reached under the counter for a gun, at which point Smith shouted something to his partner, who shot and killed the man. (There were conflicting reports as to whether Smith shouted "Get him!" or "Watch out!") Since this was a Texas case, the prosecution had to prove that this non-triggerman would "commit criminal acts of violence" in the future if sentenced to anything less than death. The prosecution presented evidence of a prior conviction for possession of marijuana, which resulted in a sentence of probation. (This minor scrape with the law was escalated by the Texas Court of Criminal Appeals to "his apparent surrender to misfortune following his marijuana conviction"; the U.S. Supreme Court inflated it still further to a "prior conviction on narcotics charges.") But the key evidence leading to a death sentence was clearly the psychiatric testimony. A local psychiatrist took the stand and confidently labeled Smith a person with a severe "sociopathic personality disorder," with "no conscience, no remorse, no guilt feelings" and a "complete disregard for another person's life." There was, he said, no treatment for this condition, and the psychiatrist was certain that Smith would commit crimes in the future.

This testimony was a masterpiece of overstatement. The psychiatrist cleverly slipped back and forth between describing Smith's personality traits and those of a "typical sociopath." He did not mention that this type of categorization is currently in disrepute among most psychiatrists. The jury was not aware that the psychiatrist had been hired by prosecutors to testify in dozens of trials, giving uniformly unfavorable reviews to defendants. The diagnosis was based on an interview lasting an hour and a half, without administering tests or checking Smith's background. The characterization as a sociopath came not from anything Smith said or did, but from what he did *not* do—he did not go out of his way to express remorse about the death of the storekeeper.

After reviewing this case and others, George Dix, a professor specializing in mental health law at the University of Texas School of Law, proposed a series of ethical standards to control psychiatric testimony. But he also concluded that the impossibility of fairly predicting dangerousness should have been enough to render the statute unconstitutional.

The seemingly endless rounds of appeals in capital cases would, one might think, ferret out every conceivable error and produce a consistent application of the law. But we must remember that appeals courts look only at points of law in dispute; they cannot question the evidence or look at evidence introduced after the trial. (It is worth noting that in most cases of mistaken identity, appeals courts had affirmed the wrongful convictions.) Frequently an appeal is lost because the defendant's lawyer failed to raise an objection to a procedural error at the proper time. And when the appeal raises a tricky point of law, the difficulty of finding the one "correct" decision is evidenced by the fact that most appeals are decided by split votes. The end result of this process is that those finally selected to die are distinguished not so much by the enormity of their crimes as by the inability of their lawyers to make sure the trial judge has made a reversible error. In *In Cold Blood*, Truman

Capote wrote that "the system of appeals that pervades American jurisprudence amounts to a legalistic wheel of fortune, a game of chance, somewhat fixed in the favor of the criminal." No matter how the odds are fixed, it hardly seems proper that luck should determine the outcome.

The Georgia and Florida supreme courts are required by law to review capital cases not just for technical errors but also to see that the standards are applied consistently. This is an admirable requirement, and it has improved the situation considerably. In Florida, the state supreme court overturned as many sentences as it upheld in the first three years under the new law. But the courts compare death penalty cases only with other death penalty cases—not with those where the jury gave a life sentence, or where the prosecutor decided to accept a guilty plea in exchange for a life sentence.

The final step of the appeals process, clemency, is the least standardized of all. The decision whether or not to commute a sentence generally rests in the hands of the governor, and his personal philosophy will determine who dies. In the past, some governors have commuted all death sentences, some none. Some were impressed by religious conversions on Death Row; others consulted the victim's family. Two New York governors routinely commuted the death sentence of any man whose appeal had been decided by a split vote. California's Governor Ronald Reagan attended the Academy Awards rather than hear a last appeal for clemency. In the end, a man's life can depend on which political party happens to be in power, or how close the scheduled execution comes to an election.

It should come as no surprise that in a system with so many uncertainties, the skill of the defendant's attorney will play a major role. This, of course, is why virtually everyone on Death Row is poor. "The poor man . . . can no more afford a really adequate defense than he can afford a year's cruise around the world on a luxury liner," Black noted. The middle-class defendant is in almost equal trouble. The ingenuity and persistence of the attorney are not the only crucial factors; it costs a tremendous amount of money to hire private investigators, conduct jury challenges, hire psychiatrists, and, in general, try to match the resources of the state. It is not that the rich buy their way out of justice, but they are able to bring out *all* the evidence favorable to them. And, of course, prosecutors are likely to think twice about taking a marginal case to trial if they know it will cost the county hundreds of thousands of dollars. Better, perhaps, to take a guilty plea and go down the hallway to another courtroom where a poorer defendant can be quietly steamrollered.

It is true that we have made great strides in the last two decades in providing legal assistance to the poor. Some public defenders are highly skilled (and, of course, many private attorneys are not). Occasionally a public-interest group will take on a case and pull out all the stops. But all too often it is an overworked, inexperienced public defender, or a private attorney who cannot afford to waste too much time on the case, who defends the poor.

In 1956 the U.S. Supreme Court declared, "There can be no fairness where the kind of trial a man gets depends on the amount of money he has." A noble principle, but no one familiar with American courtrooms would dispute that this is very much the case today.

Those people who are outraged by the concern shown here and in the courts for the rights of defendants should consider that the net effect of the death penalty may well be to increase those rights. As the Supreme Court noted, an executed person has lost the right to have rights, and before such a step is taken extra safeguards will be added. As Justice Robert H. Jackson noted in 1953: "When the penalty is death, we, like state court judges, are tempted to strain the evidence and even, in close cases, the law in order to give a doubtfully condemned man another chance." Often these precedents will eventually seep down to protect defendants in non-capital cases as well.

So far in this discussion, the arguments of the opponents of capital punishment have held sway. Those who believe in the death penalty often reply that the benefits outweigh the risks, and that on balance the process works much better than depicted here. The one legal advantage the new death penalty laws offer is that with a separate sentencing hearing, an appellate court can overturn a sentence without upsetting a conviction. This means that an error can be corrected without setting a guilty defendant free.

But their strongest rebuttal is that it really does not make a great deal of difference to the ultimate question if all the things said about the shortcomings of the death penalty as law are true. Such faults are deplorable, of course, but they infect every other court proceeding as well. Are we to give up our entire system of punishment? As Jacques Barzun put it, "What is at fault in our present system is not the sentence but the fallible procedure. . . . What the miscarriages [of justice] point to is the need for reforming the jury system, the rules of evidence, the customs of prosecution, the machinery of appeal." In other words, the solution is not to abolish the penalty but to improve the process.

Defenders of the death penalty go on to say that it does not matter if some murderers who deserve death escape it through loopholes or luck. This is essentially an act of mercy, they say; it does not give grounds for complaint to those who get what they deserve. In the *Gregg* decision, Justice Stewart wrote: "Nothing in any of our cases suggests that the decision to afford an individual defendant mercy violates the Constitution."

In his 1976 opinion, Justice White concluded that the theoretical legal arguments of the abolitionists assumed that the legal system was corrupt, and ignored the chance that the benefits could outweigh the risks:

[The] opponents have argued, in effect, that no matter how effective the death penalty may be as a punishment, government, created and run as it must be by humans, is inevitably incompetent to administer it. This cannot be accepted as a proposition of constitutional law. Imposition of the death penalty is surely an awesome responsibility for any system of justice and those who participate in it. Mistakes will be made and discriminations will occur. However. . . . I decline to interfere with the manner in which Georgia has chosen to enforce its [laws] on what is simply an assertion of lack of faith in the ability of the system of justice to operate in a fundamentally fair manner.

"Mistakes will be made and discriminations will occur." The ACLU could not have put it better. The important question here is: How often? Is this truly a standardized procedure in practice, or is it a lottery?

Such questions cannot be determined by looking at any individual case. Even an examination of all death penalty cases would not do, for they are only a minority of all murder cases.

The most comprehensive look at how murder is punished was published in 1976 as "Punishing Homicide in Philadelphia: Perspectives on the Death Penalty." It contained the results of a study conducted by Franklin Zimring, with Joel Eigen and Sheila O'Malley. They followed the first 204 criminal homicides reported to the Philadelphia police in 1970 to see what happened to them in the courts. The results were disturbing to anyone who would like to believe that the ultimate crime of murder is punished with any consistency. Out of the 204 homicides, 170 adults were eventually arrested, charged, and convicted of some crime. Only 3 received the death penalty; 14 got life sentences. But 100 received sentences of two years or less, and 48 murderers were placed on probation.

Included in the crimes were quite a few gruesome murders. The crimes usually thought most deserving of death—three rape-killings and five multiple murders—all received lesser sentences. Two of the thirty-eight people charged with murder during a felony (usually robbery) received death sentences, fifteen got life, four received sentences of six years and over. At the other end of the spectrum, eight of them got sentences of two to five years and nine were sentenced to one year or probation. The researchers investigated the facts behind the cases and found little to justify such grossly different punishments. What seemed to explain the difference was not the seriousness of the crime, but two extraneous factors: prosecutors' discretion and defendants' race. Black offenders who killed white victims were dealt with very severely; blacks who killed blacks were punished rather lightly. Zimring concluded that the legal system made only one significant distinction between crimes: whether they were "wholesale" or "retail." "Wholesale" murders (usually involving black victims) aroused little public outcry; they were disposed of quickly. But in the small number of "retail" cases where public interest ran high, the prosecutor held out for extreme sentences. What the study depicted was an amoral machine which selected a few defendants for sentences of twenty-five years or death, while the majority were punished by sentences of two years or less. Zimring concluded, "The problem is not that the punishment for murder is too harsh or too lenient; sadly, it is both."

The death penalty law then in force in Pennsylvania is now outdated, but it was similar enough to newer laws (such as Florida's) to indicate that the situation would not be greatly changed today. An even more ambitious research effort has been undertaken in Texas, Florida, and Georgia. Researchers have been trying to study all murder indictments within those states to determine whether capital cases can be distinguished from other murders according to objective criteria. At this writing, however, the results of these massive studies are not available.

One thing is clear: If these studies, and others that may be done, reveal a situation as chaotic as the one in Philadelphia—a situation that has been reflected in the infrequent executions of the last few decades—then the Supreme Court will be forced to overturn the new laws. As the Court declared in 1972, it remains a constitutional violation to impose the death penalty infrequently, inconsistently, and arbitrarily. And if the shortcomings of our legal system make this appear inevitable, we should not be ashamed to admit it; the end of the death penalty will not mean the end of punishment for murder. As Professor Black put it: "We need not fear that we will have committed ourselves to the Utopian dream of a world without any criminal justice if we conclude that our system of administering criminal justice simply will not decently do as a system for separating out those who are to die."

CHAPTER SEVEN

Death of a White Cab Driver

Profile: Jessie Lewis Pulliam

If Jessie had been white and the cab driver black, there's no question but that he would not have been given the death penalty. The case would have been worked out without a trial.

But the thing you've got to understand about these cases is that the racial background and racial undertones of the community determine not only why the punishment was given but also why the crime occurred. You've got to understand why a black person would want to rob a white cab driver. How did race and social deprivation fit into Jessie Pulliam? Into his lack of education, into his epilepsy, into his mental problems? And what part did economic disparity play? You've got to understand the economic oppression of the years of control by the cotton mills.

Once you know that, you put into the equation the way he was treated when he was arrested. Why didn't he have an attorney for ten days? If he'd had any status, certainly he would have had an attorney immediately. And if he was white and had his epileptic fits in jail, they'd immediately have gotten help.

Only then do you look at the trial. It was one of those dum-dum trials, with ineffective representation for him. And black people just don't get on juries there, except maybe for a token black they can trust. Those juries just don't value black life the same as white life.

Oh, they can say they don't have any racism, they don't have any bias. But it controls every part of the criminal system down there. And when a white person dies, it's like shooting ducks on the ground to get a death penalty for a black person.

—Millard Farmer, Director, Team Defense Project

It was duck soup. It was not a complicated case—just the cold-blooded murder of a poor, laboring white cab driver to eliminate a witness. A more open-and-shut case couldn't be found.

There was no race issue in the courtroom. I don't think I even mentioned the fact that the guy was white. Millard Farmer just does anything to divert attention away from the facts in the case.

—Billy Lee, Troup County District Attorney

Troup County, Georgia—where Jessie Pulliam was tried and sentenced to death—is not one of those backwaters where the white folk are waiting for the Confederate Army to rise from the grave and march on Washington to force the Supreme Court to overturn its 1954 school desegregation decision. It's a few miles north of the "Black Belt" of southeastern Georgia (Jimmy Carter's country), where for generations whites were in the minority and naked oppression was the order of the day. LaGrange, the county seat, was only one-third black and had largely escaped the turmoil of the civil rights movement. The schools were integrated peacefully; no police dogs or fire hoses were called out when blacks began to sit down at the lunch counters.

But while LaGrange may be moderate for Georgia, Georgia as a state probably bears the greatest burden of proving that its criminal justice system—its police, its courts, its prisons—are no longer the brass knuckles on the fist of Jim Crowism. Since 1930, Georgia has executed more people than any other state—and seventy-nine percent have been black. Georgia also leads the nation in lynchings: 491 between 1882 and 1952.

This story begins twenty miles east of LaGrange, across the Chattahoochee River, in a cluster of adjoining towns called The Valley. Millard Fuller, another Georgia attorney, describes The Valley, where he was born and raised:

The Valley's not a hard racist area. The company was very adept at keeping ahead of what it took to cause a riot—or bring in a union. In a lot of ways The Valley is harder to deal with than a place like Dawson [another small town in South Georgia, scene of a publicized trial where race was an issue], where the racism is up front. I imagine the white people over there would pride themselves on not having any race problems. But if you want to find out, get into the black community. They see what's going on.

On maps, The Valley lies in Alabama, but economically it doesn't belong to the state; it belongs to the textile mill. And the mill is in Georgia. While the rest of Alabama lives on "slow time" (Central Time), The Valley lives on "fast time"—Eastern Time, Georgia time, mill time. In income, education, and housing, the county where The Valley lies is slightly poorer than the average for the nation's second-poorest state. But the people do have jobs, jobs in the mill. The mill even hires blacks nowadays. Still, according to the 1970 census, a third of the houses were substandard; a quarter lacked indoor plumbing.

To an outsider, these are the invisible houses. You don't find them on the curved, shaded streets where the mill officials live; you don't find them even in the cramped neighborhoods of the white mill workers. Those blocks have paved streets, street lights, sewers, curbs, running water. But drive down U.S. 29 and turn onto an inconspicuous road into the country. For a mile or two you drive past scattered brick homes, overgrown pastures, collapsed barns, an occasional mobile home. You bounce over the railroad tracks and suddenly houses materialize, clustered together as if for protection. Streets branch off, but they aren't paved. There are no street lights, no sewers. The houses have no foundations; they perch on top of brick pillars; chickens and dogs wander underneath. The better houses have screens around

the sitting porch; the poorer ones have sheet tin roofs and peel-
ing tarpaper walls. Behind each house stands a little wooden
outhouse.

Welcome to Little Shawmut—"Little Shawmut" as distinct
from "White Shawmut" on the highway. Little Shawmut is
where the black community lives. Some of the people who live
in the houses have exotic, sonorous names taken from Bible in-
dexes or oral tradition: names such as Eris and Hermis, Doshie
and Coot, Etony and Arthlema, Geep and Zelpha, Lovie Luee
and Zula. Inside the houses are the obligatory magazine pictures
tacked to the living room walls: John F. Kennedy, Martin
Luther King, Jr., Robert F. Kennedy.

Willie Ramsey, store owner and general contractor, Little
Shawmut:

There hasn't been a cross burned here since the 1950s. They have
to be more discreet with the racism. Like when our school burned
down, they didn't rebuild it because they didn't want to bus any
whites from over yonder.

Most every home got a gun around here. It got pretty bad around
here. We got together and went to the D.A., asked him to tighten
down a little. Because so many blacks who killed blacks were getting
out on probation. You can kill a black and it's just a dead man
gone. But you kill a white and you're going to the chair.

Jessie? He had a problem. They used to call him a momma's pet.
He wanted to be popular. I feel he was a little weak-minded.

That one. The shack with the faucet wrapped in plastic in
the red sandy yard, the bucket hanging on the tree, the little un-
screened porch. That's where Susie Pulliam lived, and she paid
five dollars a week for those four rooms. Her husband died in
the early 1960s, leaving her alone with three girls and a boy.
She used to leave home at 6:00 A.M. and walk into White Shawmut, iron a couple of hours at one house for a dollar or two,
then move on to another house. Jessie Lewis, the boy, was
named for his father. Jessie was the youngest, and after the
others left home he stayed. Susie couldn't bear to punish him;

he did what he wanted. He was always weak and slow to learn.

When he was seven, Jessie began having fits—he'd fall down and thrash around, chomping at the air. Afterward he'd feel empty, blank, nervous. He did poorly in school and couldn't learn, but he was passed along, one grade to the next, more often than not.

A few generations ago, a light skin such as Jessie's would have been a mark of beauty among blacks; by the 1960s, with the advent of black pride, it brought ridicule. The other kids used to make fun of Jessie; "Half-White," they'd call him. He hung around with some white kids, and he would be jeered for that, too. For a while, he went to Detroit to live with his sister, but when one of his cousins back home was hurt, his mother sent for him to return to Little Shawmut. At seventeen, having finished the tenth grade (unable to read or write), he dropped out of school. He did a little construction work, hung around Little Shawmut, and looked for excitement. When he was twenty-one, he got into trouble. He was arrested for mail theft, taken into federal court, and sent to the penitentiary. He suffered a hernia there and had to have an operation before he was released, having served a year. Jessie went back to Little Shawmut, got a job working at a car wash, and returned to hanging around.

A few months later, in March 1975, at about dusk on a Sunday night, Jessie met a friend, Johnny Wilson. Johnny was only fifteen, but he got along well with Jessie; people made fun of Johnny, too, because he'd spent twelve years in a mental hospital. That night they joined someone named James; James gave them some marijuana, which they smoked. After a while, Jessie and Johnny agreed to get a taxi to carry them across the river to a club in West Point, Georgia. (The Alabama side of the river is a dry county.) Johnny couldn't dial the phone, so Jessie did, but Johnny did the talking; he ordered the cab.

William Jones, a West Point mill worker:

My brother, Sam, was a taxi driver, you know. He'd worked at the cab company about ten or twelve years. He owned his own cab.

Supported his wife and two children with it. He made pretty good money with the taxi. I got an average job at the mill and he made more money than I did.

The taxi business around here is long hours. Those mills have three shifts, and he carried help to each shift. He'd carry them to work at midnight and carry home some that got off. Then the next morning he'd have to be up to carry 'em again at eight, so it was long hours. And in between he worked to build that home for himself, with his own hands. And he wasn't a carpenter.

It happened on a Sunday night, March 9. I talked to him in the hospital and he told me what he knew about it.

He said he picked these two boys up in Alabama and drove 'em over the bridge into Georgia. He took 'em out to some little joint, a dance hall or something. They had actually planned to do it there. But one of 'em chickened out, the one that was going to do it— the one in the front seat. He was kind of retarded. They drove on and the other one took the gun from him.

Sam said he sort of got a glimpse that there was something wrong, you know. He was sort of falling over in the seat when he shot. Missed him the first time and shot the window out. Sam was sort of laying down, and he just stuck that gun over the seat and shot him laying there. Shot him in the back of the neck.

Well, the bullet cut his spinal cord. He couldn't move anything, and they thought they had killed him. But he didn't pass out. He was just helpless, he couldn't do anything.

They took his pocketbook. I believe he had sixteen dollars in it. I believe he said he had eighty or a hundred dollars up under the seat, in a cigar box, and he also had a gun under there. But they didn't get that. They just got his sixteen dollars and threw his pocketbook out in the woods. And they went and left him there.

He couldn't move at all. He couldn't move his fingers, he couldn't use his mike. But he could hear them calling him. The dispatcher had already decided there was something wrong and they kept calling him.

I believe he said two or three groups came along and wouldn't help him. They were colored, too, and they just went on. They saw him and he talked to them, asking them to help him. They passed him up. Didn't want to get involved, I guess.

I believe he said he must have stayed there about forty-five minutes. Then two small children came along. He told them, "Kids, y'all get over here and get this mike and answer." But he was laying on it or something. So he told 'em to go get somebody. In two minutes they were back with the police.

He lived ten days. He was conscious but he was paralyzed, couldn't move anything from the neck down. They operated on him on his birthday, the fifteenth, to take that bullet out. After then, he never was conscious any more. He died March 19.

My brother knew which one shot him. He knew the one in the back seat shot him. He knew both of 'em, who they was. He told the police everything.

I get sick every time I think about it. It's just so useless. I mean, it was so uncalled for. For sixteen dollars. When I think about it, I still just get sick.

Now, that was about as close to premeditated murder as you can get. Georgia, I understand, has a death penalty; it's one of the states that can. How in the world . . . how in the world can they keep holding the fella there and not do anything about it, I don't understand. For myself, I'd be satisfied just to leave him alive there, not kill him. But I hate to see that. I hate to see him spend the rest of his life over there. Because he's a young person. But I'd sure be afraid to turn him out again. If I was to tell you I thought he'd been punished enough and he was to get out of there and kill somebody else, I'd feel terrible.

It took the West Point Police, led by Lt. Arthur Carmack, only three hours to track down Jessie Pulliam and Johnny Wilson. When they arrested him in a friend's house, Pulliam had a revolver in his pants and blood on his shirt. He was taken a few miles to the Troup County jail in LaGrange to await trial.

He did not get along well there. He suffered epileptic seizures and once was beaten badly by other inmates.

The day Sam Jones died, Lieutenant Carmack went to see Pulliam in jail. He came away with a signed statement. Johnny Wilson had already given a confession.

Lt. Arthur Carmack, Detective, West Point Police Department:

Right after the man died I talked to Pulliam at the jail. And when he gave me his statement, why, it was just like Johnny talking. They fit right together.

He wasn't coerced; I had advised him of his rights. He didn't seem strange or nervous to me.

I don't think racism plays any part of the court system here today. He couldn't have gotten a fairer trial.

We don't have any racial tension here. Our ratio's about fifty-fifty in West Point. Years ago, when they started integrating the schools, things fell right into place here.

As far as I'm concerned, I think the pendulum has swung with the times. I think we're a better integrated society down here than the North. Why, the night of the incident, my phone rang constantly after midnight. People were calling to say what a good man Jones was. And it wasn't the white folks. It was black people. Everybody loved him. It was amazing to me.

Like most Southern towns, LaGrange is built about a town square—trees, grass, walkways, a statue in the center. But unlike other Southern towns, LaGrange's statue does not honor the Confederate war dead. It is a statue of Lafayette, who crossed the Chattahoochee nearby in 1825 on a tour of the South. LaGrange was named after Lafayette's home, the Château de la Grange.

The statue was donated by the Cason J. Callaway Foundation. Other remembrances of the Callaways dot LaGrange. The county health center was donated by the Fuller E. Callaway Foundation. LaGrange College has a Cason J. Callaway Building. Even the city's parking lots bear plaques: "This parking lot is furnished to the city of LaGrange rent free as a public service by the Fuller E. Callaway Foundation."

The Callaways owned Callaway Mills, one of the huge, successful textile plants that took over the destitute South in the late nineteenth century. Descendants of Cason Callaway, the founder, dominated the local scene. One of them, Bo Callaway, ran for governor against Lester Maddox and served as Secretary of the Army in the Nixon Administration.

The textile empire had been built on low wages, intimidation of labor unions, company-owned housing—and racial segregation. When the Callaway foundations gave away money, it was segregated money. Callaway Gardens, a huge, lush park a few miles from LaGrange, was not fully integrated until the 1970s. The Callaways had built a separate facility for blacks, separate but equal. Private facilities were not always covered by civil rights laws. And LaGrange depended on private money for many public services.

Thus it was that in 1975 the city of LaGrange still had segregated recreation facilities. For the whites, the Callaway Educational Association maintained groomed grass fields for baseball and football; white-columned brick buildings with gymnasiums and craft rooms; playgrounds with swings and merry-go-rounds; tennis courts; and a giant swimming pool. Lining the drives and posted on the doors glared conspicuous signs: *Callaway Educational Association*—MEMBERS ONLY. The members were all white.

Across town, the foundations had built a recreation center for blacks, separate and (almost) equal. It, too, had a few "members only" signs. Membership meant you were black.

The same was true for the library, across the street from the white recreation facilities. Its lawn, too, sprouted little signs: MEMBERS ONLY. White strangers were not questioned about their membership status. The books, at least, were not lily-white; there was quite a selection listed under "Negroes." ("Black Americans—See Negroes," read the card catalog. "Black Literature—See Negro Literature.")

In the courthouse (built by the Works Progress Administration in 1939, not the Callaways), they no longer had two separate but equal water fountains. The one integrated fountain required paper cups. A white stranger would never notice, but blacks pointed out that the paper cup system replaced the spigot when desegregation started. Apparently integration necessitated higher sanitary standards.

LaGrange has two private academies. Like most other private

schools in the South, these proudly displayed the date of their founding; it is almost part of the title on the signs in front ("LaGrange Private Academy—1970"). The dates refer to the time the public schools were integrated. The message to blacks was clear: MEMBERS ONLY.

L. W. Bailey, for twenty-six years the sheriff of Troup County:

The blacks and whites get along here. We didn't have any civil rights problems.

Yes, I think blacks were mistreated—in the North *and* in the South. But I think we treat a black person better than in the North. Of course, we don't believe in intermarriage yet. But it'll happen in this state.

A lot of people did not look at 'em as human. But I think they have a soul just like you and I. Why some of my best friends are black.

The trial of Jessie Pulliam was a modest affair. His sisters had scraped together fifteen hundred dollars to hire a private attorney, a black lawyer from Columbus, to defend him, but fifteen hundred dollars doesn't buy much. It doesn't buy private investigators to check out the police version of the facts. It doesn't buy medical examinations to see if there was any connection between Pulliam's epilepsy—his professed blacking-out— and his behavior. It doesn't buy a psychiatric examination. It doesn't buy pretrial motions. The entire proceeding was over in two days.

At the trial, the only real point of contention concerned the statement Pulliam had given in jail to Lieutenant Carmack. On the stand, Pulliam contended that Carmack had come to him in jail and asked him to sign a prepared statement that would prove his innocence. Pulliam, who at that point had been in jail ten days without seeing a lawyer, said he signed the statement immediately after coming out of a seizure and did not know what he was doing. Carmack, in rebuttal, testified that he had merely written down what Pulliam had told him, that

Pulliam had waived his right to a lawyer, and that he seemed to be in full control of himself at the time. The judge admitted the confession into evidence. In it, Pulliam said that he had fired the fatal shots.

The only evidence to contradict the prosecution's case was the testimony of Pulliam himself. On the stand, he told a somewhat disjointed tale involving mysterious strangers, implying that they had doped him up with marijuana and planted the gun on him. He was, however, sure of one thing: Johnny Wilson had fired the shot.

Pulliam's attorney brought Johnny Wilson to the stand, but Wilson's attorney stood by his side and, citing the Fifth Amendment's protection against self-incrimination, kept him from answering any questions. It was obvious, however, that Johnny Wilson was very simple-minded. (At a sanity hearing held some weeks later, Wilson was declared unfit to stand trial and sent to a state mental hospital. He was discharged within two years.)

The jury quickly found Pulliam guilty of robbery and murder.

At the sentencing hearing, which followed immediately, the prosecutor, Billy Lee, presented no additional evidence. Pulliam took the stand and talked nervously about his life. Pulliam's attorney, in his plea to the jury, noted that when Pulliam had been convicted of mail theft, the judge had recommended psychiatric evaluation and treatment. "This man is mentally ill," he argued.

In his argument for the death penalty, the prosecutor said the main issue was justice. "Is it justice to send this man off where he will be turned loose and maybe get out and do the same thing again? Is this justice?" He went on to note that the defense had introduced no psychiatric evidence to show mental illness. "I tell you what's wrong with [Pulliam]," Lee said. "He's just mean, and he's a person who has no sense of right and wrong, no idea of what he should and shouldn't do."

In his charge to the jury, the judge tried to outline the grounds on which the jury was supposed to make its decision. He indicated that there were three possible aggravating circumstances

from the Georgia death penalty law: the murder being committed during a robbery; the murder being committed for money;
the murder being "outrageously and wantonly vile, horrible, and
inhuman in that it involved depravity of mind on the part of
the defendant." An aggravating circumstance, if found, justified
death, the judge said; a lack of aggravating circumstances would
result in a life sentence. He did not mention the concept of
mitigating circumstances, or that they could offset aggravating
circumstances.

The jury returned with a verdict of death.

By law, the Georgia Supreme Court hears appeals of all death
penalty cases. In addition to whatever allegations of error are
raised by the defendant's attorney, the court is specifically instructed by the law to examine the case to be sure the sentence
was not imposed because of prejudice, and to ensure that the
sentence is similar to those imposed in similar cases.

Pulliam's lawyer prepared an appeal. In early 1976 the
Georgia Supreme Court rejected the appeal and affirmed the
death sentence. In a short, perfunctory opinion, the court concluded "that the sentence of death imposed here was not imposed under the influence of passion, prejudice, or any other
arbitrary factor." An appeal was filed with the U.S. Supreme
Court; it was rejected later that year. Pulliam was scheduled
to be executed January 2, 1977. His attorney filed another appeal and the execution was stayed, but that appeal was also rejected. A new execution date of December 5, 1977 was set.

Sally Turner, Jessie Pulliam's older sister:

It was real hard on Mother, that last execution date. We tried to
keep it from her, but they put it in the paper and some people told
her about it. She never got over it.

Jessie was my mother's baby. He got away with just anything; he
never had no one to teach him. He had a problem—he didn't seem
to think people liked him. They used to give him these names and
make fun of him. They try to get at the weak—and he was very
weak. It's the way Jessie carried himself and the crowd he followed.

All I know, if there's two nuts walking down the street, you don't free one and kill the other. That other kid's free. That's not fair.

For two and a half years, Jessie Pulliam sat alone in his cell at the Georgia State Prison at Reidsville—confused, hallucinating, suffering epileptic seizures. He was one of those nameless, faceless numbers on Death Row, forgotten by the public, forgotten in LaGrange, even forgotten in West Point. The prosecutor did not remember his name. His attorney left the state to open a new practice.

But before he left, the attorney asked Millard Farmer to take the case, and Farmer agreed. As the head of the Team Defense Project, headquartered in Atlanta, Farmer was one of the most controversial attorneys in the South. A journalist once described him as a cross "between the sensitive, principled character played by Gregory Peck in *To Kill a Mockingbird* and the cynical free spirit portrayed by Jack Nicholson in *Easy Rider*." To prosecutors, Farmer is an unscrupulous trickster who evades justice via delaying tactics, abstruse technicalities, and sheer bluster. (One frustrated district attorney publicly burned his law books on the steps of the local courthouse to protest Farmer's tactics.) Judges often feel the same. But to defendants, Farmer represents the kind of defense that only a millionaire can afford. His project, Team Defense, was started by the Southern Poverty Law Center, a public-interest group. It lives up to its name. The idea is that a trial should involve not only lawyers, but also psychologists, sociologists, students, and every conceivable sort of "expert witness" to examine the community where the trial is being held.

Team Defense gained national attention in 1976 with the "Dawson Five" case. Five young black men had been accused of robbing and killing a storekeeper in Dawson. When Team Defense entered the case, death sentences appeared inevitable— there were several confessions and an eyewitness. But Team Defense stood the trial on its head, putting Dawson itself in the docket. Defense researchers combed the area for evidence of the long-standing racial oppression there and fed it to the national news media. After many months on the front pages, the "airtight" case fell apart. The eyewitness's identification was proven to be unreliable. A former Dawson police officer testified that one of the "confessions" had been extracted by putting a cocked pistol to the head of one of the defendants and threatening to blow his brains out. Another defendant—illiterate and naive—had been connected to a lie detector and convinced he would be electrocuted on the spot if he did not say he did it. The prosecution finally dropped the charges, but only after Dawson had been depicted to the nation as a bastion of racism.

That was Millard Farmer's specialty: highlighting the racial background of Southern trials. When he took on Jessie Pulliam's case he was no stranger to race problems in Troup County. Farmer had been born and raised in neighboring Newnan, and had practiced in LaGrange for many years. A few months before, he had defended another black man, Curfew Davis, in a capital trial in LaGrange. In that case, he had questioned prospective jurors closely about their racial attitudes. Here, for example, is how he grilled one of the town's most prominent citizens, a former member of the city council and the owner of a funeral home:

Q: Mr. Martin, how long have you been a member of the Shrine Club?
A: Since 1948.
Q: Were you ever the president?
A: Yes, I was.
Q: Has there ever been a black member of the Shrine Club?
A: No, sir.
Q: Have you ever asked a black person to join?
A: No, sir.
Q: How long have you been a member of the Kiwanis Club?
A: Since 1940.
Q: Has there ever been a black member of the Kiwanis Club?
A: No, sir.
Q: How long have you been a member of the Masons?
A: Since 1946.

Q: Has there ever been a black member of the Masons?

A: No, sir.

Q: Have you, during the time that you've lived here in LaGrange, ever had a black person in your home on a social occasion?

A: No, sir.

Q: How long were you in the funeral business?

A: Forty-five years.

Q: During that time did you ever conduct a funeral for a black person?

A: No, sir.

Q: Have you ever rented any of your twenty-one apartments to black people?

A: No, sir.

Q: You are an elder of the Presbyterian Church—have there ever been any black members of that church?

A: No, sir.

Q: Do you have any prejudice or bias toward black people in general?

A: No, sir.

That was not an isolated incident. Here is another exchange that hints at the extent to which centuries of segregation had influenced the attitudes of local citizens:

Q: Mrs. Wheeler, have you ever had a black person in your home for a meal?

A: No, sir.

Q: Have you ever attended school with a black person?

A: No, sir.

Q: Have you ever worked for a black person?

A: No, sir.

Q: Your younger daughter, who is sixteen—would you allow her to date a black person?

A: No, sir.

Q: Would you allow her to bring a black male into your home for a meal?

A: On a dating basis? No.

Q: How would you feel if one of your daughters were to date a black person?

A: I would not like it.

Q: Are there any black people in your chapter of the Eastern Star?

A: No, sir.

Q: Are there black people in your church?

A: No, sir.

Q: Do you feel that you have any prejudice or bias to people who are black?

A: I do not think so.

Farmer had lost the Davis case—but he had not forgotten LaGrange.

When Team Defense took on Jessie Pulliam's case, it certainly qualified as an apparently hopeless cause. The execution date was stayed so that a new, more thorough appeal could be filed. But finding grounds for a successful appeal was more difficult. The trial attorney had seldom challenged the prosecution, and the transcript reflected the superficiality of the proceedings. The transcript of the jury questioning—where many cases are won or lost—ran only forty-seven pages (as compared with 1,253 pages in the Curfew Davis trial). The only time race was mentioned to a potential juror was this:

Q: Now, you have here a black defendant. He's alleged to have killed a white person. Would this make any difference as far as you are concerned?

A: I don't think so.

Q: You wouldn't let race enter into this case, would you?

A: I don't think so.

But Team Defense found enough in the meager transcript to support a new appeal to the federal courts, alleging forty-four errors in the trial. Many of these were trivial, but two involved major challenges. One concerned the judge's instructions to the jury. By failing to mention the concept of mitigating circumstance, Farmer charged, the judge gave the impression that the existence of one of the aggravating circumstances automatically led to the death penalty. This would appear to violate the Supreme Court's assumption that such mitigating factors would be considered. In several cases, the Georgia Supreme Court had overturned death sentences returned under similar circumstances.

The other major point did involve race. Farmer charged that blacks were systematically kept off juries in Troup County, and that the jury pool from which the jurors for Pulliam's case had been drawn seriously underrepresented blacks; there was only one black on his jury. In 1975, blacks were roughly one third of the county's population, but they comprised only 13.7 percent of the jury list. Women and young people (ages eighteen to thirty) were also underrepresented in relation to their percentages in the population. Studies have shown that blacks, women, and young people are statistically more likely to be sympathetic to a defendant; older white males are more likely to side with the prosecution. In previous cases, the Georgia Supreme Court had said that if jury pools systematically underrepresented these groups, it constituted a violation of a defendant's right to a trial by his peers.

Farmer was optimistic that one of these points would lead to a new court hearing for Pulliam, and perhaps to a life sentence. But, he conceded, perhaps he had entered the case too late. If so, all he could do was stall as long as he could—a tactic at which he is one of the nation's best.

Jessie Lewis Pulliam, sitting in the Georgia State Prison at Reidsville, looked back on his life and finally saw the prejudice. "Yeah, there was a lot of it," he said. "I had a lot of white friends, and when I get around blacks, they make me feel left out. They'd ask me why I hang around with white guys. Trying to get me upset in my mind, because I do this. Pure prejudice." (A *Washington Post* reporter who had interviewed Pulliam in 1976 noted, "The more he talks, the less convincing he sounds. The interview, in fact, has contained a series of coded questions intended to draw out whatever sympathetic qualities he might possess. Remorse. Self-examination. Worthy aspirations. Jessie Pulliam gives mostly wrong answers. He doesn't understand the code.")

Pulliam looked frail in his prison uniform: slender, with a meek voice, and a wispy, tentative mustache. He had a new pair of glasses, and to him they seemed the most important thing in his life. The prison doctor couldn't find anything wrong with his eyes, but Farmer arranged to get the glasses. They helped him see, Pulliam said. "It hit me off and on. Sometimes I couldn't see nothing but white for a few minutes."

But there were worse things to see. "Sometimes I see all kind of bugs. It seem like I see roachbugs crawling across the wall. I just blink and when I look back they won't be there. I have those problems when I get nervous.

"And since my momma died, two or three months ago, I been seeing her—walking up to me at night, when I wake up.

"Sometimes when I get nervous, I start seeing things . . . just flash; I get all upset and real hot. My nose starts bleeding. I just get out of whack. Two weeks ago I had a real bad one. I didn't see any of it. A friend of mine said I was spitting up blood. I pulled out of it, and I was laying down on the floor— with a razor blade in my hand."

Do you think those problems had anything to do with your getting here?

"No, like I said, I had those problems ever since I was small. See, I got a problem that nobody understands. My momma and my sister, they're the only ones that know the kind of problems I'm going through. My momma, she had a heart attack 'cuz of this, and she died. The guy who was in this with me [Johnny Wilson], he came by her house to talk to her. That upset her. She came to see me once but they wouldn't let her in—she didn't have no I.D. card. I could see her from the window."

Pulliam went on to talk about how he was in the front seat of the cab and didn't shoot the driver, about how "they violated my rights, did a lot of things to me they weren't supposed to." Asked to read the confession he was supposed to have given the lieutenant (". . . without promise of hope or reward, without fear or threat of physical harm, I freely volunteer the following statement to the aforesaid person . . ."), he stumbled through a few syllables, stopped, looked blankly at the page. "I'd rather pass on that," he mumbled in embarrassment.

Are you worried that they are going to execute you?

"Not exactly—'cause I got too many problems to worry about."

Too many other problems to worry about execution?

"Right. I'm trying to keep cool and calm, 'cause at any time I could blow, see? With this problem I got. See, if I got a razor blade and I go into one of my fits or something, I like to kill myself."

Are there any times you just wish it was all over with? Feel like giving up?

"Aaa-ll the time. I think about that."

Do you have anything to look forward to now?

"Nothing but another life." He gave a nervous laugh.

I meant—within the next few weeks?

"It is nothing to look for, being on Death Row."

Nothing good?

"Nothing."

Lots of bad?

"That's all."

Some months later, the Georgia State Prison was rocked by a series of disturbances—stabbings, work stoppages, melees. Many pitted blacks against whites. The worst incident came when a white prison guard was savagely killed, his body virtually stripped of its flesh by inmates' knives. The guards rebelled, and to calm things down the prison authorities segregated the prison and took all personal belongings from the inmates. Even though the Death Row prisoners, immobilized in their cells, had not caused any trouble, they, too, lost their personal items. Radios, books, calendars, pens, paper—even Bibles—were all bundled up and sent away.

At the home of Sally Turner, Jessie's sister, the little package was received with alarm. When Sally opened it and saw what was inside, she gasped. She thought it meant that they had executed Jessie.

But that had not happened—yet.

Willie Mitchell, president of a local NAACP chapter:

I remember hearing about the time they lynched Sam Hose. He and my father were close. Sam had split some white guy's head open with an ax. The mob staked out the train he was leaving on. They dragged him around the courthouse. Then they burned him. But his heart wouldn't burn. A white guy walked up and kicked it—he said, "This goddamn nigger heart won't burn."

A few years ago, a white man raped and tore up a seven-year-old black girl here. They gave him a year. They give a black guy ten years for smoking pot. When a black kills a black, they give him nothing—plea bargain and turn him loose. But if a black puts a scar on a white man, they give him the chair. And that's what it seems it's meant for—for blacks.

The Discrimination Issue: Race

Newnan, Georgia—In the presence of nearly 2,000 people, who sent aloft yells of defiance and shouts of joy, Sam Hose (a local Negro who had committed two of the basest acts known to crime)* was burned at the stake in a public road one and a half miles from here. Before the torch was applied to the pyre, the Negro was deprived of his ears, fingers and other portions of his body with surprising fortitude. Before the body was cool, it was cut to pieces, the bones were crushed into small bits and even the tree upon which the wretch met his fate was torn up and disposed of as souvenirs.

The Negro's heart was cut in several pieces, as was also his liver. Those unable to obtain the ghastly relics directly, paid more fortunate possessors extravagant sums for them. Small pieces of bone went for 25 cents and a bit of the liver, crisply cooked, for 10 cents.

—New York *Tribune*, April 24, 1899

* Hose had killed his employer after a dispute over wages. It was rumored that he had raped the man's wife, but an investigation later disclosed that this charge was false.

That barbarity took place in the last century, but equally savage lynchings occurred for decades afterward. Lynch law is the antithesis of an ordered society, but the persistence of "frontier justice" in myth and reality in this country testifies to the strength of the public's passion for revenge when hysteria prevails. Even those who most abhor lynchings often cite this passion as a justification for capital punishment. State-regulated killing, they say, is the way to defuse the problem. Justice Potter Stewart, in defending the death penalty, put it this way:

When people begin to believe that organized society is unwilling or unable to impose upon criminal offenders the punishment they "deserve," then there are sown the seeds of anarchy—of self-help, vigilante justice, and lynch law.

But lynching bespeaks more than a belief in the justice of retribution. What Justice Stewart saw as an alternative to lynching others see as the ugly fruit of the same poisoned tree: racism.

Race is a relatively new issue in the capital punishment debate. Until recently, even scholarly books on the subject mentioned only in passing the fact that blacks seemed to be executed far more often than whites in relation to their numbers. But ever since the Legal Defense Fund of the NAACP took the lead in the abolitionist fight, the racial aspects of the administration of the death penalty have become a major topic of debate. The charge is that capital punishment is aimed principally at blacks and other minorities, and that the "lottery" for distributing death sentences is not even a fair lottery, but one fixed against minorities—not just because they are poor, but because they are different.

Attention usually focuses on the plight of black people, but the problem of discrimination applies to other minorities as well—Mexican-Americans, Puerto Ricans, American Indians, and, in past decades, ethnic European immigrants. Perhaps the problem is not so much one of racism as of stereotyping. The essence of racism, after all, is to view the members of a group in terms of stereotypes and therefore to deny them their individuality, to see them as less than human, and to fear them. (As Ralph Ellison showed in *Invisible Man*, when they are not "bad" they are not seen at all.) The ugly, the deformed, the mentally ill, the "strange" people of any race can experience the same difficulty in the courtroom.

The problem of discrimination is not exclusively a Southern one. True, two thirds of American executions since 1930 have been carried out in the South, and in 1979 the South had three quarters of all those sentenced to death. But a 1976 Gallup Poll found significantly less public support for capital punishment in the South than in any other region. And many blacks have joined embattled white Southerners in proclaiming that racial attitudes are no better in the North.

Throughout history, societies have frequently used race or class as a factor in determining punishments. In ancient Rome only slaves were subject to execution; citizens could, at most, face banishment. In medieval England the "benefit of clergy" officially exempted clerics and, eventually, all literate gentry from hanging.

The American colonies frequently enacted dual criminal codes: one for white colonists, another for black slaves. In Virginia the penal code at one time listed only five capital crimes for whites but seventy for blacks. These "Black Codes" had to be rescinded after the Civil War, but an all-white court system produced the same results.

This double standard is best illustrated by Georgia's use of the death penalty to punish rape. In 1811 the law provided that while blacks could be hanged for rape, whites would be subject to a maximum of sixteen years in prison. Shortly before the Civil War, a new code introduced more complex distinctions. Rape of a white woman by a black man could be punished by death. Rape of a white woman by a white man was to be punished by from two to twenty years' imprisonment. Rape of a black woman by a white man was merely subject to "fine and imprisonment at the discretion of the court." After the Civil War these legal castes had to be dismantled, but instead juries were given the power to punish rape with either imprisonment or death at their discretion. The results remained the same: In the years from 1930 to 1958, Georgia executed fifty-eight blacks for rape but only three whites.

Only occasionally did the race issue come into the open. One of the great liberal causes of the 1930s involved the "Scottsboro Boys"—nine black teen-agers in Alabama accused of raping a white woman on a freight train. On the flimsiest of evidence, they were sentenced to death in a courtroom bubbling with racial hatred. (The prosecutor told the jury: "Get rid of these niggers, guilty or not guilty.") After several appeals to the U.S. Supreme Court, they finally won life terms; Govenor George Wallace pardoned the last of the Scottsboro Boys in 1976. Most of the time, however, the process operated in secrecy, with nameless, faceless blacks being railroaded through the white court system without a defense.

The results of the process show up in the figures for executions. Of the 3,859 persons executed from 1930 to 1967, 54.6 percent were non-white. During that time, blacks consistently represented only ten percent of the population.

The most clear-cut evidence of racial discrimination in capital sentencing involves executions for the crime of rape. Of the 455 men executed for rape since 1930, 407 (roughly ninety percent) were black. In five Southern states and the District of Columbia, no whites were executed for rape during this period, but sixty-six blacks were.

Two criminologists, Marvin Wolfgang and Marc Reidel of the University of Pennsylvania, coordinated a massive study of rape and the death penalty. They wanted to see if factors other than race could explain this imbalance. Student researchers checked all rape convictions over a twenty-year period in 230 sample counties scattered throughout the South. In the three thousand cases, they looked into the circumstances of the crime to see what factors led to the death penalty. In their conclusion, Wolfgang and Reidel wrote that nothing in the circumstances of the crime or background of the defendant could account for the disproportion except race. They computed that a black man convicted of raping a white woman was eighteen times as likely to get a death sentence as a white man.

For the crime of murder, the evidence of racial discrimination is less dramatic, but still disturbing. On the face of it, blacks and other minorities are overrepresented here as well. The 3,334 people executed for murder between 1930 and 1967 are divided roughly equally between blacks and whites. This is about five times the percentage blacks form in the population. Statistically, they also have been executed at younger ages, with less likelihood of having had their cases appealed. By and large, they have also stood a poorer chance of winning a commutation.

But we must keep in mind that throughout this period blacks have had a much higher homicide rate than whites—five to ten times as high. In recent years, half of those arrested for murder have been black—which would lead one to expect that half of those executed would be black.

Unfortunately, no studies as comprehensive as the Wolfgang-Reidel research on rape have been done regarding death sentences for murder. Numerous smaller studies have been done for different regions and times, and most of them claim to have found some evidence of discrimination against minorities. But these studies have serious shortcomings, because reliable data are not available in most states. After reviewing the data on race, sociologist William Bowers of Northeastern University concluded, nevertheless, that there seemed to be "a pattern of racial discrimination in the administration of capital punishment in America—a pattern that appears to be deeply rooted in the fabric of our society."

Despite the limitations of the research on race, even defenders of the death penalty usually admit, however grudgingly, that racial discrimination has played an ugly role in capital punishment in the past, particularly in the South. The question is whether it has been eliminated.

The way the old system worked was subtle. But the totally

discretionary system of sentencing—under which any murder could be punished with death—might well have been designed to give free rein to the racial prejudices of judges and jurors. This was consistent with the role of law enforcement in keeping minorities in their places. In the last twenty years, numerous reports have proclaimed the pervasiveness of race as a factor in every facet of the criminal justice system. In racially divided communities, the police and the courts were expected to be the frontline troops in the constant struggle to keep minorities in line. Whites were zealously protected against threats, while at the same time police ignored crimes committed against blacks. The sight of "a carful of white law" in the black community meant only one thing: trouble. And trouble followed them throughout the criminal justice process.

The most obvious focus of discrimination was in the courtroom. For most of the twentieth century, blacks, like all poor people, faced the courts without attorneys. All court officials, from bailiffs to judges, were white. Black spectators were confined to the back of the courtroom. Prosecutors and judges openly used racial epithets and slurs. The linchpin of the system was the all-white jury. Even after the formal exclusion of blacks from juries was declared unconstitutional by the Supreme Court in 1880, Southern officials discovered ingenious ways to keep the system lily-white through the 1960s.

Charles Silberman found the situation summed up in an old blues lyric:

> *White folks and nigger in great Co't house*
> *Like Cat down Cellar wit' no-hole mouse.*

Those were the formal mechanisms of racial oppression. Supreme Court decisions, changing attitudes, and the black political movement succeeded in dismantling many of them. By the 1970s, things were somewhat improved. The all-white jury is a fading anachronism. The use of coercive police techniques has been reduced. Illegally obtained evidence can be excluded from the courtroom. Lawyers are provided for impoverished defendants. The knowledge that vocal black voters would be watching their actions has made many officials watch their steps.

But even with these improvements, in 1972 the Supreme Court found that there was still too great an opportunity for racial prejudice to influence the outcome of a capital case. Several justices cited this as the major reason for declaring the existing death penalty laws unconstitutional. In response, state legislators tried to devise new laws to overcome the problem. It was hoped that by focusing the attention of the jury on specific questions such as aggravating and mitigating circumstances, racial prejudice would not influence sentencing. The Georgia law even went so far as to direct the state supreme court to examine all capital cases to see "whether the sentence of death was imposed under the influence of passion, prejudice or any other arbitrary factor."

These are commendable efforts, made in good faith. The word "nigger" no longer appears in trial transcripts. In the first seventy-five capital cases it has reviewed, the Georgia Supreme Court has not found one where a death sentence was imposed under the influence of prejudice. One might conclude that race is no longer a factor in the imposition of capital punishment.

But, as Professor Black put it, "the *unconscious* prejudice, the prejudice one thinks one has wholly overcome, is the more dangerous." It is dangerous because it is unacknowledged by the possessor—and frequently undetectable in day-to-day actions. Only occasionally can an extreme situation bring these feelings to the surface.

Provoking such situations is the specialty of Millard Farmer. That was his strategy in the 1977 trial of a black man charged with killing a police officer in the town of Lakeland, Georgia. Farmer was successful in having six different judges disqualified for their racial attitudes, after he questioned them under oath. The governor, irritated, stepped in to appoint a special judge for the case, one whom he was sure was free of the tinge of racism. Farmer promptly challenged the new judge. The judge took the stand to defend himself. Here, excerpted from the transcript of the hearing, are some pertinent exchanges:

Q: What would be wrong with playing golf with a black person?
A: I play golf with my friends.
Q: Have you ever played golf with a black person?
A: Never.
Q: What's wrong with playing golf with a black person?
A: I don't know, it's just my preference.
Q: Do you have any black friends?
A: Of course I do.
Q: Have you ever had any of them into your home for a meal?
A: Never.
Q: How do you feel about having a black person into your home for a meal?
A: I wouldn't like it.
Q: How would you like to have a black person spend the weekend with you?
A: I wouldn't like that either.
Q: How would you feel if your son came home before he was married with his girlfriend and his girlfriend was black?
A: I'd kick them out of the house.
Q: Do you realize that [the defendant's] heart is almost jumping out of his shirt when you say what you've just said?
A: I don't know anything about his heart. . . . In the twenty-one years that I have been a judge I must have tried five thousand blacks, and so far as I know I have never done any injustice to any of them.
Q: Do you realize that the statements that you've made are racist?
A: I do not.
Q: Do you think blacks have been given an equal education to whites, historically, in the South?
A: Listen, most of them don't want an education and if you can come down to Savannah I'll show you that they are walking up and down the street when they ought to be in school. I don't mean the race as a whole, of course—you find a lot of fine, educated blacks. But the majority of them apparently don't want to learn.

Q: Is the black man equal to you?
A: No, I don't think so.

The judge, needless to say, was removed from the case. The eighth judge finally conducted the trial; the defendant was sentenced to death. But any observer must wonder whether, in this atmosphere, a black defendant stands equal before the bar of justice.

Admittedly, that was an extreme example. The question is whether, on a broad scale, the new death penalty laws have diminished racial prejudice in the courtroom.

The closest examination of the national situation was made by Marc Reidel, who earlier had coauthored the rape study. Reidel wanted to see if the new laws had diminished racial disparity. He compared the 376 people under death sentences in 1976 with the 493 people awaiting execution in 1971 (who were subsequently reprieved by the 1972 *Furman* decision). Reidel found that sixty-two percent of those sentenced to death under the new laws were from minority groups; only thirty-eight percent were white. This was actually a more pronounced racial imbalance than in 1971. The greater frequency with which blacks are arrested for murder, Reidel said, did not completely explain this disparity. Reidel could only conclude that the new laws did not appear to have diminished the problem of racial prejudice in sentencing.

But many Americans have grown tired of being lectured about inherent racism, and demonstrations such as Reidel's have lost much of their persuasive force. The defenders of capital punishment have even tried to use the race issue to their own advantage with a new argument. Black people should actually be in the forefront of the crusade for capital punishment, they say, since they are eight times as likely as whites to die by murder. To quote the Nixon Administration's Solicitor General, Robert Bork, in his 1975 brief to the Supreme Court: "Abolition of capital punishment would work to the detriment of the poor and the blacks, who are disproportionately the victims of murder."

This argument rings hollow, however, when one looks at the race of the victims whose deaths are being avenged with executions. While most (fifty-five percent) of the victims of murder are black, eighty-seven percent of those on Death Rows were sent there for killing whites. In other words, while it is common for a black to kill a black, it is rare for a jury to sentence him to death. But if the victim is white, then the criminal justice system comes down with its full weight. Studies of specific crimes have shown that the higher rate of "crimes of passion" among blacks cannot account for this imbalance. In Florida, for instance, a study by Hans Zeisel showed that when a white was killed in a felony murder (murder during a robbery or rape), death sentences were meted out sixty-three percent of the time; when the victim of a felony murder was black, only fifteen percent of the convicted defendants were given the death penalty. In 1978, 104 of the 113 inmates on Florida's Death Row were sent there for killing whites.

This disturbing revelation indicates that we still have a double standard in our criminal justice system. The harshest penalties are reserved for blacks who kill whites, but, as the Philadelphia study by Zimring cited in Chapter Six shows, frequently too little punishment is given when a black person is killed. In other words, it appears as if the criminal justice system denies "equal protection of the laws" not only to black defendants, but also to black victims. As Eldridge Cleaver bitterly wrote in *Soul on Ice:* "The racist conscience of America is such that murder does not register as murder, really, unless the victim is white. . . . America has never truly been outraged by the murder of a black man, woman, or child."

This issue—that capital punishment is primarily reserved for the protection (or revenge) of the white community—is only now being raised in the courts. The research cited above should give us pause, but it is not conclusive. The numbers are too small, and the geographic area too limited. Massive studies will be required to give us a precise picture of the degree to which racism persists in the administration of capital punishment.

But a major question remains. Even if it can be proven that minorities are significantly discriminated against, does this mean that capital punishment should forever be abolished? Isn't the solution to perfect the criminal justice system?

Even some clear-thinking analysts have stumbled over this question. Harvard professor James Q. Wilson states, "If the problem of fairness does exist, however, the importance of it is not particularly clear. For if capital punishment is to be abolished because it is discriminatory, should not all forms of punishment be abolished because they are discriminatory?" And William O. Hochkammer, Jr., in an analysis of the arguments for and against the death penalty in a law journal, observed: "It would be a mistake to argue that capital punishment should be rejected because some discrimination exists. The proper approach is to remedy the defect, not abolish the system."

If the defect lies not in the system, but in our hearts and minds, then improvements in the system will not help. If the process of sentencing someone to death requires that (or is made easier if) he is viewed as less than human, then the death penalty will always be tied to race, for there is no more reliable dehumanizing factor than racial prejudice. As long as our society is tinged with even the slightest racial animosity, members of minority groups will always face a handicap in convincing juries that they should not be killed. Once they are viewed according to racial stereotypes, they have one foot in the execution chamber.

And if racial bias so easily infects our criminal justice system, then the system is not fit to decide questions of life or death. It is one thing to sentence a black person to ten years in prison where a white might have gotten seven; it is quite another to take away his life while the other lives. We *might* tolerate the former disparity even as we work to eliminate it, but those who are unfairly sentenced to death are beyond our redemption.

If blacks are the victims of most murders, why have they not joined the cry for its imposition? Polls on capital punishment consistently show blacks as opposed to it, often by margins of two to one. This is not because blacks are more tolerant of crime; frequently they appeal to judges and prosecutors for longer prison terms for those convicted of crimes against blacks. But capital punishment has a symbolic value to them. Blacks look at three hundred years' experience in this country and see the gallows as a tool of oppression. They look at the regions of the country and see that the South has been the most vigorous in using executions. They look at the courts and see that black victims arouse little sympathy. They look at the world and see that among Western-style nations, only South Africa executes a significant number of people—almost all of them black. The message is not an admirable one. Given our past, we should be able to understand why minorities might look with skepticism on the claim that, henceforward, capital punishment will be administered without regard for race, creed, or national origin.

CHAPTER EIGHT

The Man Who Killed Halloween

Profile: Ronald O'Bryan

It rained in Houston on Halloween in 1974. The rain had made him late, Ronald O'Bryan explained to his friend Stan Carr, who sat watching the evening news. He had left work at four-thirty, O'Bryan said, but it had taken an hour and a half to fight the snarled traffic of Houston's rush hour to reach Carr's home in the suburb of Pasadena.

Carr glanced up to see O'Bryan brushing raindrops off the blue smock he wore at his job dispensing eyeglasses for an optical company. It was too bad about the rain—it would dampen the trick-or-treating for the kids.

"Marilyn! Ken! Look what I brought for you," O'Bryan called out. The two Carr youngsters, aged eleven and eight, dashed up to him. So did O'Bryan's own children: Timothy, eight, and Nancy Star, five, who had arrived earlier with their mother. The father pulled two plastic plaques out of his pocket.

One read "Marilyn's Room," the other, "Ken's Room"—gifts for the Carr children.

Out in the kitchen, Sheila O'Bryan and Lois Carr were fixing supper. A pork roast simmered in the oven, and vegetables were on the stove. It was natural for the two families to share Halloween. Timmy O'Bryan and Ken Carr were classmates together at Carpenter Elementary School; Ron and Stan attended the same church, and worked together on a busing program to bring children to Sunday school. A week before Halloween, Ron had asked Stan if he could bring his kids over to Pasadena for trick-or-treating, and Stan thought it was a fine idea.

Pasadena is a blue-collar suburb of Houston, with quite a bit of heavy industry. The Bowling Green subdivision, where the Carrs lived, was a new development, surrounded by vacant fields that would soon be smothered by even newer developments. The streets of Bowling Green were all named after famous racehorses, and even the streets themselves were shaped like horseshoes. The houses were new brick and wood structures picked from a catalog so they didn't all look the same. Each house seemed to have a pickup truck parked next to a station wagon. O'Bryan had parked his station wagon, a five-year-old Ford Falcon, out front; Carr's truck was in the driveway.

After supper, Stan Carr stepped out on the little front stoop and scowled at the weather. Not only did it threaten the fun, it also meant that he faced a miserable night of work. He worked on a crew for Houston Lighting and Power Company, and his shift started at ten. Carr went out to his truck to get a yellow rain slicker for O'Bryan to wear while they were trick-or-treating. He would carry an umbrella.

The children crowded onto the front porch. Timmy and Nancy Star O'Bryan (people called her Star) were wearing *Planet of the Apes* costumes that their father had purchased at a Woolworth's. Marilyn Carr looked up at the drizzle and turned back to the door. "Daddy, it's raining too hard," she said. "I'm going back."

"Maybe we really shouldn't go," said Carr. But he took a

look at the younger children and realized they would be too disappointed.

The Carrs lived near the middle of the horseshoe-shaped street. The group set off down Citation Street, one leg of the horseshoe. Carr huddled under an umbrella with a camp lantern, picking out houses that seemed prepared for trick-or-treaters and flashing the light up the walks. "That one's okay," he would say. "Run up there." O'Bryan, in the heavy raincoat, accompanied the children to the door. They worked their way around one leg of the horseshoe, then across Alabama Street, which cut off the legs of the horseshoe. When they came to the other leg leading back toward the Carr house, Carr decided to speed things up by working only one side of the street. But an exception had to be made a few houses down for Mrs. Good's house. Every year she dressed up as a witch; when little goblins knocked, she would come to the door and offer them a cup of "witches' brew"—fruit drink served from a cauldron. The kids didn't want to miss that. Most of the other houses gave out the usual small treats—packs of gum at one house, foil packets of Sour Tarts (fruit-flavored tablets) at another, Pixy Stix (ten-inch polyethylene straws filled with granulated candy) somewhere else.

After partaking of the witches' brew, the party crossed back to the even-numbered side of the street. They only stopped at houses with their lights on. At one house, a porch light was lit but no one answered the first knock. The children, impatient and excited, scampered across the lawn while O'Bryan knocked again. The kids were already at the next house when he emerged from the portico waving several long flexible sticks. He switched them back and forth. "You've got rich neighbors," he yelled jubilantly at Carr. "Look what they're giving out!" The prizes were giant Pixy Stix; they cost ten cents each and were twenty-one inches long, half an inch in diameter, with colored stripes running the length of the tube. "I don't know how they afford that," Carr joked. "This is really the ghetto."

When he caught up with the three youngsters, O'Bryan

waved the Pixy Stix. "I've got them—who wants them?" Of course the youngsters wanted the large candies. O'Bryan passed them out, but then took them back; they were too big for the rain-soaked candy bags.

At the last house next to his, Carr saw the children bantering with his neighbors, so he went inside, yelling at the children to come home when they were through. O'Bryan followed, but said he had to stop at his car. He came into the Carr house about the same time the kids did. He gave out the special treats he had brought from the car: giant Life Savers suckers. He also gave out the Pixy Stix. There was an extra Pixy Stix, which O'Bryan took with him to the door when the bell rang. Another group of trick-or-treaters was outside. O'Bryan held up the tube of candy. "Who wants this?" he asked. Barney Ronson, eleven, jumped up and down, yelling, "Me, me—I go to your church!" O'Bryan gave him the Pixy Stix, and told the group that they could get more down the street.

Shortly afterward, the O'Bryan clan gathered together and set off for their home in Deer Park, a few miles away. Sheila drove home in her car with Timmy; O'Bryan took Star back in the station wagon. It had been a successful evening.

At home, after taking his bath, Barney Ronson decided to eat some of the giant Pixy Stix. He got a knife and tried to cut it open, but his father announced firmly that it was bedtime. Barney took the tube to bed. There, he tore off the paper label at one end and tried to get into the tube, but it was stapled shut, and he couldn't pry the staples loose. He fell asleep without eating any candy.

Back at the Carr house, Ken also wanted some of the Pixy Stix. He tore off the paper. "Mother, I'm going to eat this candy," he said. Lois Carr took one look at the tube of candy and another look at the kitchen floor, where she had just finished mopping up the mud tracked in by the trick-or-treaters. "No, you aren't," she declared. "That's 'outside' candy. You can eat it out-of-doors tomorrow." Ken went to bed without any Pixy Stix.

It was about nine o'clock when the O'Bryans got home. Ron took the wet costumes off Timmy and Star and let them wander around in their underwear. Sheila set down the sacks of Halloween candy on the dining room table and announced that she had to leave. She had to go to Alice's and she was very determined about it. Alice was Alice Powell, a friend of Sheila's who ran a flower shop in Pasadena. Ron was used to these absences, but he wasn't very happy about them. Alice exercised a strong influence over Sheila; she was a charismatic Christian, and lately Sheila decided that her life needed a total emotional involvement with Jesus Christ. Ron felt he was a pretty strong Christian and active member of the Baptist Church, but he worried that his wife was carrying things a bit too far. She had started writing little slogans—"Praise the Lord!" or "He is good!"—on their checks, for instance. But he didn't interfere with these visits to Alice.

As O'Bryan later recalled the evening, he was the one who gave the children their bath—one at each end of the tub, so he could keep an eye on both of them. Then they were allowed to watch a few minutes of television, but only a few minutes since Friday was a school day. Soon O'Bryan announced that it was bedtime. "What about the candy?" they asked plaintively. "We want a piece of candy!" O'Bryan gave in.

"You can have one, just one. Run and get in bed and I'll bring it to you."

The children scampered to their bedrooms. O'Bryan went into the kitchen to fetch their medicine. They both took Actifed, a common antihistamine. Timmy took it as a pill; Star as a liquid. When O'Bryan went into Star's room he brought the bottle of medicine and a glass of fruit drink. She swallowed her medicine and took a swallow of the fruit drink to wash away the taste. "What about the candy?" she said. O'Bryan replied that he would bring it after Timmy was squared away. The little boy took his pill with the fruit drink; he, too, asked about the candy. O'Bryan set down the glass and went out for the candy. He went to Star's room first. She rummaged through her sack and pulled out the foil packet of Sour Tarts. She ate one, gave one to her father, ate another, and asked O'Bryan to "take one in to Bubba"—her brother.

Carrying the small gift and Timmy's own bag. O'Bryan went into his son's room. Timmy went through his sack and came up with the big Life Savers sucker his father had given him. "No, that's too big," O'Bryan said. "If you unwrap it and lick it a little bit, how are you going to keep it?"

Another foray into the sack. "Can I have some of that?" he asked, pointing to the Pixy Stix. O'Bryan said he could, since the stick could be resealed with a clothespin, then tore off the paper and pulled out the staples. "Just one bite," he warned. "You can have the rest tomorrow." Timmy raised the tube and tilted it into his mouth, then he set it down with a disappointed look. "I didn't get any," he complained. O'Bryan looked inside; apparently moisture had seeped into the tube and packed the candy together. He rolled the tube back and forth between the palms of his hands and gave it back to his son. The boy took a mouthful, swallowed, and made a face. "Ugh, that tasted bad," he said. O'Bryan gave him the glass of fruit drink to wash out the sour taste. Timmy drained it, lay down and smiled. O'Bryan kissed him good night, got up, and turned out the light.

Back in the dining room, O'Bryan had no sooner put the sacks of candy back on the table before he heard footsteps. Behind him stood Timmy. "What are you doing up, young man?" he asked sternly.

"I feel sick—my tummy hurts," the boy complained. He hurried into the bathroom, with O'Bryan following. Timmy rushed over to the toilet, leaned over, and vomited. He vomited so hard he buckled. His father grabbed him around the waist. The boy threw up again and collapsed. Then he started gasping for breath and going into convulsions. O'Bryan checked the boy's throat to see if he were choking on something, but his windpipe was clear. He ran out and called the police. "Send an ambulance right away," he said. "Please hurry!"

When the ambulance came, O'Bryan bundled a coat around his daughter and brought her along. The ambulance attendants asked what Timmy had eaten and O'Bryan told them: pork roast, vegetables, one Sour Tart, medicine, some Pixy Stix. They brought the Pixy Stix with them. At the hospital, the boy was rushed into the emergency room, where his stomach was pumped and doctors performed other emergency measures. "Oh, God! Don't let my boy die!" O'Bryan yelled at one point. He recovered enough to call the Carr house, and he spoke to Lois. He was at the hospital, he said; Timmy was very sick after eating that Pixy Stix candy. He asked Lois Carr to get in touch with Sheila at Alice Powell's since he didn't have that phone number.

Sheila drove to the hospital. Twice O'Bryan went into the bathroom and threw up. Doctors offered to pump his stomach, in case he had been poisoned by the same thing as his son, but O'Bryan, who was troubled by a bleeding ulcer, refused. Then a doctor came out of the emergency room and solemnly told the parents that Timmy was not going to make it. O'Bryan turned to the wall and beat his fist on it. "Oh, God—why did an eight-year-old boy have to die?" he wailed.

It was a cold, silent, shocked ride home. After his wife and daughter had gotten out of the car, O'Bryan drove off by himself.

Sheila was furious; she didn't have the housekeys with her and had to force her way into the house. When her husband returned about a half-hour later, she asked where he had been. He said he had driven a little way down the block. "I had to be alone," he said. "I just rolled the windows up and screamed."

The screaming was over when friends and relatives began to trickle in to offer consolation. To some, O'Bryan was quite composed, but others thought that, in a quiet way, he seemed totally devastated.

Human beings have poisoned each other ever since they discovered that unclean arrowheads could be fatal even if they only scratched their target. Poisoning flourished in the Middle Ages and Renaissance, especially in court intrigues such as those that gave the Borgias a bad name among dinner guests. But poisoning lost popularity as a means of murder when firearms became common, and in the twentieth century the advent of autopsies and medical examiners have further discouraged would-be poisoners. In 1974 less than one percent of all U.S. murders were attributed to poison.

When people do resort to poisoning, they often turn to the cyanide compounds. Cyanides have important industrial uses in electroplating, gold extraction, and fumigation. But they are dangerous and are classified as "supertoxic" along with strychnine, pure heroin, and nicotine. Sodium cyanide, dissolved in hydrochloric acid, produces hydrocyanic gas—the lethal agent used in gas chambers. Potassium cyanide, KCN, came to the minds of Texas prison officials when they had to find a fatal substance to use in injection executions, but they decided to use an overdose of a conventional drug instead.

It only takes .2 to .3 grams of potassium cyanide—about the same weight as the tip of a pencil—to kill a human being. Within minutes of being swallowed, the cyanide induces violent nausea, clogs the lungs, and stops all motor functions in the brain.

Dr. Joseph Jachimczyk, the Harris County chief medical examiner—an attorney as well as a doctor, and one of the country's leading experts on the causes of death—took personal charge of the autopsy on the body of Timothy O'Bryan. In the lungs, Dr. Jachimczyk found an abundance of "red-gray frothy material." The brain glowed with an unusual shade of red. When the contents of the stomach were tested, they confirmed the doctor's suspicions: cyanide.

The medical examiner took the partially eaten Pixy Stix that had accompanied Timmy to the hospital. Two things were unusual about it: first, the top end of the plastic tube, normally melted shut, had been sliced open and then stapled closed. And second, the top two inches of the Pixy Stix had contained enough potassium cyanide to kill several people.

Early Friday morning, the O'Bryans went to a funeral home to make arrangements for Timmy's burial. O'Bryan signed over a bank insurance policy on Timmy, face value one thousand dollars, to pay for the services. Then he called his insurance agent to inform him of the death and arrange for payment on other insurance policies. Much of the rest of the day was spent with the police—in the station house and walking around the neighborhood, trying to remember the house where the Pixy Stix came from.

Feeling ran high in Bowling Green. The Carrs were furious; someone had tried to poison their children. Neighbors looked at each other with suspicion and hatred. Where had the candy come from? Carr and O'Bryan could only remember the general area. Finally, after much prodding, O'Bryan thought he remembered a door being opened at one house after the children had scurried away. He described the house. A balding man had thrust the Pixy Stix out without a word, O'Bryan told the police. The man had hairy arms. At least O'Bryan thought he remembered. His certainty wavered, but once he pointed the man out in a crowd of neighbors. The man, however, had an alibi, and the police continued their investigation.

The day after Halloween, Deer Park and Pasadena police urged parents to bring in all their children's candy for inspection. The police collected only four more giant Pixy Stix—from the O'Bryan daughter, the two Carr children, and Barney Ronson. All of the Stix had potassium cyanide in the top two inches; one that was measured contained .68 grams of it. Other Halloween sabotage was found. Some Tootsie Roll "Midgies," given out in the same general area, contained one-and-a-half-inch needles. In Houston, two straight pins were found in a candy bar, and a razor blade had been stuck into a Three Musketeers bar. Except for Timmy O'Bryan, no other children were hurt.

It was, of course, a big story, followed by newspapers across the nation. "Deer Park Boy Dies After Eating Trick-or-Treat Candy," blared the headline in the morning *Houston Chronicle*. On Saturday, there was a front-page interview with O'Bryan: "Poisoned Son Suddenly 'Went Limp in my Arms.'" O'Bryan cried as he told the reporter, "He was all boy. He loved football, basketball, anything. But I have my peace in knowing that Tim is in heaven now." A $10,000 reward was offered for information leading to the arrest of the killer.

At Saturday's funeral, the news cameras were there again. At the end of the service O'Bryan stood up and made an unusual plea for those in attendance to devote their lives to God and join the church. The cameras snapped his picture as, teary-eyed and wiping his nose, he walked away from the gravesite.

Later that evening, O'Bryan's brother-in-law came by to offer his condolences. To him, O'Bryan seemed unusually animated—he had collected all the newspaper stories on Timmy's death and he chattered incessantly about the tragedy. The brother-in-law thought O'Bryan occasionally crossed the bounds of taste in his conversation, such as when he speculated on what he would do with the insurance money from his son's death. He said he was thinking of making a donation to the church, or putting up a flagpole at the school in his memory. Or maybe he should use it for the family.

A special memorial service was held on Sunday. Outside the church, Stan Carr spoke to O'Bryan. Carr was furious that the killer had not been caught. But O'Bryan already seemed resigned to the prospect that the police would never solve the case. During the services, O'Bryan rose to sing a special solo. It was a Baptist hymn, "Blessed Reassurance." "This is my story, this is my song; praising my Savior all day long," the hymn went. But O'Bryan, singing with great force and feeling, changed the words. "This is Tim's story, this is Tim's song," he sang.

The police, by this time, were feeling a great deal of pressure. The big lead in the case—O'Bryan's description of the man who had given out the Pixy Stix—fizzled. There was indeed a balding man with hairy arms who lived on Donerail Street, but investigation proved that he could not possibly have been at home that night. The man worked as an air traffic controller at the Houston airport and was on duty Halloween night. Dozens of co-workers vouched for his presence, and the airport kept meticulous records.

Early Monday afternoon the police got a break in the case. They had spoken with O'Bryan's insurance agent, and he had given them some unusual information. In September, he said, O'Bryan had arranged for twenty-thousand-dollar life-insurance policies on each of his children, had paid for them in cash, and specified that his wife not be told. The agent was suspicious.

O'Bryan and his wife came down to the Deer Park police station at five o'clock that evening. Detectives separated them for questioning. Six hours later, the prosecutor handling the case called Houston and asked the district attorney, Carol Vance, to come in. Vance came in, reviewed the evidence, and gave the go-ahead. Shortly afterward, Ronald Clark O'Bryan was arrested for the murder of his son. He was also charged with the attempted murder of Nancy Star O'Bryan, Marilyn Carr, Ken Carr, and Barney Ronson. The police believed that O'Bryan expected that several children would be killed, and that this somehow would have focused less attention on him.

What evidence did the police have on O'Bryan? From the evidence later produced at the trial, it appears to have been a sketchy case at that point. No witness had actually accused O'Bryan of the crime. The information about the insurance, however, was suspicious—especially since O'Bryan had called his agent to arrange for payment immediately after Timmy's death. And when detectives told Sheila O'Bryan about the insurance, she uttered only three words: "Oh, my God." From that moment on, she apparently believed her husband to be a murderer. She said he was sick, and told police that some years before, he had collected insurance money from some suspicious fires when they were living in Maryland. Then there was the matter of debts; O'Bryan owed money to a lot of people. He had borrowed to buy his cars, to repair his teeth, and the family habitually spent more money than it took in. The detectives also felt that O'Bryan had been evasive and untruthful during six hours of questioning.

The most titillating evidence probably came from a search of O'Bryan's house, authorized by Sheila during the questioning at the police station. Inside the house, detectives found two pairs of scissors, a knife, and a letter from a credit company demanding payment. They took vacuum sweepings from both cars. But the clincher was the little medicine bottle of white powder they found in the kitchen. This, along with the scissors and knife, was sent to the F.B.I. crime lab in Washington, to be checked for traces of cyanide.

O'Bryan responded in shock and outrage to the arrest. He struggled to convince the police that they were making a monstrous mistake. He had explanations for everything, and he even offered to take a lie detector test. But the police were not interested; they were sure they had their man.

When news of O'Bryan's arrest was made public, the Halloween murder made even bigger headlines. "A cloud of suspicion has been lifted," sighed one resident of the Bowling Green neighborhood. Pictures of O'Bryan—a pudgy man of thirty whose lack of eyebrows gave him a perpetually inquisitive look—and recordings of interviews he had given over the weekend were broadcast throughout Houston and the rest of the nation.

After the story broke, other people began to recall strange things about O'Bryan. He certainly seemed to have been interested in cyanide. A man for whom O'Bryan had fit glasses Halloween afternoon said that O'Bryan had asked him what he knew about cyanide. A chemist friend of O'Bryan's said that O'Bryan had called him up out of the blue and, under the pretext of being enrolled in a college chemistry course, had grilled him about what would be a lethal dose of cyanide.

When asked about this, O'Bryan admitted calling the man but gave a different account of the conversation. He had been intrigued by a segment of the television program "Emergency," he said, in which a boy got cyanide poisoning from a peach pit, and had called his chemist friend to see if it could be true. It was ironic, O'Bryan went on, that his son had been poisoned by cyanide, because it had been in the news recently, and the school had sent home a pamphlet warning parents about poisonous substances.

Law enforcement officials were not impressed with O'Bryan's explanations, but their case was not airtight. No one had seen O'Bryan purchase cyanide or Pixy Stix. And they received disappointing news from the F.B.I. crime lab: The objects from O'Bryan's home sent for analysis contained no cyanide. The white powder in the bottle that they had hoped would be the proverbial "smoking gun" turned out to be glitter, something used for Christmas decorations.

Texans are proud of their criminal justice system. It fits the image of the state: sprawling, rough, proud of its size, almost proud of the bizarre wickedness of its spectacular crimes. Flamboyant defense lawyers like Percy Foreman and "Racehorse" Haynes flourished there; so did prosecutors who could make Pope John XXIII seem like a Mafia godfather. A major trial in Houston amounted to a spectacle—some would say a circus.

The Honorable Frank C. Price, of the 209th Criminal District Court in Houston, wasn't going to let the O'Bryan case turn into a circus. Neither was he going to let the pair of crack prosecutors—Mike Hinton, a boisterous, aggressive bulldog in front of a jury, and Vic Driscoll, a scholarly and meticulous researcher—impale a debt-ridden defendant. He appointed two experienced and respected lawyers to represent O'Bryan: Richard Harrison of Dallas and Marvin Teague of Houston. Teague had a reputation as one of the best criminal appeals attorneys in the state.

The trial of Ronald O'Bryan stands in marked contrast to those of several other defendants described in this book—one- or two-day juggernauts in which overworked, inexperienced legal

aid attorneys were squashed by the weight of the state's resources. In O'Bryan's case, the *voir dire* examination of potential jurors, in which they were questioned to see if they were
unbiased, took ten days by itself. Some seventy-two jurors were
examined in detail about their attitudes toward law enforcement, their opinions regarding the death penalty, how much
they had seen or heard about the case. It was taken for granted
that everyone had read something about the case; a juror who
had not would have been most unusual. The trial itself took
twelve days; 150 exhibits were presented; the transcript ran
5,413 pages.

It is an axiom of modern legal practice that trials are often
won or lost before they begin, in the pretrial hearings. Teague
and Harrison presented a sheaf of motions to exclude evidence
or forbid certain tactics. They lost all the important motions—
especially one to quash the testimony of a man named Richard
Jarvis.

Jarvis, thirty, was as close to the "smoking gun" as the prosecution could get. He had been discovered by the Deer Park
police the week following O'Bryan's arrest. They had been
making the rounds of all the wholesale chemical dealers in the
Houston area, trying to tie O'Bryan to the purchase of cyanide.
It was not illegal to sell cyanide to an individual, but it was not
common, either. They went to the half-dozen companies that
deal in chemicals in Houston without luck. Finally, at Curtin
Matheson Scientific Company in Houston, they found something. Both the manager and the desk clerk said they had had
no inquiries about cyanide. But a shipping clerk, Jarvis, occasionally worked in the desk area with customers.

After several rounds of questioning Jarvis said that yes, he did
remember someone coming in and asking about cyanide. The
police showed him a picture of O'Bryan. Was that him? "That's
Mr. O'Bryan, isn't it?" Jarvis responded. He, too, had seen the
television and newspaper stories. He then identified O'Bryan
as the man who had come in and asked about cyanide. At first
Jarvis remembered little about the incident, but by the time of

the trial his recollection was quite precise, down to his thinking he remembered an insignia on the pocket of O'Bryan's aqua-colored smock.

The defense attorneys fought to keep Jarvis off the stand. He had changed his story repeatedly, they said, and many of the details he "remembered" about the alleged visit were first supplied by the questioning police officers. The defense attorneys also attacked Jarvis's credibility, trying to show that he was not a man who could be believed.

It didn't work. The judge decided that his testimony would be allowed.

The prosecution's first witnesses were the Carr family. While they provided no direct evidence against O'Bryan, the fact that they were willing to testify for the prosecution made it clear that they were satisfied that the police had solved the crime. In addition to describing the events of Halloween night, Stan Carr recalled two damaging conversations he had with O'Bryan in the weeks before the murder. Both times, Carr testified, O'Bryan had mentioned that he was thinking of buying a house "because he would be coming into some money after the first of the year." Both times, he said, O'Bryan cautioned him not to mention it to his wife.

Barney Ronson testified next. A few minor witnesses were called, including a nurse, police officers, and an ambulance driver, to describe O'Bryan's conduct the night Timmy died. Even the president of the Pixy Stix company, flown in from St. Louis, was called to the stand. During the questioning of Dr. Jachimczyk, the prosecution introduced—over vociferous objections by Harrison and Teague—its most graphic exhibit: a picture of Timothy O'Bryan's body, laid out naked on a table waiting for the autopsy. The defense attorneys argued this was too gruesome a picture to be used for identification purposes, and that it would needlessly inflame the emotions of the jurors. But the exhibit was allowed.

Then the state introduced a number of witnesses who portrayed O'Bryan as a man constantly in debt. One bank account was traced in detail. It showed a deposit of $6,000—the proceeds from the sale of the O'Bryan house before they moved into rented dwellings—in the summer of 1974; within a few weeks the account had dwindled to $413.59. O'Bryan owed money to several financial institutions, and was delinquent in the payments on his car. In late October he begged more time from one of his creditors by saying that he would soon be coming into a large sum of money. Another finance company rejected his application for a loan. O'Bryan received a repossession notice on his car that month.

O'Bryan's insurance agent then testified that O'Bryan had first purchased insurance from him in 1971—$20,000 coverage on himself, $2,000 on his wife, $1,000 on each of the children. The amount on his wife was later increased to $20,000. But O'Bryan let the policies lapse for nonpayment of premiums. In 1973, O'Bryan again purchased insurance; again he let it lapse. In September 1974, the agent testified, O'Bryan called him to say he needed additional insurance on his children. The agent testified that he had recommended a special policy for juveniles with an initial coverage of $5,000 escalating to $25,000 by the time the child was twenty-three. O'Bryan said he wanted to think it over and talk to his wife about it. He called back to say they had decided on a straight policy of $20,000 each. The agent met O'Bryan at work on October 3 and again tried to sell the escalating policy but O'Bryan said he preferred the flat policy. He paid the premium in cash, $108 for a quarter of a year—unusual for O'Bryan, who usually paid by the month. In the week of October 21, the agent continued, the policies were returned by the company because they lacked Mrs. O'Bryan's signature and Social Security number. O'Bryan provided the number and signed his wife's name. At that time, the broker testified, O'Bryan had no insurance on himself.

Ten months earlier, O'Bryan had joined a special savings club at a bank that provided a $10,000 insurance policy on each child—over his wife's objections that it cost too much.

When Sheila O'Bryan took the stand to testify against her

husband, the drama increased. Photographers snapped pictures of her in the corridors; they even took a telephoto picture of her on the witness stand through a keyhole in the door. Cool and collected, she recounted her life with O'Bryan and pictured him as a man who couldn't hold a job and exaggerated to the point of being a chronic liar. Their financial condition, she said, was "very poor." She recalled the events of Halloween evening, and recounted what O'Bryan had told her of the events leading up to Timmy's death. O'Bryan had never told her about the recent insurance polices on the children, she said; he did tell her he was going to put more insurance on himself. Of her husband's relations with the children, she said, "He was more lenient and partial to Star."

Sheila had given no solid information that was very damaging to O'Bryan's cause, but as with the Carrs, it was not what she said so much as it was the fact she was willing to testify against her husband. O'Bryan's attorneys could imagine how likely a jury would be to believe a man whose own wife thought him a murderer. But they could not keep her from testifying, even about privileged conversations, because it was her child who had been killed.

When Sheila took the stand, the defense attorneys made the best of it. On cross-examination, she described how active O'Bryan was in church activities. She conceded that the money from the sale of the house had not been squandered, but had been used to pay off past debts. That fall, she admitted, they were in better financial shape than they had been for some years. She also described watching the "Emergency" television show involving cyanide.

The prosecution called O'Bryan's boss at the optical company. He said that in August, O'Bryan had asked if he could obtain some cyanide with which to polish gold eyeglass frames, an old-fashioned use for the substance. He said he told O'Bryan it was too dangerous and that safer substances would do a good job. But, he said, O'Bryan had pressed the matter again a couple of weeks later.

The next witness was Jarvis, the chemical company employee who thought he had seen O'Bryan in his store. The account he gave was this: A man had come into Curtin Matheson Scientific Company at about four o'clock on a rainy day. He was a heavy-set man with a soft, high-pitched voice; a man who had virtually no eyebrows. He was wearing an aqua-colored smock with an insignia on the pocket. "Do you stock potassium cyanide?" the man asked. Yes, Jarvis replied—in quarter-pound, one-pound, and five-pound containers, both in an impure and a pure grade. He went back to check the stock and returned to tell the man that only the five-pound container of pure cyanide was in stock, at a cost of more than fifty dollars. Jarvis suggested two other chemical outlets to the customer and the man left. That man, Jarvis said, was Ronald O'Bryan.

Harrison and Teague, who had fought hard to keep Jarvis off the stand, did their best to poke holes in his testimony. They read from his earlier affadavits, and got him to admit that he remembered the incident only after the police had suggested details and shown him a picture of O'Bryan. They pointed out inconsistencies from his earlier statements. It was strange, they implied, that he could remember in such great detail an incident that was only a hazy memory eight months before. And some of the detail was spurious—O'Bryan did not own a smock with an insignia on the pocket, a fact of which Jarvis had been sure.

But the biggest gap they opened was in the timing of the incident. In an earlier statement, Jarvis had been sure that the man had come in between the twenty-eighth and the thirty-first of October, very likely on the thirty-first. But O'Bryan's attorneys had been able to prove that O'Bryan had been working until five-thirty on Halloween; he had even walked the boss's daughter to her car in the rainstorm. At the trial, Jarvis said that he had been mistaken; the visit was sometime in the latter part of October, not necessarily on the thirty-first. The prosecutors subpoenaed O'Bryan's work records and showed that on the Wednesday of the week before, O'Bryan had taken off from work at one o'clock. This, they implied, was when he had gone shopping for cyanide.

The next witness was O'Bryan's chemist friend, who described the strange telephone call about cyanide. After being made to believe that O'Bryan was having an argument with the instructor in his college course (O'Bryan was not taking any such course, the prosecution proved), the man testified that O'Bryan "asked me if [cyanide] could be obtained reasonably easy."

The man said yes, probably at some large chemical company.

Prosecutor: And after that, did you have an occasion to have any further conversation about its effects on the human body?

Witness: Yes, he asked what concentration would be fatal to a human.

Prosecutor: All right, sir. And what was your reply to this?

Witness: Well, I asked him, I said, "I don't know. What do you want to know for?"

Prosecutor: And his reply was?

Witness: Just curious.

The last prosecution witness was a man who had been a customer, on October 31, of the optical company where O'Bryan worked. He said that from the parking lot he had seen O'Bryan walking from a store toward the office holding a stapler. He testified that inside the office the following conversation took place:

"He asked, 'What do you know about cyanide?' And my response was, 'Well, try me. What do you want to know about it?' And he said, 'I'm taking a course and I'm having an argument with the instructor. He says that one small grain of cyanide will kill, and I say it won't.' And I said, 'Well, I'm no expert, but what I know about cyanide, one grain will kill.' "

Upon cross-examination, the witness denied that he had applied for the reward in the case.

By now the prosecutors had built a formidable case, but it was not impregnable. For one thing, it consisted entirely of circumstantial evidence. And there were a few gaps. They could not prove that O'Bryan ever purchased, owned, or possessed cyanide. They could not prove that he had put the cyanide in the Pixy Stix, or that he had forced his son to eat it. They could not prove that O'Bryan disliked his son.

The major points of evidence that looked bad for O'Bryan were these:

1. The events of Halloween night—the fact that O'Bryan had appeared with the Pixy Stix and had distributed them.

2. The recent purchase of insurance coverage.

3. His inquisitiveness about cyanide.

4. His poor financial condition.

5. The alleged visit to Curtin Matheson Scientific Company.

6. The recurring theme, emphasized by the two prosecutors, that O'Bryan was a liar and a wild schemer.

The first three points could be explained as coincidence. The conversations about cyanide were probably the most damaging evidence, but Teague and Harrison could show that O'Bryan was an inquisitive man, intrusively so, and likely to talk about anything at all with no real thought behind it. In cross-examination, the attorneys had brought out the fact that O'Bryan had recently paid off many of his debts, and also that he had been fiddling with various insurance policies for several years. They brought O'Bryan's father as a witness to testify that he had lost his wife to a lingering illness without insurance coverage, and had spent the next twenty-five years paying off the bills. He had, he said, repeatedly warned his sons never to be caught without plenty of insurance. And it was clear that for many years O'Bryan seemed to be preoccupied with maintaining insurance.

The testimony of the chemical company employee seemed damaging, but his story had been shaken during cross-examination. To further discredit Jarvis, the defense lawyers called his co-worker who supposedly had been present during the conversation with O'Bryan; he remembered no such incident. They called the boss's daughter to testify that O'Bryan had taken her out to her car in the rain, proving that O'Bryan could not have gone to the company on the thirty-first. To counter the allegation that the visit had been made during the previous week on O'Bryan's afternoon off, they called several people to testify that at five o'clock O'Bryan had been at his son's school presiding over a meeting of the Parent-Teachers Organization, of which he was president. It was impossible, the lawyers pointed out, to be at Curtin Matheson (on the other side of Houston) at four o'clock and make it to Deer Park through rush-hour traffic by five. All of O'Bryan's afternoons in late October were accounted for.

These witnesses served a purpose more important than demonstrating that O'Bryan did not visit Jarvis on his afternoon off. They were able to show that he was active in his son's school affairs and in church groups. This was vital to the central task: to erase the picture of O'Bryan painted by the prosecution as a conniving, untruthful, selfish man. They needed to replace it with a portrait of a deeply religious man, a pillar of his church and his community: president of the P.T.O.; active in church affairs; treasurer of the Kiwanis club. A naive, inquisitive man, the attorneys implied, but not a killer. O'Bryan might live beyond his means, he might want too much for his family, but —Harrison and Teague planned to show—he lived *for* his family. A man who, in short, had been victimized by a few coincidences, by overzealous police work, and a sensation-seeking press.

If the jury was to accept this portrait, if it was to believe that much of the evidence against him was innocent coincidence, then it had to believe O'Bryan himself. He would have to confront his accusers.

O'Bryan spent three hours on the stand. In his testimony, he was prompt and solicitous in answering his attorney's questions. He began by outlining his upbringing: how he went to a local high school, served in the military, and suffered a minor injury in the service. He described how he and his wife sold their house to pay off debts. To make sure they didn't get in trouble again, he said, he had cut up all of his credit cards except one. He denied ever going to Curtin Matheson Scientific Company, denied having a conversation about cyanide with the optical customer. The other conversations, he said, were innocent ones given a sinister twist by subsequent events. He gave a step-by-step description of what happened on Halloween night.

O'Bryan's attorney tried to keep things low-key, but O'Bryan seemed obsessed with giving long, convoluted explanations, and with flaunting his sincerity. Finally at the end of his questioning, the attorney looked him in his eye and asked, "Mr. O'Bryan, did you murder your son, Timothy, for insurance?"

O'Bryan replied, trying to stay calm, "No, sir."

Mike Hinton, the prosecutor, rose for the cross-examination eager to dissect his adversary. He asked about the insurance, he asked about the conversations about cyanide, he asked about the debts and his statements that he was soon to come into a large sum of money. O'Bryan denied any sinister implications, and denied that some of the conversations had taken place.

Finally, Hinton asked, "Isn't it true that from the very beginning of your marriage you have lived beyond your income; that you are a dreamer and an exaggerator?"

"Yes, I have lived beyond my income," O'Bryan replied. "I always wanted my wife and children to live well. Yes, I dream. I dream of the very best I can for me and my family. And yes, I exaggerate—like any normal human being."

It was, perhaps, too much. On his second chance at questioning his witness, Harrison tried to bring his client back to earth:

"Mr. O'Bryan, I want you to look at these jurors. Look directly at these jurors. I want you to answer my question, sir. Did you kill your son, Timothy, Mr. O'Bryan, by giving him a Pixy Stix that you knew contained cyanide?"

"No, I did not."

"Did you know those Pixy Stix on October 31, 1974, contained cyanide?"

"No, I did not."

"Did you mix those Pixy Stix and did you put any cyanide in any Pixy Stix ever in your life?"

"No, I did not, Mr. Harrison."

"Did you cause the death of your son for insurance proceeds by giving him a Pixy Stix containing cyanide?"

"Lord, no."

In closing arguments prosecutor Driscoll began by pointing out how Mr. Carr (host of the trick-or-treat evening) had testified that O'Bryan said he left work at four-thirty on Halloween when he had actually escorted the boss's daughter to her car at five-thirty. "This is the first clue of many," he said, "that you have seen that establishes the whole pattern of this man's lifetime. The truth is not in him even when the truth would do better."

That was the beginning of Driscoll's assault on O'Bryan. He went on to highlight other aspects of the evidence—how O'Bryan held twenty-one jobs in the space of a few years, how deeply he was in debt, how interested he was in cyanide. The prosecutor summed up his case with a ringing call to arms. O'Bryan, he said, "used his friends, his church, his community. . . . [But] this jury will say to Ronald Clark O'Bryan, you are guilty of *the worst crime in the history of this community, perhaps of mankind,* and we know it. We will not be used by you."

Marvin Teague, in his summation, started where the prosecutor left off. Yes, he said, O'Bryan stood accused of "perhaps the most heinous, dastardly crime known to man, and this is killing his own son for money." But the enormity of the charge, Teague said, should not overwhelm the jury's objectivity. The prosecution had not proven that O'Bryan did anything illegal, Teague said; his client should not be convicted merely because of a few coincidences. "My client might be a dreamer," he concluded. "He might be bad off financially. He might be an exaggerator. But I submit to you, ladies and gentlemen, this man is not a murderer."

The jury deliberated for about an hour. Its verdict: Ronald O'Bryan was guilty of the murder of his son Timothy.

Even though O'Bryan had been found guilty of "the most heinous, dastardly crime known to man," there was some question whether he was even eligible for the death penalty. Texas law provided capital punishment only for certain types of murder, and killing one's own son was not one of them. But the prosecution argued that the case fell into another category: "The person committed the murder for remuneration or the promise of remuneration." On the face of it, this clearly refers to gangsters, "hit men," and third-party killings. But the Texas courts had interpreted the provision to permit the jury to invoke it in any case where money was part of the motive.

And that was precisely what O'Bryan's jury did. The verdict specified that O'Bryan was guilty of murder for remuneration—capital murder.

Although Texas law called for a separate hearing to determine whether O'Bryan should be sentenced to life imprisonment or death, the jury's verdict had sent him two thirds of the way to the execution chamber. The law required the jury to consider three questions, but the answers to two of them—whether the murder had been deliberate and whether the victim had provoked the crime—were preordained. Thus the only substantive question for the jury to decide was this: "whether there is a probability that the defendant would commit criminal acts of violence that would constitute a continuing threat to society."

At the penalty hearing, which took place the day after the verdict was returned, the prosecution presented no witnesses. The state would rest on the evidence presented in the trial itself. O'Bryan's attorneys moved to have the proceedings voided immediately, but the judge ruled that the trial evidence could be sufficient.

Teague and Harrison presented ten witnesses, all acquaintances or relatives of O'Bryan. The questioning was brief and pointed, as the attorneys sought to hammer home the notion that O'Bryan was not really dangerous. The defense attorneys asked each witness the same question: Did he or she, knowing Ronald O'Bryan as a family man, a churchgoer, a civic figure, think he would commit acts of criminal violence in the future? Each time the answer was no. Each time the prosecuting attorneys rose to ask the same questions. Did the witness hear all the evidence in this case? No? Then how could he or she sit there and say that a man who would murder his own son would never hurt a stranger?

The closing arguments reflected these themes. Teague and Harrison dwelled on the testimony of O'Bryan's acquaintances that he did not pose a threat. Harrison started describing a gruesome execution scene, but the judge stopped him. He then reiterated his belief in O'Bryan's innocence, reminding the jury that death was an irrevocable punishment. He ended by saying, "I think a life sentence would be appropriate."

The prosecutors were considerably more flamboyant. Driscoll called the murder the "high-water mark of shame in this community." Addressing the question of future criminal behavior he said, "Once he's done it—crossed that line—what else can he do? None of the men who testified are in danger, not from him, but what about the women and the little children?" Hinton occasionally shouted to the jurors, and he declared that O'Bryan "ought to be damned for what he did." On the question of dangerousness, he asked, "You tell me, if a man would kill his own flesh and blood for money, how easy would it be for him to kill a stranger for money? . . . I think we have a duty to the future innocent victims to carve this cancer out of this community and out of this society forever. Do it. I'm not ashamed to ask for it."

This time the jurors debated for an hour and twenty minutes. From statements later made by several of them, it seems they did not confine themselves to the three specific questions. As might be expected, they discussed the larger issues lurking behind their answers: how long O'Bryan might spend in prison under a "life" sentence; whether he "deserved" to live or die. Only one vote was taken; it was unanimous.

When the jury returned to the courtroom, the foreman handed the judge a slip of paper. Underneath each question was written the answer: Yes. O'Bryan was officially dangerous. He was sentenced to die.

Looking back on the case, Marvin Teague said he was not surprised by the verdict or the sentence. "There are some cases," he sighed, "where all the prosecutor has to do is read the indictment and rest."

It was sensation, he argued, that convicted O'Bryan—that portrayed him in the media as a killer, and that overwhelmed any "reasonable doubt" standard in the court room. A horrible crime had been committed, and someone had to pay for it; the finger was pointed at only one person. It was sensation, he said, that accused O'Bryan in the first place. Teague's theory was that the police were desperate to find a suspect after four days of fruitless investigation amid heavy public pressure. The insurance change aroused their suspicions and when they found the vial of white powder in O'Bryan's house they were sure they had their man. When the vial turned out to be innocuous, Teague said, "All their beautiful police work went to pot," so they started pressuring people into remembering things that might not have happened, like the visit to Curtin Matheson. And once the finger of accusation was pointed at O'Bryan, Teague said, people began to see him in a new light. To these conservative, simple people, Teague said, it would be blasphemy to suggest that the police had made a mistake. So their memories gave innocent statements by O'Bryan a sinister twist.

But still, in the face of the evidence, how could Teague maintain that O'Bryan was innocent? Teague replied that it was not that hard to believe. O'Bryan was a curious man by all accounts, boyishly inquisitive. He was likely to inquire about cyanide if it cropped up in the news, and it had, several times. Accept that view of O'Bryan's character, accept him as a chronic exaggerator, accept the revision of the insurance policies as part of his continuing struggle to maintain coverage—then, Teague said, the case against him falters. Throw out the statements about cyanide by Jarvis and the customer at the optical company as the result of police pressure and media suggestion—and the case falls apart.

Teague's faith in O'Bryan's innocence was really grounded in his character. The portrait of O'Bryan as a schemer, he said, was false. "In cases like this, you look into a man's background to see something there that would indicate he could do it. Nothing. Not one iota of evidence. You could say O'Bryan lived in a quasi-dream world, living beyond his means—but the man didn't even smoke."

This belief is what buoys up the many people who still believe in O'Bryan's innocence. Dr. John Graham, a friend of the family and a former employer of O'Bryan, said in an interview: "He just adored and worshipped kids. You could beat him in the head with an ax and he wouldn't hurt a child."

All this speculation was balderdash, replied Mike Hinton. In an interview he said, "The man has been lying all his life. This case shows how a circumstantial evidence case can be stronger than one depending on eyewitness testimony." Hinton called O'Bryan "a total sociopath," one society was better off without. "This was the most overwhelming case of circumstantial evidence I've ever seen."

A year after the death of Timothy O'Bryan, there were few Halloween trick-or-treaters. Many children accepted only pennies or scrip; no food. A newspaper article quoted Hinton calling O'Bryan "the man who destroyed Halloween."

And what of Sheila O'Bryan? Did she ever have any doubts about her husband's guilt?

Divorced now, trying to raise her daughter by herself, she declined to be interviewed. "The Lord has put a protective shield around me and I don't want to take it down," she said.

On Death Row at the Ellis Unit of the Texas State Prison, the other inmates had a nickname for O'Bryan: "The Candy Man." According to the universal inmate code of every prison, O'Bryan ought to fear for his life, for the code dictates that a man who will injure little children is the lowest of the low. Often such criminals are victimized by other inmates. But O'Bryan seemed to get along well with his neighbors on Death Row. Several of them said they truly believed he was innocent.

And they said so convincingly, in a way that indicated polite disbelief in other inmates' strident protestations of innocence.

Teague had described O'Bryan as "his own worst witness," because of his overzealous way of minimizing every connection between himself and the events leading up to his son's death. "He's an overselling salesman," Teague said, "and he tries to outdo himself in whatever he's selling."

Months on Death Row hadn't changed O'Bryan—"not one iota," Teague said. In several conversations, held over small tables in the day room next to Death Row, O'Bryan seemed obsessed with refuting each and every element of the case against him. Unlike most inmates, he was eager to be confronted with the evidence against him. He wanted to tell his story, to tell how he was framed. Point by point he went over the case, repeating what he told the police, what he told on the witness stand. The conversations about cyanide, he said, stemmed from the "Emergency" television show, and he should have been allowed to show the segment to the jury. (His attorneys had obtained a copy of the film, but the judge did not allow them to show it.) The insurance on the children was the result of his father's sermons on the consequences of being caught without it. He could not possibly have visited Curtin Matheson on any day in October—his work records showed that. "They impressed the jury with one fact, and one fact only: Halloween and a little boy's murder, and all the atrocities that always happen on Halloween." He saw himself as a scapegoat.

O'Bryan was a convincing salesman, maintaining steady eye contact while he talked. His voice was gentle, soft, very slow, with a pleading quality to it. He didn't seem bitter, or outraged, or resigned. He did seem hurt.

But despite his insistence on discussing the evidence, O'Bryan said he had "quit trying to convince everybody of my innocence. Now I'm to the point where all I want them to do for me—and for my dad and my brother and everyone else out there—is to say that we can prove with factual evidence that Mr. O'Bryan poisoned and killed his son, because here is where he bought the cyanide, or—so they've got something that proves I did something." In other words, he thought the state should produce the "smoking gun" before it executed him.

Every Halloween since 1974, he said, "just shatters me"—made him think about Timmy. What did he remember? "I think the one specific thing that sticks in my mind is an experience at his school. Occasionally I would take off and eat lunch at his school. You could do it, just tell the teacher. This always made Tim real happy. He'd tell the kids, 'My daddy's coming to eat with me.' We'd go sit in the cafeteria with forty thousand other kids and eat lunch together. He'd just love that."

O'Bryan said he never got away from thoughts of his boy. Or from thoughts of impending death. But, he said, worse things could happen than to die. "You take a man and kill him, that's no punishment. Nobody has ever come back from the dead to tell us it was punishment. For me it would not be punishment, because I'm a Christian. If I die, I know I'm going to heaven. And that's no punishment for me. If you really want to punish a man for what he's done, you lock him up for a number of years, and you keep him away from his children. He can't hug 'em, he can't touch 'em, he can't see his wife except through a glass window with bars in between. You separate him from society. I can tell you that's punishment. Because it punishes me."

Did O'Bryan really think he could be executed?

"Of course, of course. Sure it could happen. For it not to happen, I would have to say that no innocent man has ever been convicted. Let me say this: No one wants to die. I think that anybody who tells you they want to die is crazy. It's ridiculous. The most precious gift you have is your life."

At the conclusion of the last interview, after going over the case in all its details, O'Bryan pressed for an outsider's opinion of his case. It was an uncomfortable moment. I hedged a bit, then gave up and told him what I had told someone else the night before: "If I stand up and say I'm sure you're innocent, then I've got problems, because there's a lot of evidence against you. It's hard to believe that so many witnesses were all wrong. But, on the other hand, if I stand up and say you're guilty, there are other problems. The principal one is, how can some one with a background like yours try to kill, not just his own son, but five children? For such a small amount of money? And botch it so badly?"

The warden indicated it was time to go. O'Bryan, rising, had one last plaintive reply: "But they wouldn't kill a man for that, would they? Would they? Just so they could have a scapegoat for Halloween?"

Conclusion: Punishing Murder

"Some like chocolate, some like vanilla; I believe in the death penalty." The Florida judge put it crudely—but a choice must indeed be made. Do we need to punish some murderers with death, or can we settle for imprisonment?

It should be apparent by now that I find the arguments in favor of resuming executions inadequate. We must abandon capital punishment. I take this position with some misgivings, for the evidence is not all on one side and none of the alternatives are attractive. Other honorable and intelligent people may come to the opposite conclusion. But I find too many problems associated with the death penalty, and not enough advantages.

If our paramount concern is with increasing public safety here and now, it appears to make no difference whether we execute convicted murderers or imprison them. On a statistical basis, the murderer, once caught and put behind bars for a substantial length of time, will not kill again. The rare exceptions are tragic, but they cannot be reliably predicted. And when we look for the deterrent value of executions as a threat to potential murderers, it cannot be found. The conclusion that capital punishment fails to act as a significant deterrent to murder does not fit in with some of our assumptions about human behavior; on the surface, it flies in the face of common sense. But, as Charles L. Black, Jr., points out, "One of the first axioms of 'common sense' is that it looks for and acknowledges *evidence*." And the evidence is convincing that any effect capital punishment might have on the murder rate is so subtle that it cannot be measured by today's most sophisticated researchers. Yes, the remote threat of execution will probably deter a potential murderer here or there—but in the minds of other, less rational killers, it will serve as an incentive.

But what of the alarming rise in homicides from the 1960s to the early 1970s? Are we to believe that it was merely coincidence that the number of murders skyrocketed just as executions were abandoned?

Let us take a second look at the social science research cited in Chapter Four. Brian Forst, who studied this very question, assigned numerical values to the social trends of the 1960s and concluded that the moratorium on executions was not a factor in rising homicide rates. What was? If we think seriously about crime, we should not be surprised at the answers Forst and others have found: poverty, youth, migration to urban areas, racial tensions, rapidly rising affluence in some sectors of the population while others remained poor. I do not mean to imply that scholars have finally discovered the missing link of social science: the Cause of Crime. But doing something about these problems certainly offers more hope of reducing crime rates than reviving capital punishment.

One of these factors deserves special attention, because it has been too widely ignored. Unfortunately, it is something we can do nothing about: the post-war Baby Boom, which began in 1946, peaked in 1951, and tapered off slowly thereafter. We know that young people between the ages of fourteen and twenty-four are responsible for more than half of all violent crimes. Their number increased tremendously in the late 1960s and early 1970s. Not only did this population bulge provide a much larger pool of potential criminals, it also exacerbated other factors (increase in unemployment, decline in respect for elders) that contribute to crime. So crime *rates* went up as well.

This explanation does not lend itself to political rhetoric, and any police chief who tried to calm his frightened town-folk by advising them to hide under their beds until the Baby Boom subsided would be run out of town. But now the bulge has passed through its crime-prone years—and the crime rate has stabilized. While murders increased eleven percent in 1971 and five percent during each of the next three years as the youth boom reached its peak, they dropped slightly in 1975, 1976, and 1977. Fear of crime, as measured by public opinion polls, has subsided a bit.

It is too early to proclaim the end of the murder boom or of public paranoia about crime, particularly since birth rates in the inner cities remained high for many years and since unemployment among black youths has been allowed to remain at the forty-percent level. But the worst may well be over.

This is not to say that punishment has no role to play in our attempts to reduce crime. One of the factors identified by the researchers as partially responsible for the increase in homicides was that the certainty of punishment declined during the 1960s. Forst noted that only thirty-five percent of all murders in this country are punished with any imprisonment at all. That is an astounding figure—a true scandal by anyone's figuring. The same point was made by Franklin Zimring in his study of homicide in Philadelphia. Among the 170 convicted murderers included, a change in policy from a maximum penalty of death to a maximum of life imprisonment would have affected only 1.8 percent. But raising the minimum sentence for murder to five years—hardly a Draconian proposal—could have increased punishment for seventy-six percent of the criminals. That end of the spectrum, I submit, is where the cheapening of life—especially black life—is occurring.

Even if capital punishment is not necessary to protect us, however, it can still be defended on the grounds of justice, retributive justice. As the Supreme Court put it, "some crimes are themselves so grievous an affront to humanity that the only adequate response may be the penalty of death." The sense of outrage that lies behind retributive justice is honorable, part of the glue that holds civilization together. It offers emotional consolation to some relatives of murder victims. Those who call for the death penalty because their sense of justice will be offended by lesser punishments are taking a defensible position with a long history. We may not regard them as moral dwarves. In the long run, they may be right.

But justice requires more than proportionality. It also demands equity, fairness, consistency. And this is where capital punishment runs into trouble. Society long ago decided that *all* murders did not have to be punished with death. For the past century, the number of murders for which death sentences have been deemed appropriate has been in a steady and rapid decline. We are now at a point where death is being demanded for only a small fraction of killers, about one percent. Lawmakers have tried to aim the death penalty at the one percent of "worst" murderers. But it appears to be beyond the competency of our institutions to determine just who belongs in this group. The laws have proven to be impossible to apply consistently.

Look at the cases in this book. Who can say whether Clifford Hallman's crime was "especially atrocious, heinous or cruel" when compared to 1,180 murders in Florida that same year? Who can say whether Charles Proffitt's striking of Pam Margolis constituted "a great risk of death to many persons"? Whether a heritage of segregation and racism affected Jessie Pulliam's jurors? Whether Ronald O'Bryan, after spending two decades in prison, would still present a danger to the public? Whether George Vasil at fifteen is old enough to be executed? In each case in this book, it is easy to imagine other judges and jurors reaching exactly the opposite conclusions on vital questions of law.

But these questions of law did not, in most cases, really

determine the outcome of the case. The single outstanding characteristic that most of these defendants share is the superficiality of their defense. I do not mean to impugn their attorneys as incompetent or nonchalant, although a more aggressive and effective defense would certainly have been mounted had the defendant been wealthy. But in most cases, the defendants were almost entirely unknown to their jurors. In five cases, no defense witnesses were called by the defense in the first stage of the trial. Only two of the defendants ever spoke in front of their jurors. They stood before the jury box as enigmas, known only by the gory particulars of one terrible act, described in minute detail. They stood as creatures beyond comprehension, virtually gagged and masked in preparation for the execution chamber.

In giving the states permission to resume executions, the Supreme Court envisioned an "informed, focused, guided, and objective inquiry" to decide each person's fate. But, with rare exceptions, these proceedings are better characterized as uninformed, vague, capricious, and subjective.

When we look at the broad range of those murderers who receive death sentences and those who do not, it seems that we are snaring not the "worst" one percent, but the unluckiest. In too many cases, their bad luck centered on being born poor and black. Despite the procedural improvements of the new death penalty laws—and they are improvements on the pre-1972 system—the results show that the "new" death penalty is basically the same as the old one. As Hugo Adam Bedau declared after the Supreme Court revived capital punishment: "In this country, today, it is simply not possible to have a death penalty applied with uniform, predictable, rational impact all across the land. Instead, we can have capital punishment only if it is unpredictable, arbitrary and infrequent in its application. . . . Retributive justice of this sort is simply not justice at all, because it is inequitable."

If this is the case, then eventually—after a few unappealing losers in the lottery have been executed—the Supreme Court will have to consider again the constitutionality of the death penalty. The 1976 decision was, after all, grounded in theory, not in practice. If social scientists can persuasively demonstrate that there is no rational basis to distinguish condemned murderers from murderers serving a life sentence, then the Court will have no choice. It will have to declare the death penalty unconstitutional on the same grounds it did in 1972.

We could then try once more to write new laws. Certainly some improvements could be made to reduce abuses. Legislators could eliminate vague non-standards such as "heinousness" and "dangerousness." They could require a higher standard than "reasonable doubt" for death sentence decisions. They could set up sentencing commissions to examine murder sentences for uniformity, and special legal aid bureaus to provide expert defense.

But this is mere tinkering; further refinement would only lead to new problems of definition and newly irrational discriminations. If the elaborate machinery of two-stage trials and specified circumstances did not do the trick, then the death penalty will probably be beyond legislative resuscitation. If unfairness persists, then the defect is not in courtroom procedures or legal language, but in the nature of the decision to terminate human life. Any penalty that can be stomached only in rare instances, and only for crimes against the dominant race, is well on its way to extinction. The death penalty may remain on the books for treason, and perhaps for special crimes such as terrorist killings and assassinations (although these are crimes for which it would probably serve as an incentive, considering the drama a capital trial would hold for suicidal political fanatics or deranged loners)—but for all practical purposes, execution will be permanently retired to the museum of "cruel and unusual punishments."

What will that leave us with?

In the past, criminals were often banished or sent into exile. But we have no new continents to populate, and no Siberias in which to build our own Gulag Archipelago. Fantasies of rocketing criminals to space colonies are implausible.

In the not-so-distant future (but well after 1984), science will probably hold out dramatic innovations in behavior control. Already research is being done on some powerful ways of modifying violent behavior. Most center on the brain: drugs to reduce aggression, electronic implants to buzz out antisocial impulses, psychosurgery. When perfected, they will seem to be a humane alternative to executions or imprisonment. The most apparent danger is that they will be used before crime occurs, not just afterward. But we should be more concerned with the ethical aspects of forcibly tinkering with the essence of human choice. Criminologist John Conrad, a humane realist on the subject of punishment, counsels: "Let us hope that when science offers criminal justice a foolproof drug or surgical procedure to stop criminal behavior, we will be principled enough to reject it."

This leaves us with the unhappy alternative of imprisonment.

Certainly the current "life sentence" has been debased in many states to the point where it is a legal fiction. In California, a person sentenced to "life" is frequently eligible for parole after seven years. The public—and many prison inmates—have come to equate the minimum with the sentence; "life equals seven years." In practice, parole boards are generally quite stingy with their favors. But the "mythical time" handed out in the courts for all offenses under indeterminate sentencing laws has contributed enormously to disrespect for law (as well as to support for capital punishment). And the public is rightly outraged by the thought that serious murders will be punished with the same penalty as lesser murders, armed robberies, or, as in Texas, a third offense of passing bad checks.

The alternative proposed by most abolitionists is "life without possibility of parole." This (in itself a form of exile) would, in theory, offer society as much protection from future criminal activity as an execution. It would also represent an escalation of punishment from the current "life sentences."

Such a sentence cannot be as ironclad as it sounds. The governor always retains his power to pardon an offender and order his release. In states where such sentences have been used, commutations are generally considered after the murderer has served a very long period of time—but they are not easily granted, and sometimes they never are. Such a sentence does seem to offer an adequate amount of protection for the public. California had "life without parole" for murder and kidnapping during the 1950s. Of ninety-five such sentences handed down, fifteen inmates remained in prison in 1977 or had died there. The other eighty had been released, but only seven returned to prison for new crimes.

A life sentence offers some advantages over capital punishment. It can be mitigated if a mistake is discovered, and it allows for the possibility of atonement and rehabilitation. While this is not our primary objective in punishing murder, it is worth considering. Even Nathan Leopold, responsible for one of the most publicized brutal murders of the twentieth century (the Leopold-Loeb case, involving the kidnap-slaying of a young boy for a thrill), managed during his decades in prison to inspire many convicts and officials with his rehabilitation. After he was released to do charity work in Puerto Rico, he was able to contribute a great deal to society.

The nature of imprisonment must change as well. Both our sense of justice and our sense of human dignity should make us want the inmate to work in prison—not pounding rocks, but doing socially productive work. The serious offender must be allowed—even forced—to contribute to the welfare of the society he has injured.

The adequacy of a true life sentence depends on its being reserved for a very small number, the way the death penalty is used now. It cannot be used to put away everyone we are afraid of, from bank robbers to check forgers. Since taking away a man's future is not a much easier decision than taking away his life, perhaps the two-stage trial procedure and the consideration of aggravating and mitigating circumstances should be required before it could be imposed.

Even the addition of the stiffest life sentence, however, will not appease an ill-informed public that is frightened about its safety and convinced that crime can be stopped if only we are tough enough with criminals. By abandoning capital punishment, we are losing the ability to make a dramatic demonstration of that willpower. We are admitting that human institutions are too fallible to make irrevocable judgments. We are hoping that even the most troubled segment of society will respond better to the example of preserving life than it does to the threat of death. We are conceding that there is no final solution.

We are conceding something clse as well: that the world is not starkly divided into good and evil. And neither are people. This dichotomy, often reflected in primitive religions, inspires us to eliminate evil by eliminating evildoers. I believe that, as a motivation for capital punishment, this way of looking at people may go deeper than the fear of crime, the desire for retribution, or even the lust for revenge. It was stated forthrightly in a 1978 newspaper interview by the chief justice of the Georgia Supreme Court, Hugh Nichols, who shares responsibility for the fate of Georgia's condemned inmates:

You know, you don't put up a mad dog and feed him and take him home—you get rid of him. What good are they to society? They are incorrigible. Scientists prove now beyond any question that they are just born that way. You can't correct them. It's genetic. They're animals. There's no way you can do anything about them.

As the language above demonstrates, this belief lends itself to dehumanization of the murderer, to the conclusion that those who kill are not part of the brotherhood of man—perhaps not even human at all.

That, I believe, is the real key to the cases in this book. Some individuals appeared to their jurors to be dangerous, others as *deserving* death for the enormity of their crimes. But each, I believe, was viewed as fundamentally and irretrievably evil.

This is a choice I cannot make. These men have been convicted of awful deeds; perhaps they will never be able to participate in a free society. Certainly they deserve stiff punishment. But while I do not pretend to understand these people, or to have the right to forgive them, I am not willing to assume the power to deny them their humanity. By looking at the murderer the way he looked at his victim, we set the wrong example.

Many of these conclusions became clear in the process of making a practical choice that I found excruciating. At one point while I was working on this book, a flurry of execution dates were being set around the country. As a reporter, I might well be assigned to witness an execution. Would I go? Could I stand to look in the eyes of a man in his underwear as he was strapped in the electric chair? Could I stand impassively and watch, without feeling compelled to make some futile demonstration of protest? Could I successfully smother my horror with more horror, visions of the crime this man had committed? Or would I just have two nightmares to haunt me?

After some agony on my part, I finally decided that I could attend, with appropriately solemn demeanor. *But not if I knew the inmate.* So long as he was unknown—a name, a crime, a label—I could watch. But if he was one of the people I had interviewed—people whose crimes I have visualized in all their gore dozens of times—I could not.

I had failed my test. I could not look the condemned man in his eyes and tell him he had to die. Reluctantly, I turn to his victims and say that he must be allowed to live—not for his sake, but for ours.

Acknowledgments

Whatever pleasure I received from this enterprise came not from the work itself, but from the reminder that there are so many people who care. Their trust carried me through many dark hours. Their good faith has earned them clemency for any errors that may appear here, which are my responsibility.

I first must thank the individuals whose private nightmares are told here—victims, inmates, families—for their cooperation in a painful venture. The inmates' attorneys frequently went far out of their way to assist me. Many public officials—police officers, prosecutors, judges, court clerks, prison staff—were gracious to me, even when their viewpoint differed from mine. The Florida Attorney General's office and the Florida Department of Corrections were particularly helpful.

Much material in the story of Luis Monge was taken from a masterful series of articles by Samuel H. Day, published in the *Intermountain Observer* (Boise, Idaho) in 1971. I thank Mr. Day for permission to draw from his labors and for the tone he set in his reporting.

Grateful acknowledgment is made to *The Floridian*, Sunday supplement to the *St. Petersburg Times*, for permission to use material from "The Death Routine of the Electric Chair. You Are There," by James McClendon, August 19, 1973.

David Powell did valuable research in Florida on two cases, Charles Proffitt and Clifford Hallman. David Fritze provided background material, ideas, and phrases in telling the story of Richard Hager.

Richard Kwartler, then editor of *Corrections Magazine*, was the first person to see the makings of a book in this material, and he cajoled and threatened me when I shrank from continuing.

Philip Spitzer kept faith in this project when others had lost interest. Robert Levine of Macmillan, who also believed, did his best to keep me on deadline and off the soapbox.

My colleagues and friends at *Corrections Magazine* and *Police Magazine* made this book possible by their generosity with time, resources, and advice. David Anderson and Michael Serrill (who also did initial research on the O'Bryan case) helped to keep bad writing and sloppy thinking to a minimum. Rob Wilson kept me going whenever I tried to back out. Thanks also to Kevin Krajick, Louise Fraza, and Rhela Moskowitz. The story of George Vasil first appeared in *Corrections Magazine* (September, 1976), and permission to use it here is gratefully acknowledged.

Henry Schwarzschild and Deborah Leavy of the American Civil Liberties Union provided contacts, information, and constructive criticism. At the NAACP Legal Defense Fund, David Kendall, Joel Berger, and Jack Boger took time from their work to guide me through the intricacies of the legal maze.

Advice, encouragement, lodging, research, and brainstorming came from many sources. Doug Underwood deserves special gratitude. I also thank Marvin Barrett, Shirley Barry, Jonathan Beard, John Conrad, Todd Engdahl, Dewitt Rogers, Rollie Rogers, and Charles M. Young. Melvin Mencher, my teacher, provided the sobering biblical admonition that hung over my typewriter: "Who is this, that darkeneth counsel by words without knowledge?" As my reprieves were running out, Kathleen Dimmick came to the rescue.

A final note of gratitude to Janet, who gave space, sympathy, and understanding beyond measure.

Bibliography of Quoted Sources

This includes only materials from which direct quotations were taken.

Allen, Edward J. "Capital Punishment: Your Protection and Mine." *The Police Chief,* June 1960.

Barzun, Jacques. "In Favor of Capital Punishment." *The American Scholar,* vol. 31, no. 2, Spring 1962.

Beccaria, Cesare. *On Crimes and Punishments,* 1976 Quoted in Sellin, *Capital Punishment.*

Bedau, Hugo Adam. "Capital Punishment." *The Nation,* August 28, 1976.

————, editor. *The Death Penalty in America.* Chicago: Aldine Publishing Company, 1967.

————, and Pierce, Chester M. *Capital Punishment in the United States.* New York: AMS Press, Inc., 1975.

Bennett, James V. *I Chose Prison.* New York: Alfred A. Knopf, Inc., 1970.

Black, Charles L., Jr. *Capital Punishment: The Inevitability of Caprice and Mistake.* New York: W.W. Norton and Company, Inc., 1974.

————. "The Crisis in Capital Punishment." *Maryland Law Review,* vol. 31, p. 289, 1971.

————. "The Death Penalty Now." *Tulane Law Review,* vol. LI, no. 3, April 1977.

————. "Due Process for Death: Jurek v. Texas and Companion Cases." *Catholic University Law Review,* vol. 26, Fall 1976.

Blumstein, Alfred; Cohen, Jacqueline; and Nagin, Daniel, eds.

Deterrence and Incapacitation: Estimating the Effects of Criminal Sanctions on Crime Rates. Washington, D.C.: National Academy of Sciences, 1978.

Bork, Robert. *Amicus curiae. Brief filed in Gregg v. Georgia.* Quoted in Carrington, *Neither Cruel nor Unusual.*

Bowers, William J. *Executions in America.* Lexington, Mass.: D.C. Heath and Company, 1974.

Camus, Albert. "Reflections on the Guillotine." In *Resistance, Rebellion and Death.* New York: Alfred A. Knopf, 1961.

Capote, Truman. *In Cold Blood.* New York: Random House, Inc., 1965.

Carrington, Frank. *Neither Cruel nor Unusual: The Case for Capital Punishment.* New Rochelle, N.Y.: Arlington House Publishers, 1978.

Chessman, Caryl. *Trial by Ordeal.* Englewood Cliffs, N.J.: Prentice-Hall, Inc., 1955.

Cleaver, Eldridge. *Soul on Ice.* New York: McGraw-Hill Book Company, 1968.

Coker v. Georgia 433 U.S. 584 (1977).

Conrad, John, and Dinitz, Simon. *In Fear of Each Other.* Lexington, Mass.: Lexington Books, 1977.

Darrow, Clarence. "Is Capital Punishment a Wise Policy?" In Arthur Weinberg, ed., *Attorney for the Damned.* New York: Simon and Schuster, 1957.

Dix, George E. "Administration of the Texas Death Penalty Statutes: Constitutional Infirmities Related to the Prediction of Dangerousness." *Texas Law Review,* vol. 55, no. 8, November 1977.

————. "The Death Penalty, 'Dangerousness,' Psychiatric Testimony, and Professional Ethics." *American Journal of Criminal Law,* vol. 5, no. 2, May 1977.

Duffy, Clinton T. "My Views on Capital Punishment." Press Release. *See also* Clinton T. Duffy and Al Hirshberg, *88 Men and Two Women.* Garden City, N.Y.: Doubleday and Company, Inc., 1962.

Ehrlich. Isaac. "The Deterrent Effect of Capital Punishment: A Question of Life or Death." *American Economic Review,* vol. 65, p. 397, 1975.

Ellsworth, Phoebe C., and Ross, Lee. "Public Opinion and Judicial Decision Making: An Example from Research on Capital Punishment." In Bedau-Pierce, *Capital Punishment in the United States.*

Eshelman, Byron. *Death Row Chaplain*. Englewood Cliffs, N.J.: Prentice-Hall, Inc., 1962.

Forst, Brian. "The Deterrent Effect of Capital Punishment: A Cross-State Analysis of the 1960s." *Minnesota Law Review*, vol. 61, no. 5, May 1977.

Furman v. Georgia. 408 U.S. 238 (1972).

Gerstein, Richard E. "A Prosecutor Looks at Capital Punishment." *Journal of Criminal Law, Criminology and Police Science*, vol. 51, no. 2. Northwestern University School of Law, 1960.

Gregg v. Georgia, and companion cases: *Proffitt v. Florida, Jurek v. Texas, Woodson v. North Carolina, Roberts v. Louisiana*. 408 U.S. 238 (1976).

Greider, William. "The Return of the Death Penalty." *The Washington Post*, November 28, 1976.

Griffin v. Illinois. 351 U.S. 12 (1956).

Halliwell v. State 323 So. 2d. 557 (Florida, 1975).

Hochkammer, William O., Jr. "The Capital Punishment Controversy." *Journal of Criminal Law, Criminology and Police Science*, vol. 60, no. 3, 1969.

Jackson, Justice Robert. *Stein v. New York*. 346 U.S. (1953).

Kemmler v. New York. 136 U.S. 436 (1890).

Koestler, Arthur. *Reflections on Hanging*. New York: Macmillan Publishing Co., Inc., 1957.

Kohlberg, Lawrence, and Elfenbein, Donald. "The Development of Moral Judgments Concerning Capital Punishment." *American Journal of Orthopsychiatry*, vol. 45, no. 4, July 1975.

Lehntinen, Marlene. "The Value of Life—an Argument for the Death Penalty." *Crime and Delinquency*, vol. 23, no. 3, 1977.

Lockett v. Ohio. 57 L. Ed. 2d. 1978.

McCafferty, James A., ed. *Capital Punishment*. Chicago: Aldine-Atherton, Inc., 1972.

McClendon, James. "The Death Routine of the Electric Chair. You Are There." *The Floridian*. Magazine supplement to *St. Petersburg Times*, August 19, 1973.

McWhirter, Norris. D., and McWhirter, A. Ross, eds. *Guinness Book of World Records*. New York: Bantam Books, 1976.

Massie, Robert. "Death by Degrees." *Esquire*, April 1971.

Mead, Margaret. "A Life for a Life: What That Means Today." *Redbook*, June 1978.

Meltsner, Michael. *Cruel and Unusual: The Supreme Court and Capital Punishment*. New York: William Morrow and Company, 1974.

Menninger, Karl. *The Crime of Punishment.* New York: Viking Press, 1968.

Miller, Gene. *Invitation to a Lynching.* Garden City, N.Y.: Doubleday and Company, Inc., 1975.

————. Articles in the *Miami Herald.* September 19–20, 1975.

Morris, Norval, and Hawkins, Gordon. *The Honest Politician's Guide to Crime Control.* Chicago: University of Chicago Press, 1970.

Mueller, Ed. "Musings of a Death Row Chaplain." *Life on Death Row.* Printed version of videotape. Bearsville, N.Y.: Video Project, 1976.

Nichols, Hugh. Interview with Beau Cutts. *Atlanta Journal and Constitution,* August 13, 1978.

Reid, Don, with Gurwell, John. *Eyewitness.* Houston, Tex.: Cordovan Press, 1973.

Reidel, Marc. "Discrimination in the Imposition of the Death Penalty: A Comparison of the Characteristics of Offenders Sentenced pre-Furman and Post-Furman." *Temple Law Quarterly,* vol. 49, 1976.

Rovere, Richard. Review of *Reflections on Hanging. The New Yorker,* September 14, 1957.

Royal Commission on Capital Punishment. *Report.* London: H.M.S.O., 1953.

Sellin, Thorsten. *Capital Punishment.* New York: Harper and Row, Publishers, Inc., 1967.

Shakespeare, William. *Romeo and Juliet,* Act V, Scene III, 1. 157.

Silberman, Charles E. *Criminal Violence, Criminal Justice.* New York: Random House, 1978.

Smith v. *State* 540 S.W 2d 693 (Texas Crim. App. 1976) cert. denied, S.Ct. 1341 (1977).

Tillich, Paul. Quoted in Daniel H. Benson, "A Christian View of Capital Punishment." Washington, D.C.: *e/sa forum-30;* United Methodist General Conference.

Turnbull, Colin. "Death by Decree." *Natural History,* May 1978.

United States Law Week. "Arguments Before the Court." Washington, D.C.: Bureau of National Affairs, Inc., April 6, 1976.

Van den Haag, Ernest. *Punishing Criminals.* New York: Basic Books, Inc., 1975.

West, Dr. Louis J. "Psychiatric Reflections on the Death Penalty." *American Journal of Orthopsychiatry,* vol. 45, no. 4, July 1975.

Wilson, James Q. *Thinking about Crime*. New York: Basic Books, Inc., 1975.

Witherspoon v. *Illinois*. 391 U.S. 510 (1968).

Wolfgang, Marvin, and Reidel, Marc. "Rape, Racial Discrimination, and the Death Penalty." *The Annals of the American Academy of Political and Social Science*, vol. 407, May 1973.

Zeisel, Hans. "The Deterrent Effect of the Death Penalty: Facts v. Faith." *The Supreme Court Review*. Chicago: University of Chicago Press, 1976.

Zimmerman, Isidore. Interview with *Fortune News*. The Fortune Society, New York, June–July, 1976.

Zimring, Franklin E. "Policy Experiments in General Deterrence: 1970–75." In Blumstein, Cohen, and Nagin, *Deterrence and Incapacitation*.

———; Eigen, Joel; and O'Malley, Sheila. "Punishing Homicide in Philadelphia: Perspectives on the Death Penalty." *University of Chicago Law Review*, vol. 43, 1976.

Index

Index

E

F

G

W

Warren, Earl, 26
Washington, 30, 163
Weil, Simone, xxi
West, Dr. Louis J., 94, 123, 160
White, Byron, 29, 194
Whitman, Charles, 12
Wilson, James Q., 153, 226
Witherspoon v. *Illinois*, 27
Wolfgang, Marvin, 219, 220
Women and crime, xix

Y

Youth and crime, 127, 133, 258

Z

Zeisel, Hans, 118, 225
Zimmerman, Isidore, 95
Zimring, Franklin, 188, 195, 196, 259